THE LIFETIME READING PLAN

THE LIFETIME READING PLAN

Third Edition

CLIFTON FADIMAN

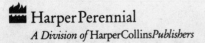

HarperPerennial

A Division of HarperCollins*Publishers*

FOR
Mortimer J. Adler

WHO FIRST TAUGHT ME,
AND HAS NEVER CEASED
TEACHING ME,
HOW TO LISTEN TO
THE GREAT CONVERSATION

Designed by C. Linda Dingler

The Library of Congress has catalogued the previous versions of this book as follows:

Fadiman, Clifton, 1904–
    The lifetime reading plan.

    Bibliography: p.
    Includes index.
      1. Bibliography—Best books.   2. Books and reading.
I. Title.
Z1035.F29   1988   011'.7   87-46135
ISBN 0-06-055066-X
ISBN 0-06-273064-9 (pbk.)   94 95   RRD   10 9 8 7 6 5 4 3 2

Contents

CONTENTS

THE MIDDLE AGES

PLAYS

NARRATIVES

CONTENTS

CONTENTS

PHILOSOPHY, PSYCHOLOGY, POLITICS, ESSAYS

CONTENTS

Preface to
the Third Edition

This book was first published in 1960, twenty-seven years ago at this writing. A revised and expanded edition appeared in 1978. The book you are now reading is further revised, corrected, enlarged, and updated. A great many inelegancies and ambiguities have, I hope, been removed. I have modified a number of judgments. The Bibliography has been simplified and updated. The Suggestions for Further Reading have been enlarged and updated.

The approach and purpose however remain unaltered. They are discussed in the Preliminary Talk with the Reader following these remarks.

In the main text seven writers have been added to those treated in the expanded 1978 edition. They are: Samuel Beckett, Gabriel García Márquez, Saul Bellow, George Orwell, Fernand Braudel, Virginia Woolf, and Anton Chekhov. Of these the first three have deservedly won Nobel Prizes. Orwell's reputation since his premature death in 1950 has steadily risen. Braudel is perhaps the greatest historian of our time. As for Woolf and Chekhov, mea culpa. It seems that a quarter-century was needed for me to improve my judgment. One of the advantages of a long life is that you are given a chance to change your mind.

The commentary on George Eliot now includes a brief discussion of her masterpiece *Middlemarch*. That on Herman Melville recommends a reading, in addition to *Moby Dick,* of his classic short story "Bartleby the Scrivener."

The book's basic structure has been slightly modified. Its main text, commentaries 1–103, deals with "original communications," a term explained in the Preliminary Talk. There I also discuss the purpose of commentaries I–VI, a group headed Annex, which occupies pages 227–37. In earlier editions Whitehead's *Science and the Modern Mind,* the Durants' *Story of Civilization,* and Morison's *Oxford History of the American People* were included in the main text. Subsequent reflection has led me to transfer them, I believe more usefully and appropriately, to the Annex. The Annex has been enlarged by the addition of William H. McNeill's *The Rise of the West* and Page Smith's *A People's History of the United States.*

Without the conscientious and patient work of my assistant, Siu Zimmerman, the preparation of the revised (1978) edition would have been far more onerous. I wish to thank her.

A Preliminary Talk
with the Reader

This book contains a *Lifetime* Reading Plan. The books here discussed may take you fifty years to finish. They can of course be read in a much shorter time. The point is that they are intended to occupy an important part of a whole life, no matter what your present age may be. Many of them happen to be more entertaining than the latest best-seller. Still, it is not on the entertainment level that they are most profitably read. What they offer is of larger dimensions. It is rather like what is offered by loving and marrying, having and rearing children, carving out a career, creating a home. They can be a major experience, a source of continuous internal growth. Hence the word *lifetime*. These authors are life companions. Once part of you, they work in and on and with you until you die. They should not be read in a hurry, any more than friends are made in a hurry. This list is not something to be "got through." It is a mine of such richness of assay as to last a lifetime.

The aim is simple. The Plan is designed to help us avoid mental bankruptcy. It is designed to fill our minds, slowly, gradually, under no compulsion, with what some of the greatest writers of our Western tradition have thought, felt, and imagined. Even after we have shared these thoughts, feelings, and images, we will still have much to learn: all of us die uneducated. But at least we will not feel quite so lost, so bewildered. We will have disenthralled ourselves from the merely contemporary. We will understand something, not much but something, of our position in space and time. We will know how we have emerged from three thousand years of history. We will know how we got the ideas by which, unconsciously, we live.

Just as important, living in an age which to its cost has abandoned the concept of the hero, we will have acquired models of high thought and feeling. We will feel buoyed up by the noble stream of Western civilization of which we are a part. This book, then, is a small act of faith, faith in the notion that many Americans, despite all the pressures inducing them to do so, have no desire to remain All-American Boys and Girls.

Does this sound schoolmasterish? Let it. The school is a far greater invention than the internal combustion engine. A good schoolmaster is a far more useful citizen than the average bank president, politician, or general, if only because what the schoolmaster transmits is what gives meaning to the life of the banker, the politician, and the general. We survive precisely as primitive people survived, by force and cunning. But we *live* by ideas and faiths of which they had hardly a premonition.

I do not wish to claim too much for *The Lifetime Reading Plan*. It is not magic. It does not automatically make you or me an educated man or woman. It offers no solution to life's ultimate mysteries. It will not make you happy—such claims are advanced by the manufacturers of toothpastes, motorcars, and deodorants, not by Plato, Dickens, and Hemingway. It will simply help to change your interior life into something a little more interesting, as a love affair does, or some task calling upon your deepest energies.

Like many others, I have been reading these books, off and on, for most of my life. One thing I've found out is that it's easy enough to say that they enlarge you, but rather difficult to prove it in advance. Perhaps a better metaphor is that they act like a developing fluid on film. That is, they bring into consciousness what you didn't know you knew. Even more than tools of self-enhancement, they are tools of self-discovery. This notion is not mine. You will find it in Plato who, as with many other matters, thought of it first. Socrates called himself a midwife of ideas. A great book is often such a midwife, delivering to full existence what has been coiled like an embryo in the dark, silent depths of the brain.

For whom is this Reading Plan meant? Not for the highly educated or even (not always the same thing) the very well read. They would find nothing new in what I have to say. The titles here listed would be perfectly familiar to them. Indeed, they could add many more, and quarrel quite legitimately with some of my choices.

In general the Plan is meant for Americans, from eighteen to eighty plus, who are curious to see what their minds can master in the course of their remaining lifetime, but who have not met more than ten percent, let us say, of the writers listed. It is meant for college graduates who were exposed to many of these books during the undergraduate years but who successfully resisted their influence. It is meant for the college graduate—his or her name is legion—to whom most of these writers are hardly even names. It is meant for the high school graduate who might well have profited from a college education but did not have the chance to do so. It is intended for that great and growing army of intelligent men and women who in their middle years are penetrated by a vague, uncomfortable sense that the mere solution of the daily problems of living is not enough, that somewhere worlds of thought and feeling call out for exploration. It is intended for the eager young man or woman of modest means (many of these books can be bought for little money) for whom the thrills of business competition or homemaking, while valid, are inadequate. It is intended for the retired elderly who have found that growing roses or looking at television does not leave them mentally exhausted. It is intended for teachers (college teachers too, in some cases) who would like to deepen and extend their knowledge and sensitivity, and so deepen and extend the nonmaterial rewards of their noble vocation. In its small way *The Lifetime Reading Plan* is a contribution to the solution of the problem of that imminent Leisure Era which may prove either an opportunity or a horror.

A word about the titles.

This is not in any absolute sense a list of the "best books." There are no best books. All we can say is that, over three thousand years of Western history, there has gradually accumulated a body of what have been called "original communications." The schoolroom term is *classic*, and that is all right with me if we add Carl Van Doren's definition: "A classic is a book that doesn't have to be rewritten." "Literature," says Ezra Pound, "is news that stays news." The list of books that stay news changes, though not radically, with each generation. No two scholars would compile identical lists, and no single scholar (I am not one) would find my own list satisfactory in all respects. A Frenchman would include more French books. I, an American, find myself stressing books in my own language. Also,

3

while there is considerable agreement on the original communications up to perhaps the year 1800, there is diminishing agreement as we near our own era. That, Time being the great sifter, is natural enough.

You will at once note omissions. I have not listed the Old and New Testaments. The Bible of course is more important than any book on the list, influencing constantly and deeply the lives of all Westerners, including those, such as the Communists, who claim to be atheists. But I have assumed that anyone who would read this book is already familiar with the Bible. In any case I assume you own one—and the practical purpose of the Plan is to induce you to *add* to your library.

The great books of the East are not to be found here. Why not?

First, we are Western men and women. Up to almost yesterday our minds were molded by Western ideas and images, plus those supplied by the Bible. A hundred years from now, even fifty years from now, this may no longer be true. But it is reasonably true today; and this book is for now. Besides, to familiarize ourselves with the Western tradition whose children we are is a project big enough for any ordinary lifetime.

Second, I have no competence in any tradition other than my own. It's easy enough to fake competence, but the purpose of this book is not to exhibit the erudition of the writer (limited enough in any case) but to be of service to the reader.

Third, the Eastern classics that I have read (I confess this with some embarrassment) simply light no fire within me. Limited outlook? Probably so. I have tried Lady Murasaki and the Koran and the *Arabian Nights* and the Bhagavad Gita and the Upanishads and *All Men Are Brothers* and perhaps a dozen other Eastern classics. Unable to read them with much enjoyment, I cannot write about them with much honesty. Those wishing to find their way in the vast world of Oriental literature are referred to *The Guide to Oriental Classics* (Columbia University Press), edited by William de Bary and T. Embree.

But many Western classics are also omitted. How about Aristophanes, Ariosto, Tasso, to name three that happen to jump to mind? The difficulty here is one of translation. Even the best versions seem to me to convey too small a proportion of what must be great originals. Read them if you can, by all means. Where they might well be in this book there stands some other title that in my fallible judgment has more to offer. How about Gibbon's masterpiece? It *is* a masterpiece but I don't think I could induce you to go through so much undergrowth in order to come from time to time upon his magnificences. Perhaps I am wrong: add *The Decline and Fall of the Roman Empire* to my list if you wish. How about philosophy? I have included as much as I thought the reader could well digest. But I am making you up, I do not know you, perhaps you can take much more. I have had to drop some names: Spinoza, for example, Hegel, Kant. Some seem to me too difficult except for the professional. Some write so badly that they cannot stir most minds.

Poetry posed a painful problem. The only non-English-writing poets I have suggested for extended reading are Homer, the Greek tragic dramatists, Virgil, Lucretius, Dante, Molière, and Goethe. In these cases the best translations give a good idea of the original, and anyhow the men are so overshadowing that they must be included. But I know that Baudelaire is every whit as great a poet as Coleridge. I am quite willing to admit on the authority of scholars I respect that Pushkin may be greater than either. But there is simply no use in claiming that Baudelaire and Pushkin can be read intensively in English with great pleasure. Robert Frost defines poetry as what is lost in translation, and there is much sense in the statement.

And of course there are other omissions—Plutarch, the *Song of Roland,* Malory, Bacon, Pepys, Racine, Corneille, many others. I could not include all. I had to call a halt at a given point. I hope that, roughly and generally speaking, the titles included give an adequate sense of the mainstream of Western thought and imagination. I am aware that others have valid claims. I will not quarrel over them.

The most glaring omission is that of a whole large field, science. A dozen or more masterpieces, from Euclid to Einstein, have contributed vastly to the mental world we inhabit. But to include them in a book of this sort would be little more than an act of academic piety. They are accessible only to the highly prepared mind or to the specialized student. However, I assume that you would like to get a general idea of the total impact of science, as well as of its underpinnings, mathematics. You will find in the Annex two readable books that may be of help. They are both by Whitehead: *Science and the Modern World* and *An Introduction to Mathematics.* They will open the door to the sciences.

I have mentioned the Annex. The Annex lists and discusses eight titles. *Science and the Modern World* may perhaps claim to be an original communication. The others cannot. They are useful, well-written secondary sources. Those by the Durants, McNeill, Morison, and Smith are intended to give us a surface knowledge of world history and of our own country, so that we may sense the larger background out of which our original communications emerged.

While books are our main concern, the Western tradition of course includes the arts. *The Story of Art* by E. H. Gombrich offers a sound introduction, as far as the printed page can provide one, to the arts of painting, sculpture, and architecture. But there is no real substitute for what your eyes can do for you.

The last title in the Annex might well be read first. It is a guide, not to all kinds of reading, but to the kind of reading with which this book is concerned.

We come now to the structure of the book, its angle of approach, the way to use it.

I have arranged the entries in a manner that seems reasonably interesting and convenient. We begin with twelve classics, listed chronologically according to type, from Greece and Rome. We continue with three, chronologically arranged, from the Middle Ages. If the reader wishes to work on these fifteen first, well and good; a certain useful view of our origins is obtained in that way. But there is no compulsion to do so.

I then talk about eight great dramatists of the Renaissance and modern world, arranged in order of date, and reflecting eight different eras or national cultures. If you have a special interest in drama, or would simply like to get an overall view of the peaks in this field, these eight may be read as a unit. Again, such rigor is not of the essence. Following these discussions is a note on a four-volume anthology, a reading of which will make you familiar with much of the modern theater.

The largest portion of the book is devoted to prose narratives of all kinds and from many countries. Within each country, the writers are grouped chronologically. The same arrangement is followed in the next section (comprising philosophy, psychology, politics, and essays) and in the section on English and American poets. Two anthologies of poetry are recommended. The pattern is slightly broken in the section on history and biography.

Perhaps, viewing the contents as a whole, it would have been simpler to follow a straight chronological order. But by grouping the books not only by date, but also by country and kind, I hope I have made it possible for the reader to approach the list in various ways and work out personal combinations.

Throughout the commentaries I use a device that may at first seem a bit irritating. Example: talking of Thucydides, I say, "He is the first historian to grasp the inner life of power politics. Hobbes (71), Machiavelli (78), and Marx (75) are, each in a different way, his sons." The purpose of the parenthesized commentary numbers, showing that these three men are discussed elsewhere, is not to make you turn at once, or indeed at all, to these references. The purpose is to stop you for a split second. It is to make you realize that the Western tradition is what Robert Hutchins called it, a Great Conversation, in which hundreds of powerful or noble or delightful minds are talking with each other, reinforcing each other, praising each other, refuting each other, recalling each other, or prophesying each other. In that one sense, all these men and women are contemporaries. Our writers are not islands. They are parts of a vast continent. They connect mutually, and finally they connect with us. Those little parenthetical numbers are there to point up this fact whenever it is legitimate to do so, and only then. Before rereading or reviewing these books, I thought I knew many of them, not well, but somewhat. But I was astonished to find something I had not before perceived—that great writers, consciously or unconsciously, are always making gestures toward their peers. Deep calls unto deep: Santayana looks back toward Plato, not La Mettrie; Dante glances into the future toward T. S. Eliot, not Vachel Lindsay.

As to the comments themselves: they are simply brief talks with you, my imaginary reader. They are not true essays, hardly rounded judgments, least of all compendiums of essential facts. What then are they? They are cards of invitation. Using from four hundred to twelve hundred words, I have tried to seduce you into reading the book I talk about. That is all; but it is also all I have in mind. My own work is valueless if it does not make you read the book discussed. This is not a critical volume of scope or depth or originality. It is not put forward as such. It is at best a key to open doors. Not the key, but what lies back of the door is what counts. I hope earnestly that these talks are readable and even interesting, and I can at least say that I have tried to pack a good deal into a few words. But their essential job is to be of service to the reader.

And so, in order to seduce you, I have not hesitated to use any method I thought might do the job. Sometimes I have stressed a writer's life or personality. Sometimes I have advanced critical judgments. Sometimes I have summarized a writer's whole work. Sometimes I have quoted the opinion of a great authority. Sometimes I have warned the reader against common misconceptions. Sometimes I have tried to show a familiar figure, Dickens for example, in a somewhat less familiar light. Sometimes I have stressed the modernity of a writer who might too easily be considered stale and dusty. Always I have tried to point out, not always directly, what we late-twentieth-century Americans can gain from a given book.

Why *should* you read Dante? Jane Austen? Lucretius? Voltaire? Because they are great? That is no answer. Their greatness is what we feel *after* we have read them, often years after. I have tried to give a more concrete, less lofty answer to a natural and proper question.

The judgments expressed are largely what is called "received opinion." This is not a book of personal crotchets, though I have allowed an occasional prejudice to show through. But where my own judgment is given, that fact is clearly signposted, and the reader is free to ignore me. In any attempt, however, to interest a general, nonexpert audience in some hundred or so books, most of them acknowledged masterpieces, one is duty bound to explain why people over many generations have so acknowledged them. Therefore scholars or critics will find not a word in this book of the slightest interest. They have heard it all before. I am not talking to them, although I have learned from them. I am talking to beginners, which is what we are all at some point in our serious reading lives. These brief conversations with the reader are little more than icebreakers. They help to make it possible for you to set forth on your own adventures among masterpieces.

You may read this book from first page to last before starting out on your Lifetime Reading Plan; or you may read it in sections, should those sections correspond to the titles you propose to cover as a kind of unit; or you may read the numbered commentary corresponding to the single title you have in mind. I have tried, as I advanced from Homer to our own day, to give some sense of whatever evolution and development we can legitimately detect.

Hence this book may be a little more profitable if read from beginning to end. The essential thing, however, is the use you make of it. If you do no more than read it, you have wasted your time and money. While it is true that it contains a certain amount of information, many famous names, and hundreds of thumbnail judgments, its aim is not educational, but practical. That is, it is intended to spur you to action. Any one of the books it discusses may alter your mind profoundly; but the only alteration this book can effect is in your will. It aims to direct your steps to the bookstore or library.

In what order should these books be read? Any that you prefer. The order in which I list them has nothing sacrosanct about it. You may wish to start with the moderns and work backward; a fresh perspective is gained that way. You may wish to concentrate for a while on a single group, the poets or the philosophers. You may elect to read the Greeks first, as a whole. You may rove about virtually at random. The Lifetime Reading Plan *is* a plan, not a course. You are not required to pass an examination in it, any more than you are required to pass an examination in your knowledge of your children or parents. If you try a book, say Hobbes's *Leviathan,* and find it too difficult, put it aside for a year or so. Then take it up again. You will find that the other books you have read in the meantime will somehow have made Hobbes a little easier. That is one of the marvels of this kind of reading: each original communication helps us to extract a bit more from all the others.

Remember also that these books are not only to be read. They are to be reread. They are not like a current novel. They are inexhaustible. Plato read when you are twenty-five is one man, Plato read at forty-five still another. It is not entirely frivolous to say that any great work of art is without question the cheapest thing you can ever buy. You pay for what seems a single object, a book or a picture or a record. But actually each such object is many objects; the works of Shakespeare do not consist of thirty-seven plays, but more nearly of three hundred seventy plays, for *Hamlet* changes into something else as you change into someone else with the passing of the years and the deepening of your sense of life.

Can you read these books without having gone to college? Yes, if you are willing to take pains. But only then. Says Walt Whitman: "Books are to be called for and supplied, on the assumption that the process of reading is not a half sleep, but in the highest sense, an exercise, a gymnast's struggle; that the reader is to do something for himself." There it is: the reader must *do* something. Reading is not a passive experience, except when you're reading trash or the news. It should be, and is, one of the most vigorous modes of living. A good book, like healthy exercise, can give you the pleasant sense of fatigue that comes of having stretched your mental muscles.

On the other hand, these books, however carefully read, are not to be studied as if they were school tasks. Do not try to exhaust their meaning. If you or I can absorb ten percent of what Plato has to offer us, we will have done well enough. It happens to be a fact that even a surface familiarity with most of these books will leave your mind better furnished than are the minds of ninety-nine out of a hundred college graduates. But that is a minor argument for the Lifetime Reading Plan. We are not competing with others, we are trying to excel ourselves.

Throughout this book I have tried to be realistic. When a book is hard, I've said so. When a book is so odd that it presupposes a preliminary adjustment of your mind, I've said so. When in a few cases a book is dull, I've said so. Remember that part of the pleasure we get from this kind of reading depends on the attitude with which we approach it. Herodotus can be enjoyed in an informal mood; Thucydides gains if you gird your mental loins in advance. Furthermore, these works cannot all be read at the same tempo. Just as you slow down at curves, so you are forced to slow down at Aristotle or Dewey. You can handle *Candide* in a single pleasant evening, but you may find it worthwhile to spend an equal amount of time over a single short poem such as Yeats's "Sailing to Byzantium." In any case there's no hurry; you have a lifetime.

A word about the two book lists you will find at the end of the volume.

The first, called the Bibliography, is meant as a buying aid. It gives the title, author, and publisher of each of the titles discussed. Furthermore it frequently lists other titles by the same author, to supplement the titles suggested in the Plan. In the great majority of cases, only paperback editions are listed. This is important; for the first time in the history of civilization the great classics of that civilization are within reach of the average purse. Paperback books are easy to buy and easy to shelve. I have made no exact estimate, but I would guess that eighty percent of our list could be purchased for a total sum of about four hundred dollars, or forty dollars a year over a ten-year period. But of course mass market paperbacks are perishable and you cannot expect the page to be quite as readable or handsome as is apt to be the case with the more carefully produced hardcover and quality paperback editions. Keep in mind, however, that used-book stores often sell older hardcover books at prices lower than those of new paperbacks.

With respect to translations I have occasionally added a comment indicating which version I have found most satisfactory. But this is a matter of taste and you need not be rigidly guided by my preferences. Other things being equal, however, choose a modern rather than a Victorian or pre-Victorian version. Ours happens to be a superb age of translation, possibly even greater than the Elizabethan-Jacobean age.

There are few hobbies more satisfactory than the gradual accumulation of good books. They are timeless; that is, they will be as useful to your descendants to the third or fourth generation as they are to you. No money spent on a good book can ever be wasted; somehow, sometime, somewhere that book will be read, if not by you, then by your children or your friends. And there is a certain satisfaction in completing the purchase of these titles (or others of comparable value). It is like seeing your entire past, three thousand years of it, ranged in order on your shelves. But—don't let your past stay there; make it part of your present.

The second list of books at the end of this volume is headed Suggestions for Further Reading. It consists of biographies of the authors mentioned, critical books or essays about them, and related reading aids. It is not only incomplete, it is hardly more than suggestive. But it is enough to start you off in the event that you want to find out more about, let us say, John Donne, after you have become acquainted with his work. Some Great Books teachers decry the use of secondary material. I taught such classes for many years, so that I am not without experience, and I must state that I do not agree. These secondary works should not be used as a substitute for your own opinions. That is why it is better to read them *after* you have read the original. But they are often most enlightening, and frequently works of art. I have tried, as far as possible, to list critical and biographical material by writers who are fine thinkers and stylists, themselves parts of the Great Conversation. Many happen to be available in cheap paperback editions, within reach of the purses of most of us. Some, however, can be secured only through your library. I should stress again that these Suggestions for Further Reading are not for scholars or specialists, who will find them woefully inadequate. They are for beginners or almost-beginners.

This has been a long and rambling talk with the reader rather than a formal Introduction. It is that by design. Its tone is informal because the Plan is informal. I would like you to find the Lifetime Reading Plan an exciting adventure of the mind, as well as a discipline. If I have communicated to you any of my own enthusiasm (which has persisted and grown over a period of more than sixty-five years) you are ready to sit down for a lifetime of conversation with some of the liveliest talkers our civilization has produced. In the next pages I will start pointing them out to you. That is all I can do. You must make friends with them by yourself.

THE BEGINNING

1

HOMER
(probably 9th or 8th century B.C.)

The Iliad

The *Iliad* and the *Odyssey* are two long, ancient Greek narrative poems called epics. They are the first as well as the greatest epics of our civilization. Every time we refer to a siren or Achilles' heel or compare a lovely woman to Helen of Troy we are borrowing from these poems that are perhaps three thousand years old.

I say perhaps. We do not know when Homer lived—maybe between 800 and 700 B.C., maybe earlier. As a matter of fact we do not even know *whether* he lived. We do not know whether the stories were written by one man named Homer; or, as the old joke has it, by another fellow of the same name; or by a syndicate; or even, as Samuel Butler thought in the case of the *Odyssey,* by a woman. These questions are for scholars. The poems are for us.

Originally, it is supposed, they were listened to rather than read. Homer, whoever he or she was or they were, recited them.

The *Iliad* tells the story of some fifty days of the last of the ten years' siege of Troy (or Ilium) by a number of tribes we loosely call Greeks. This siege resulted in the capture and firing of Troy's "topless towers," which we know to have actually existed. To find out how Troy was taken, see Virgil's *Aeneid* (11).

The *Iliad* is probably the most magnificent story ever told about man's prime idiocy: warfare. The human center is Achilles. The main line of the narrative traces his anger, his sulkiness, his savagery, and the final assertion of his better nature. He is the first hero in Western literature; and ever since, when we talk of heroic qualities, Achilles is somewhere in the back of our minds, even though we may think we have never heard of him.

You can look at the *Iliad* through a diminishing glass. Then it becomes the story of a trivial scuffle, marked by small jealousies and treacheries, fought by long-dead semibarbarians who had hardly advanced beyond the sticks-and-stones era. The wars of the *Iliad,* compared with our splendid planetary slaughters, are petty stuff.

Strangely enough, when you actually start to read the *Iliad,* the lens of this diminishing glass changes and becomes a magnifier. The scale of the war becomes unimportant; the scale of the men and the gods enlarges. The essential quality of the *Iliad* is nobility. Nobility is a virtue connected with magnitude; there are no small nobilities. General Eisenhower's *Crusade in Europe* was a useful book, portraying the largest single military and naval exploit in all history. Yet, compared with the *Iliad,* recounting a local struggle of little historical importance, it lacks magnitude. This is no reproach to General Eisenhower. He was no Homer.

And there never has been another Homer. If a reading of the *Iliad* and the *Odyssey* does nothing else for us, it makes us reflect on the difference between art and science. There has been "progress" in the latter; there is none in the former. All imaginative artists, but only if they are great enough, seem contemporaries. That is the way to read them.

2

HOMER
(probably 9th or 8th century B.C.)

The Odyssey

The *Odyssey* is a kind of sequel to the *Iliad.* It tells what happened to the Greek heroes after the sack of Troy. More especially it follows the fortunes of one of them: Odysseus, King of Ithaca, also known as Ulysses. It describes what happened to him during his ten years' long voyage home; the search of his son Telemachus for his father—a theme repeated in hundreds of novels since, such as Joyce's *Ulysses* (39); the arrogant wooing by the suitors of his patient wife, Penelope, during his absence; Odysseus' return; and his bloody revenge on his enemies. The story is well known even to those who have never read it. Like the Bible, it is less a book than part of the permanent furniture of our minds.

When we take up the *Odyssey* after the *Iliad*, we step into a different world. Even its sound is different. That of the *Iliad* is clangorous with the clash of arms; that of the *Odyssey* murmurous or thunderous with the myriad-mooded sea.

But the difference is more basic. The *Iliad* is tragic. It announced a theme repeated in Western literature ever since, and one that obsesses our own private minds: the limitations of even the noblest minds in the face of a world seemingly governed by unchangeable Fate. But the *Odyssey* is not tragic. It stresses not our limitations but our possibilities. Its theme is not courage in the face of death, but intelligence in the face of hardship. It announces another of the great themes: the power of intelligence, a theme to which we moderns readily respond. Though Odysseus is brave enough, his heroism is of the mind. He is not outsized in passion, like Achilles, but of human size, like us.

The tone of the *Odyssey* corresponds to this more homely conception of man. While full of fairy-tale episodes, it impresses us as does a realistic novel; indeed it is the first of all realistic novels, as it is the first of adventure stories, and still perhaps the best.

It is in this spirit that we may read it today, as a narrative of adventures that happened to an unusual man whose mind never stopped working. The mood of the *Odyssey* is more relaxed than that of the *Iliad*. And so should ours be as we read it.

3

HERODOTUS (ca. 484–ca. 425 B.C.)

The Histories

Of Herodotus we know mainly that he was born of good family in Halicarnassus, a city in Asia Minor, originally a Greek colony, but under Persian control for half his life. We know also that he traveled widely throughout the entire Mediterranean world, presumably amassing the materials that went into his *Histories,* a word which in the original Greek means inquiries or investigations. His work was famous during his lifetime and has never ceased to be so.

Herodotus states his purpose: to preserve "from decay the remembrance of what men have done" and to prevent "the great and wonderful actions of the Greeks and the Barbarians from losing their due meed of glory." The latter part of his book fulfills his purpose. It gives us as full and objective an account of the titanic struggle between Persia and Greece as was possible for this pioneer historian. With these "actions" we associate such glorious names as Marathon, Thermopylae, and Salamis, battles in a war in possible consequence of which we are today a part of Western rather than Asiatic culture.

But the earlier portions of the book, while all leading up to this grand climax, are really a kind of universal cultural history, mingling fact, anecdote, and myth, of the entire known world during the time immediately preceding and contemporary with Herodotus's own period.

In a manner sometimes confusing, sometimes enchanting, he mixes journalism, geography, ethnography, anthropology, fables, travelers' tales, and marketplace philosophy and moralizing. Though he writes in prose and about real rather than legendary events, he is nearer to Homer (1, 2) and to art than to the modern historian and so-called scientific history. The later Roman critic Quintilian said he was "pleasant, lucid, diffuse." All three adjectives are precise.

Hence the beginning reader should not seek in him a clear and, by present-day standards, correct account of the Greek-Persian Wars. He should be read, at least at first, in great long gulps, almost carelessly. He should be read for the stories, the digressions, the character descriptions, the fantastic oddments of information about the manners and customs of dozens of ancient peoples. And he should be read for the pleasure of meeting Herodotus himself—sometimes gullible, sometimes skeptical, always humane, humorous, curious, and civilized. Don't worry overmuch about who is who and what is where. The absorption of specific facts is less important than immersing yourself in the broad, full, buoyant Herodotean river of narrative. The Greek critic Longinus, who said of him, "He takes you along and turns hearing into sight," gives us our cue—just to go along and see things.

4

THUCYDIDES (ca. 470/460–ca. 400 B.C.)

The History of the Peloponnesian War

Called by Macaulay "the greatest historian that ever lived," Thucydides belonged to a highly placed Athenian family and saw Athens at its height under Pericles. He was himself involved as a general in the war he chronicled. In 424 B.C., as a consequence of his failure to relieve the Thracian town of Amphipolis, he was removed from his command and banished, enduring twenty years of exile before being pardoned. In his history he refers to this crucial episode with brief, cold, third-person detachment. During these twenty years he traveled about in Sparta and elsewhere seeking and verifying the facts that form the material of his book. A tradition states that he was assassinated, perhaps in 400 B.C.

Never finished (it breaks off in 411 B.C.) but somehow a satisfying whole, his history records the great Greek Civil War between the imperial forces of Athens and the coalition headed by Sparta. The emphasis is almost entirely on the second half of the war, of which in his mature years Thucydides was a contemporary. This phase began in 431 B.C. and ended in 404 B.C. with the defeat of Athens and the breakup of the most hopeful civilization the world has ever known and to whose purely intellectual eminence we have never since attained. Thucydides knew he had a great tragic subject. He devoted to it limited but magnificent talents of whose worth he was quite aware. With calm confidence he states that his work will remain "a possession for all times." So far he has not been proved wrong.

Though Thucydides and Herodotus are partially contemporary, they have little else in common. Thucydides does his best to be what we now call a scientific historian. He believes the proper ordering of sufficient facts plus the exercise of a powerful mind can explain historical processes. He rejects entirely all fuzzy explanations, such as Herodotus's childlike notion of an avenging Nemesis, ever alert to punish arrogance like that of the Persians. He scorns omens, oracles, and prophecies; he does not need the gods. He analyzes the motives, rarely idealistic, that impel leaders and so precipitate great events. He supplements his extraordinary psychological insight with notable understanding, considering his time, of the demographic and economic forces that underlay the Peloponnesian War.

Where Herodotus is gossipy and digressive, Thucydides is austere and unified. He is not a cultural historian, but a politico-military one. He is skeptical, charmless—and, let us admit, difficult. He cannot be read except with one's full attention and is one of those writers who yield more with each rereading. Finally, he is the first historian to grasp the inner life of power politics. Hobbes (71), Machiavelli (78), and Marx (75) are, each in a different way, his sons.

Despite his severity and aristocratic denial of emotion, he grips the serious reader. Of the forty speeches he puts into the mouths of his historical personages, at least one, Pericles' Funeral Oration (Book II), is a supremely great dramatic monologue. Masterpieces also, though of differing kinds, are his accounts of the plague at Athens (Book II), the Melian dialogue (Book V), and the terrible Sicilian expedition (Books VI and VII) that signal the end of Athenian dominance.

PLATO (ca. 428–ca. 348/7 B.C.)

Selected Works

Plato is less an author than a world of thought. He is probably one of the half-dozen most influential minds in Western civilization. It has even been said—by Whitehead (III, IV)—that all Western philosophy consists of a series of footnotes to Plato, an exaggeration (or minimization), but not entirely untrue. The beginning reader cannot hope to explore the entire Platonic world, nor should he attempt it. The readings suggested below enable us to make his acquaintance and that of his master Socrates. And that is all.

A wealthy Athenian who lived through his city-state's great and also declining days, Plato experienced one supremely crucial event in his long life: his meeting with Socrates. (Compare Boswell and Johnson [101].) He had many talents, and was drawn, for example, toward both poetry and politics; but Socrates determined him to a life of thought, undertaken on many fronts.

The result of this life of thought was a series of "dialogues," long and short, some very beautiful, some dull, and most of them spotlighting his master Socrates. The "Socratic method" was part of the atmosphere of the period. Socrates questioned all things, and particularly the meanings men attached to abstract and important words, such as justice, love, and courage. The questioning was real; the truth was finally approached only through the play of minds, that give-and-take we call "dialectic." This mode of thought is exemplified and perfected in the dialogues. They are not mere exercises in mental agility (except occasionally) but works of art in which all the resources of a poetic and dramatic imagination are called into play. The reader of Plato, like the reader of Shakespeare, is reading an artist.

You should keep in mind three central Platonic notions. The first is that, as Socrates says, "a life without inquiry is not worth living." That lies at the heart of everything Plato wrote. The second notion is that virtue is knowledge; the sufficiently wise person will also be sufficiently good. The third notion has to do with the kinds of knowledge most worth having. Plato believed in "Ideas," invisible, intangible archetypes or prototypes of things and actions and qualities. These latter, as we know them on earth through the distorting veil of the senses, are but faint reflections of the heavenly Ideas. We call this mode of apprehending the universe Idealism; and Plato is its father.

His philosophy, however, is not a consistent whole, and in many respects it changed as he grew older and lost faith in humanity's ability to govern itself wisely. I suggest therefore that the dialogues be read, not as systematic expositions of dogma, but as the intellectual dramas they are, full of humor, wit, mental play, unforgettable extended similes called myths, and particularly full of one of history's most fascinating characters, the ugly, charming, mock-modest Socrates.

It might be best to begin with the *Apology,* in which Socrates defends himself against the charges of atheism and corrupting the youth. As we know, his defense was a failure— he was executed, by self-administered poison, in 399 B.C. The dialogue—it's really a long speech—has, however, been a success for almost twenty-four hundred years.

Follow that with the *Crito.* Here Socrates gives us his reasons for refusing to escape from prison. Then perhaps the *Protagoras,* in many ways the most sheerly brilliant of the dialogues, and the perfect exemplification of Plato using all his talents. Some may wish to try the *Meno,* recording Plato's famous doctrine of recollection. Then comes the *Symposium,* practically a drama in its movement and structure. This deals with love in all its phases, including that accepted Greek passion, homosexuality. It deals also with drunkenness, as well as with more exalted matters.

After this perhaps the *Phaedo.* The sections on immortality may be skimmed or skipped, but the last few pages, describing Socrates' noble death, are required reading. Many good judges have felt them to be the finest short piece of narrative ever written. Finally, absorb as much as you can of Plato's most ambitious and rather difficult work, the *Republic,* which outlines his highly conservative ideal state and is the ancestor of all the Utopias and Dystopias—see (42) and (43)—that have since appeared.

So many of our notions and ways of thought go back to Plato (including some fantastic and even harmful ones) that knowing nothing of him means knowing less about yourself. To discover Plato is not merely to discover a masterly intellect. It is to come face to face, if you are an inheritor of the Western tradition, with much of the hitherto unsuspected content of your own mind.

6

ARISTOTLE (384–322 B.C.)

Ethics, Politics

Aristotle tells us that education is accompanied by pain. An education in Aristotle himself certainly involves, if not pain, at least difficulty. Unlike his master, Plato, he is charmless. Furthermore, the fact that we do not possess his original works but only what has come down to us as probably students' notes, does not make for readability. You are warned not to expect from Aristotle the pleasure Plato offers, except that pleasure which comes from following the operations of a supreme brain.

Aristotle's intellect was one of the most comprehensive, perhaps *the* most comprehensive, on record. He wrote on everything, from marine life to metaphysics. While it is unwise to say that all these writings (many of merely anti-quarian value today) can be related under a single system, it is true that Aristotle was a systematizer in the sense that Plato was not. He believed in the collectability and relatability of all knowledge. He spent his life collecting and relating. Our idea of an encyclopedia, a most fruitful notion, goes back to him.

Today we would say he was of upper-middle-class origin. At seventeen or eighteen he left his small native town of Stagira for Athens. Here for twenty years he studied at Plato's Academy. The influence of Plato (5) is marked in his work (often by disagreement or development), but we know nothing about the personal relations between the two greatest philosophers of antiquity.

After Plato's death Aristotle sojourned for five years in Asia Minor and Lesbos, possibly engaged in biological research, for his mental bent was scientific and investigative, rather than artistic and speculative. In 343/2 B.C. he went to Macedon to tutor the future Alexander the Great. There is no evidence, despite all the sentimental romancing, that he greatly influenced Alexander's mind. The one great Alexandrian idea, that of a world imperium, is not Aristotelian.

In 335/4 B.C. Aristotle returned to Athens; organized his own school, the Lyceum; taught, wrote, investigated. In 323 B.C., perhaps because of his suspect connections with the Macedonian party, he found it expedient to exile himself from Athens. A year or so later the mere man Aristotle died in Chalcis, in Euboea. His influence, however, though it has had great downward swoops, has never died.

We cannot comment here on his crucial pioneering in logic—he is credited with inventing the syllogism; or in scientific method; or in the biological and cosmological sciences; or in esthetics—his *Poetics,* an analysis of classic Greek tragedy, has had a profound and continuing effect on literary criticism. In general we may say that his whole approach to life is more earthbound than Plato's, less utopian, certainly more geared to the actual nature and abilities of the ordinary man or woman.

This is borne out by a reading of the *Ethics* and the *Politics.*

The *Ethics* tries to answer the basic question, What is the Good? It involves an inquiry into happiness and the conditions that attend it; and into virtuous actions, thought of as means between two extremes of conduct. The "Golden Mean" is an Aristotelian catchword.

Ethics is a part of politics, for to Aristotle (and the Greek citizen in general) the individual cannot be thought of fruitfully except as a social and political animal. The *Politics* deals specifically with men in association. Much of our twenty-four hundred years of speculation as to the best form of government, whether ideal or contingent upon circumstances, traces back to ideas found in the *Politics.* This is not to say that Aristotle gives us universal political "truths"—for example, his views on slavery are conditioned by his era. But his classification of the forms of government; his sense of the state as a *development*, not an imposed system; and his notion that the state must have a moral aim beyond that of a mere freezing of power: all this makes him alive and pertinent today.

The serious reader (and for Aristotle no other kind is possible) can handle all of the *Ethics.* Take it slowly. You might concentrate on Books I, II, III, VI, and X. Of the *Politics* possibly the first and third of the eight books are the easiest of access.

7

AESCHYLUS (525–456/5 B.C.)

The Oresteia

(Ancient Greek tragedy is so different from the plays we are familiar with that the beginning reader will do well first to study some standard book on the subject; or to consult the relevant chapters in a history of Greek literature; or at least to read carefully the notes and introductions usually accompanying the translations. He or she might also look up the myths associated with the names of the chief personages in the recommended plays. See Suggestions for Further Reading, The Beginning.

Classic Greek drama was written in verse, usually in an elevated and formal style. It was presented in the open air at the yearly festival at Athens in honor of the god Dionysus. That means the plays were part of a religious ceremony, attended, as a civic duty, by all or most of the citizens. The plays were given as trilogies, followed by a shorter play of a comic nature, and the dramatists competed with one another for the laurel of victory. Aeschylus's Oresteia *is the only complete surviving trilogy.*

It is hard for us to visualize these ancient Greek sunlit productions. They incorporated music, dance, and choral song, and doubtless words were declaimed or chanted in a manner quite dissimilar to our modern realistic convention. As the plots were usually reworkings of famous legends, they offered no suspense; everyone knew the story in advance. Two features, among others, that seem strange to us were: the Chorus, which acted as a kind of commentary on the action; and the Messenger, who recounted offstage events, particularly if they were of a violent kind. As we approach Greek drama we must try to keep in mind that it is religious in origin and partly so in effect; and that its language and action are not in our sense "realistic.")

Though he did not "invent" Greek tragedy, Aeschylus is generally considered its earliest leading practitioner and so the ancestor of all Western tragic drama. He lived through the great days of the growth of the Athenian democracy and himself helped in its ascendancy, for he fought at Marathon and perhaps at Salamis. Born in Eleusis, near Athens, he spent most of his life in and around Athens, dying in Gela, Sicily, from the effects, says an improbable story, of a tortoise dropped by an eagle on his bald head. Of his ninety plays, seven survive.

His best surviving work is the trilogy known from its central character as the *Oresteia*. Its theme is one frequently encountered in Greek legend, family blood-guilt and its expiation. The *Agamemnon* is a play about murder, the murder of the returned hero Agamemnon by his faithless wife, Clytemnestra. The *Choephoroe* (*Libation-Bearers*) is a play about revenge, the revenge taken on Clytemnestra by Orestes, Agamemnon's son. The *Eumenides* (*Furies*) is a play about purification: the tormenting of Orestes by the Furies and his final exoneration by a tribunal of Athenian judges, plus the goddess Athena. The entire trilogy is a study in the complex operations of destiny, heredity, and pride, which produce a tragic knot untied by the advent of a higher conception of law and order.

As the word for Homer is noble so the word for Aeschylus is grand. He cannot be read as modern plays are read. His language is exalted and difficult; it struggles magnificently to express profound ideas about guilt and sin, ideas that have become part of the world of imaginative literature right up to our own day with Faulkner (59) and O'Neill (22). Aeschylus is much more akin to the author of the Book of Job than to even the best of our contemporary dramatists. He must be approached in that spirit.

SOPHOCLES (ca. 496–406 B.C.)

Oedipus Rex, Oedipus at Colonus, Antigone

Sophocles was born in what we would call a suburb of Athens, of upper-class family. He held high office; he was a constant victor in the dramatic competitions; he developed in various ways the relatively primitive techniques of Aeschylus; he lived long and, it appears, happily; and he was one of the greatest ornaments of the Periclean Age. Of his more than one hundred twenty plays we possess seven. But these suffice to place him among the few great dramatists of all time.

Formulas are treacherous. But it is not entirely untrue to say that the beginning reader may best see Aeschylus as a dramatic theologian, obsessed with God and his stern edicts. Sophocles may be seen as a dramatic artist, concerned with human suffering. Euripides may be seen as a playwright-critic, using the legends as a vehicle for ideas current in his skeptical and disillusioned era.

The three recommended plays of Sophocles are all about the same family, that of King Oedipus, but they were not written as a trilogy. The order of their composition is *Antigone, Oedipus Rex, Oedipus at Colonus.* (The last, written by a very old man of undiminished powers, was produced in 401 B.C. after Sophocles' death.) If you wish, you may read them in the order of the chronology suggested by their action: *Oedipus Rex, Oedipus at Colonus, Antigone.* Together they are often called the Oedipus Cycle or the Theban Plays.

In his *Poetics,* which you might try if you find Greek tragedy interesting, Aristotle (6) tells us that Sophocles said he portrayed people as they ought to be, Euripides portrayed them as they are. He might have added that Aeschylus portrayed people as demigods driven by single outsize passions.

Aristotle considers *Oedipus Rex* the ideal play, admiring it especially for its plot and construction. Today we might stress other qualities. There is no doubt, however, that it is the most influential Greek tragedy in existence, the one most often revived, the one most universally studied. Its basic myth, that of a man who killed his father and married his mother, suggested to Freud (77) the name for the Oedipus complex. (Max Beerbohm called the Oedipuses "a tense and peculiar family.")

After reading the *Oedipus,* you may find yourself asking two profound questions that continue to be asked down to our own day: First, Is man free or bound? Second, If the intelligence brings tragedy, to what degree is it good? Technically the effect of the play depends in large part on the masterly use of dramatic irony—the device whereby the audience is in possession of crucial facts hidden from the protagonist.

Oedipus at Colonus is a difficult play, even for the learned reader. Unlike *Oedipus Rex,* it is not well knit; its interest does not lie in its plot. Perhaps it should be approached as a kind of miracle or mystery play, a study of a man more heavily burdened with guilt and knowledge than is normal, whose life is at last vindicated and given meaning by both the gods and the city of Athens. In the end Oedipus becomes a kind of transcendent hero, like King Arthur, and also like him comes to a mysterious end.

The *Antigone* is psychologically the most complex of the three plays. It has been viewed as a study of the conflicting claims of convention and a higher law of conduct, or, differently phrased, of the state and the individual. It is also one of the many Greek plays about hubris, or excessive pride—in this case, the pride of Creon—and the ruin that attends such immoderacy of feeling. The reader may already have met this notion in Herodotus (3). Before you start the *Antigone* keep in mind that to the ancient Greeks the proper burial of the dead was a matter of overwhelming importance. Also you must accept the Greek idea (or at least Antigone's idea) that a husband or child is replaceable, a brother never.

In the Oedipus Cycle, Sophocles deals with the downfall of greatness. But he is inspired as much by the greatness as by the downfall. We might say that the special Sophoclean emotion is born of the tension resulting from his sad recognition of man's tragic fate on the one hand and his admiration for man's wondrous powers on the other.

9

EURIPIDES (ca. 484–406 B.C.)

Alcestis, Medea, Hippolytus, Trojan Women, Electra, Bacchae

Though possibly fewer than fifteen years junior to Sophocles, Euripides inherited a different Greek world, torn by intellectual doubt and civil strife. His work seems to reflect the change. In Sophocles' sense of tragedy there is a certain grave serenity; not so with Euripides.

He was born at Salamis, where the famous naval battle was fought. He appears to have led a retired, perhaps even an embittered life. One story has him living alone in a cave by the sea. Of his possibly ninety-two plays, nineteen survive, if the *Rhesus* is genuine. Though they were popular, he won the prize, according to one account, only five times to Sophocles' eighteen.

Of the three great Attic tragedians, Euripides is the most interesting in the sense that his mental world is least alien to our own. A son of the all-questioning Sophists, swayed by the irony of Socrates, he, like us, felt the uncertainty of all moral and religious values. His later career contemporary with the suicidal Peloponnesian War, he too lived in a crisis period marked by fear, pessimism, and political confusion. The development of his genius was irregular and his thought is not consistent, but we can say that his outlook was rationalistic, skeptical, and, though not in the exalted Sophoclean pattern, tragic. He would understand without difficulty certain existentialist and vanguard writers of today.

His plays are generally, though not always, marked by theatricality, even an operatic luridness; by exaggerated coincidence; by the employment of a knot-resolving "god from the machine"; by dialogue that is often debate and oration

29

rather than impassioned speech; by a mixture of tones (Is the *Alcestis* a serious or a comic play?); by unconventional, even radical ideas—the *Trojan Women* empties war of its glory, *Medea* can be taken as a feminist tract, other plays portray the gods as either delusive or unlovely; by a remarkable talent for the depiction of women—Phaedra and Medea are miracles of feminine psychology; and finally by a pervading interest, not in the relations between human beings and some supernal force, but in the weaknesses and passions of our own natures. As a psychologist and vendor of ideas, Euripides is the ancestor of Ibsen (19) and Shaw (20).

And yet he eludes formulas. His plays at times seem to be the broken record of a search for certainties that were never found. He can write realistic, even down-to-earth dialogue—but also choruses and speeches of rare beauty. Plutarch tells us that certain Athenians, taken prisoner at Syracuse, were freed because they recited so enchantingly some passages from Euripides. He seems often to be a skeptic, almost a village atheist; yet in his masterpiece, his last play, the *Bacchae,* he delves profoundly and with strange sympathy into humanity's recurrent need for irrationality, even for frenzy. Euripides is not of a piece. Perhaps therein lies part of his fascination for a time which, like ours, specializes in damaged souls.

I have suggested six plays. They are arranged in the probable order of their composition or at least representation. But many others repay study, among them *Heracles, Hecuba,* and *Andromache.*

As you read Euripides, see whether you can understand why Aristotle (6) called him "the most tragic of the poets."

10
LUCRETIUS
(dates uncertain; first half of 1st century B.C.)

Of the Nature of Things

Of Lucretius we know virtually nothing. A tradition states that he was driven mad by a love potion and that he ended his own life. This note of violence is at least not contradicted by the vein of passionate intensity running through his great and strange poem, *De Rerum Natura.*

We do not today cast our explanations of the physical and moral world into hexameters. But in classic times poetry was often the vehicle of instruction and propaganda. Lucretius's poem is such a vehicle.

His temperament was original, his thought less so. As he proudly avers, he borrowed his system from the Greek Epicurus (341–270 B.C.), who in turn derived parts of his theory from two earlier Greek thinkers, Democritus and Leucippus. The Epicurean philosophy has little in common with our modern use of the phrase. Acknowledging pleasure (or, more accurately, the absence of pain) as the highest good, it rests its ethics on the evidence of the senses. But the pleasures Epicurus recommends are those flowing from plain living and high thinking.

Denying the existence of any supernatural influence on men's lives, Epicurus holds that the world and all things in it are the consequence of the meeting and joining of refined but quite material atoms. Lucretius expounds this materialism systematically, explaining everything from optics to ethics in terms of atoms. He empties the world of God; his gods are do-nothing creatures living in the "interspaces," caring nothing about men. In effect he is an atheist. He attributes the origin and behavior of all things to the movement of the atoms composing them. Free will is saved by the idea of the "swerve" of some atoms, a break in the general determinism. To Lucretius, the soul dies with the body. He exhorts the human race to live without the fear born of superstition. *Of the Nature of Things* is pioneer rationalist propaganda.

The "atomic theory" of Lucretius was less absurd than many other early Greek explanations of the universe, but in all truth it has little resemblance to our modern atomic theory, and too much should not be made of the anticipation. On the other hand, Lucretius foreshadows much of our own thought in the fields of anthropology, sociology, and evolution. Like Euripides he would have been quite at home in our century.

As we should expect, his poem is knotty and difficult, for physics and cosmology do not translate easily into verse. It is remarkable that he should have succeeded as well as he did. While there are many opaque stretches, they are worth struggling through in order to come upon the frequent passages of intense eloquence and beauty. These flow from Lucretius's ability, unmatched until we meet Dante, to hold in his head a complete vision of things and to body it forth in concrete, sometimes unforgettable images.

In Virgil's (11) famous line, "Happy is he who knows the causes of things," the reference is probably to Lucretius: It is Lucretius's passion for knowing causes, his stubborn refusal to be fobbed off with myth and superstition, together with his uneven but powerful art, that commend him to our modern temper. No matter how wrong he was in detail, it was a titanic achievement to build a universe out of nothing but matter and space.

11

VIRGIL (70–19 B.C.)

The Aeneid

The poet called by Tennyson "wielder of the stateliest measure ever moulded by the lips of man" used that measure to celebrate Rome's high destiny, yet was no Roman but a Gaul. He was born near Mantua, situated in what was then called Cisalpine Gaul. His quiet life was marked by study in Rome and by years of contemplation and composition at his Mantuan farm and later on at his residences in Campania. His relatively brief life span may point to the fragile physique of which we have other evidence. The great Maecenas, minister of the greater Emperor Augustus, was his patron, as he was that of Virgil's friend, the poet Horace.

Labor on his masterwork occupied his entire last decade. He felt the *Aeneid* to be unfinished and, dying, ordered its destruction. This was prevented by Augustus, however, whose gesture seems odd to us in an age when heads of state are not only ignorant of literature but in some cases not even particularly literate.

Homer may be said to have begun European literature, Virgil to have begun one of its subdivisions, the literature of nationalism. The *Aeneid* was written with a deliberate purpose: to dramatize, through the manipulation of legend, the glory and destiny of that Rome which had reached its high point in Virgil's own Augustan Era. The *Aeneid* is no more an "artificial" epic than is the *Iliad*. But it is a more self-conscious one. Writing it, Virgil felt he was performing a religious and political duty. Aeneas is called "pious," by which is meant that he was not merely orthodox in religious observance but faithful to the idea of Roman supremacy. The *Aeneid's* political center of gravity may be located in the famous lines of Book VI, in which the spirit of Anchises is showing forth to his son the glorious future of Rome: "Romans, these are your arts: to bear dominion over the nations, to impose peace, to spare the conquered and subdue the proud."

Because this nationalist (but not at all chauvinist) ideal is one of the keys to Virgil's mind, the reader should be aware of it. But for us it is not the important thing. The *Aeneid* today is a story, a gallery of characters, and a work of art.

Its story is part of us. We may not have read Virgil but nonetheless a bell rings if mention is made of Dido or the death of Laocoön or the Harpies or the Trojan Horse. The personages of the *Aeneid,* particularly the unhappy Dido and the fiery Turnus, have also remained fresh for two thousand years. Its art, hard to summarize, is not always immediately felt. It is based on a delicate, almost infallible sense of what words can do when carefully, often strangely, combined and juxtaposed and subdued to a powerful rhythm. It is this that has made Virgil among the most quoted of all poets. And back of the story, the characters, the art, there vibrates Virgil's own curious sense of life's melancholy, rather than its tragedy, his famous *lacrimae rerum*. The Virgilian sadness continues to move us though the Rome he sang has long been dust.

One word of counsel: the *Iliad* (1) and the *Odyssey* (2) influenced Virgil decisively. Indeed the *Aeneid*'s first six books are a kind of Odyssey, the last six a kind of Iliad, and Homeric references are legion. But Virgil is not as open as Homer. He requires more effort of the attention, he does not have Homer's outdoor vigor, and for his master's simplicity and directness he substitutes effects of great sublety, many, though not all, lost even in the finest translation.

12
MARCUS AURELIUS (121–180)

Meditations

Marcus Aurelius Antoninus, ruler of the Roman Empire from 161 to his death, is the outstanding, perhaps indeed the only, example in Western history of Plato's (5) Philosopher-King. His reign was far from ideal, being marked by wars against the barbarian Germans, by severe economic troubles, by plague, and by the persecution of Christians. It will be remembered not because Marcus was a good emperor (though he was), but because, during the last ten years of his life, by the light of a campfire, resting by the remote Danube after a wearisome day of marching or battle, he set down in Greek his *Meditations,* addressed only to himself but by good fortune now the property of us all.

The charm, the sweetness, the melancholy, the elevation of the *Meditations* are his own. The moral doctrines are those of the popular philosophy of the time, Stoicism, as systematically expounded by the Greek slave (later freed) Epictetus (ca. 55–ca. 135). Its ethical content is roughly summed up in Epictetus's two commandments: Endure and Abstain. Stoicism passed through many modifications, but in general it preached a quiet and unmoved acceptance of circumstance. It assumed a beneficent order of Nature. Humanity's whole duty was to discover how it might live in harmony with this order, and then to do so. Stress was laid on tranquillity of mind (many of our modern inspirational nostrums are merely cheapenings of Stoicism); on service to one's fellows; and on a cosmopolitan, all-embracing social sense that is a precursor of the fully developed Christian idea of the brotherhood of man. Stoicism's watchwords are Duty, Imperturbability, Will. Its tendency is puritanical, ascetic, quietistic, sometimes even escapist. Though a philosophy peculiarly suited to a time of troubles, its influence has never ceased during almost the whole of two thousand years. It seems to call out to men irrespective of their time and place—see, for example, Thoreau (84).

We find it at its most appealing in the *Meditations*. This is an easy book to read. We seem to be eavesdropping on the soliloquy of a man almost painfully attached to virtue, with a firm sense of his responsibility, less to his empire than to the Stoic ideal of the perfect man, untouched by passion, generous by nature rather than by calculation, impervious both to ill and good fortune. Says Marcus, in one of the saddest sentences of a book shadowed throughout by melancholy, "Even in a palace life may be lived well."

Through the years the Golden Book of Marcus Aurelius, as it has been called, has been read by vast numbers of ordinary men and women. They have thought of it not as a classic but as a wellspring of consolation and inspiration. It is one of the few books that seem to have helped men and women directly and immediately to live better, to bear with greater dignity and fortitude the burden of being merely human. Aristotle we study. Marcus Aurelius we take to our hearts.

THE MIDDLE AGES

13

SAINT AUGUSTINE (354–430)

Confessions

Autobiography would seem to be the easiest of all literary forms, for what could be simpler than to talk of one's own life? Yet, though the Lifetime Reading Plan abounds in great poems and novels, it suggests only four autobiographies: those of Yeats (93) Rousseau (100), Henry Adams (102), and Saint Augustine. Of all the autobiographies ever written, perhaps the most powerful and influential is the *Confessions*.

In passing from Marcus Aurelius to Augustine we meet a deeper, if less attractive mind. The profundity of Augustine's intellect can be felt only by those willing to spend some time in the vast and obscure forest of his works, particularly his masterpiece *The City of God*. But its intensity, its obsession with God, and its tortured concern with sin and salvation can be felt by anyone who reads at least the first nine books of the *Confessions*.

This Roman citizen, born in North Africa, who became the bishop of Hippo, is probably the most effective defender the Church has had in its long history. Yet, as he tells us, he came to Catholicism only in his thirty-second year, after he had tasted the delights of the flesh (including thirteen years with a mistress who bore him a son); after he had dabbled in the heresy of Manichaeism; after he had sampled the classical doctrines of Platonism (5) and Skepticism as well as Neoplatonism. Readers of the *Confessions* will note the many influences, especially that of his revered mother Monica, that led him at last to his true vocation. The moment of his conversion in the garden, as described in the twelfth chapter of Book VIII, is one of the pivotal moments in the history of

Christianity as well as a crucial instance of the mystical experience.

There is a great deal of theology and Christian apologetics and biblical exegesis in the *Confessions,* notably in the last four books, dealing with memory, time, the nature of temptation, and the proper expounding of the Scriptures. But the power of the book is exerted even on the nonbeliever. The *Confessions* was originally written to bring men to the truth. For us it is rather a masterpiece of self-revelation, the first unsparing account of how a real man was led, step by step, from the City of Man to the City of God. To the psychologist, to the student of what William James (85) called the varieties of religious experience, it is endlessly interesting. But beyond this, it grips us because we cannot shut our ears to the terrible humanness of Augustine's voice. He is trying desperately to tell us the truth, about the events not only of his external life, but of his soul. The *Confessions* is the classic spiritual autobiography. In all our literature there is nothing quite like it.

14

DANTE ALIGHIERI (1265–1321)

The Divine Comedy

Like his era, the life of Dante was disordered, but his masterpiece is the most ordered long poem in existence. During his lifetime his native Florence, and indeed much of Italy, was divided by factional strife. In this struggle Dante, as propagandist and government official, played his part. It was not a successful part, for in 1302 he was banished. To the day of his death, almost twenty years later, he wandered through the courts and great houses of Italy, eating the bitter bread of exile.

To our modern view his emotional life seems no less unbalanced. He tells us that when he was nine he first saw the little girl, Beatrice; and then nine years later saw her again. This is the extent of his relationship with the woman who was to be the prime mover of his imagination and whom, in the last canto of the *Paradiso,* the third part of *The Divine Comedy,* he was to place beside God.

Dante called his poem a *comedy* (the adjective *divine* was added by later commentators) because it began in Hell, that is, with disaster, and ended in Heaven, that is, with happiness. To the beginning reader it at first seems almost impenetrable. To daunt us, there is first its theology, derived from the great thinker Thomas Aquinas (1224/5–1274). There is its complex system of virtues and vices, in part stemming from Aristotle (6). There is the fact that, as Dante tells us, the poem is written on four levels of meaning. There is its constant use of allegory and symbol, not a mere device with Dante, but part of the structure of his thought. And finally, the poem is stuffed with contemporary references, for Dante was one of the few great writers who constantly worked with what today we would call the materials of journalism.

And yet, despite these and many more impediments, Dante can still move the nonscholarly reader. Perhaps it is best, as T. S. Eliot (94) advises in his famous essay (see Suggestions for Further Reading), to plunge directly into the poem and to pay little or no attention to the possible symbolic meanings. Its grand design can be understood at once. This is a narrative, like Bunyan's *Pilgrim's Progress* (25), of *human* life as it is lived on earth—even though Dante has chosen to make our earthly states vivid by imagining a Hell, a Purgatory, and a Paradise. We too live partly in a state of misery, or Hell. We too are punished for our sins and may atone for them, as do the inhabitants of Purgatory. And we too, Dante fervently believed, may, by the exercise of reason—personified in Dante's guide Virgil (11)—and faith, become candidates for that state of felicity described in the *Paradiso.* Dante's moral intensity, though exercised on the life of his time and within the framework of the then dominant scholastic philosophy, breaks through to the sensitive reader of our own century. Dante is as realistic, as true to human nature, as any modern novelist—and far more unsparingly so.

Furthermore, the poem is open to us *as* a poem. The greatest poetic imaginations are not cloudy, but hard and precise. Concision and precision are of the essence of Dante's imagination. He is continually creating not merely vivid pictures, but the *only* vivid picture that will fully convey his meaning. These we can all see and feel, even in translation: Dante is a great painter. Similarly we can all sense the powerful, ordered, symmetrical structure of the poem: Dante is a great architect.

One last word. I would qualify Eliot's advice to this extent: no harm, and much good, will result from a reading of the introduction to your edition, for Dante's poem and his life and time are inextricably interwoven. Furthermore, most editions contain notes explaining the major references. A good way of trying Dante is to read a canto (there are one hundred in all) without paying any attention to the notes. Then reread it, using the notes. Do not expect to understand everything— eminent scholars are still quarreling over Dante's meanings. You will understand enough to make your reading worth the effort.

15

GEOFFREY CHAUCER (ca. 1342–1400)

The Canterbury Tales

As Dante's masterwork is called the Divine, so Chaucer's has often been called the Human Comedy. It is a fair distinction. Dante loved God; Chaucer loved human beings, including the imperfect and even sinful ones. Dante fixed his eye on those paths leading to perdition, purification, and felicity; Chaucer fixed his on the crowded highway of actual daily life. Both wrote of journeys. Dante's is a journey through three symbolic universes. But Chaucer takes thirty-odd Englishmen and Englishwomen of the fourteenth century on a real journey, on a real English road, starting at a real inn at Southwark, then just outside of London, and ending at the real town of Canterbury. Though Chaucer was greatly influenced by Dante (14), the two supreme poets of the Middle Ages could not have been more unlike in temperament.

Their careers too, parallel in some respects, turned out

differently. Like Dante, Chaucer was a civil servant. Serving under three kings he held various posts, many quite important, as economic envoy, Controller of Customs, Clerk of the King's Works, Justice of the Peace, and others. He seems to have met with one or two brief periods of disfavor, but on the whole his life was lived close to the centers of English power. He rose steadily in the world, and all the evidence suggests a successful career, marked by lively contacts with the stir and bustle of his day, and sufficiently relaxed to allow time for the composition of a great number of works in both verse and prose.

He lacks Dante's depth, bitterness, intensity, vast scholarship, and complexity of imagination. Instead he offers more ingratiating if less overwhelming talents: broad humanity, humor, a quick but tolerant eye for the weaknesses of human nature, an unmatched gift for storytelling, a musical gift of a lower order than Dante's but nonetheless superb, and most of all a certain open-air candor that makes us at once eager to claim him as a friend.

As the *Prologue* indicates, *The Canterbury Tales* was originally conceived as perhaps one hundred twenty narratives of all kinds, held together by the ingenious device of having a band of pilgrims, bound for Thomas à Becket's shrine, tell stories to while away the tedium of travel. Chaucer completed twenty-one of these, with three left unfinished or interrupted. Several are dull exercises in sermonizing and are well skipped. The *Prologue* of course must be read; it is perhaps the most delightful portrait gallery in all literature. The tales most generally admired are the ones told by the Knight, the Miller, the Prioress, the Nun's Priest, the Pardoner, the Wife of Bath (Chaucer's greatest single character, and comparable to Shakespeare's supreme achievements in comic portraiture), the Clerk, the Merchant, the Squire, and the Canon's Yeoman. I suggest you also read the various prologues, epilogues, and conversations that link the stories. Many readers prefer them to the Tales themselves.

Chaucer is a perfect yarn spinner, the founder of English realism, and an entrancing human being. He is also full of interesting information. He paints an immortal picture of Catholic medieval England, with all the warts left in, in colors as freshly and lively as though applied only yesterday. He can be read without any scholarly apparatus at all, though most editions supply a handful of notes explaining those customs and manners peculiar to his day. His book is an open book, like the *Odyssey* and unlike *The Divine Comedy*. He makes you feel that a clear-eyed man of the world has taken you by the arm to tell you about the men and women of his time—and, lo, they turn out to be oddly like the men and women of ours. There are no mysteries in Chaucer. Even when he is allegorical, he is plain and forthright.

If you are lucky enough to have an exceptional feeling for English words, you may find it quite possible to read a good deal of Chaucer in the original Middle English—at any rate the *Prologue*. But most of us need a translation, either a sound prose version (I like Lumiansky's) or the verse renderings by Coghill or Wright.

PLAYS

16

WILLIAM SHAKESPEARE (1564–1616)

Complete Works

Enjoying Shakespeare is a little like conquering Everest: much depends on the approach. Let's clear away a few common misconceptions.

1. He was a man, not a demigod. He was not "myriad-minded," even though Coleridge (92) said he was. He does not "out-top knowledge," even though Matthew Arnold said he does. He was not infallible—merely a genius, one of many the race has produced. He was also a practicing theater craftsman, a busy actor, and a shrewd, increasingly prosperous businessman. A genius may live a quite conventional life, and Shakespeare (unless you are terribly shocked at his leaving his young wife and children for some years) did so.

2. He is our greatest English poet and dramatist. But he is not always great. He often wrote too quickly, with his eye not on posterity but on a deadline. Some of his comic characters have lost all power to amuse, and it is best to admit it. His puns and wordplay are frequently tedious. He can be obscure rather than profound.

3. He is not a great original thinker. Few poets are—that is not their business. Those who seek ideas that have changed the world should not go to Shakespeare; they will be disappointed.

4. Finally, we all (including this writer) think we "know" Shakespeare, when what we probably know is merely what we are supposed to think about him. Hard though it is, we must try to clear our minds of the formulas inherited from the average high school or college English class. Approaching the plays as "classics" is less fruitful than approaching them with

the fresh expectancy with which we attend the opening performance of a new play.

This brief note therefore does not at all suggest what to look for. Even if you are not looking for anything in Shakespeare you will find something.

Read, do not study him. And of course reread him, for the simple approach I have advised will disclose only a part of a complex artist. Many men have spent almost their entire lives on Shakespeare and felt no regret.

To read all of Shakespeare is well worth, let us say, a half-year out of the ordinary three score and ten. Yet few of us possess the necessary curiosity. Judgments vary, but of the thirty-seven plays the following dozen may be recommended as minimum reading, to be done not as a block but in the course of your lifetime: *The Merchant of Venice, Romeo and Juliet, Henry IV* (Parts 1 and 2), *Hamlet, Troilus and Cressida, Measure for Measure, King Lear, Macbeth, Antony and Cleopatra, Othello, The Tempest.*

Shakespeare also wrote a sonnet sequence, some of the poems being clearly addressed to a young man, others to an unidentified "Dark Lady." Though the whole forms a kind of loose progression, the sonnets may be read singly with perfect satisfaction. Some of the more famous: numbers 18, 29, 30, 33, 55, 60, 63, 64, 65, 66, 71, 73, 94, 98, 106, 107, 116, 129, 130, 144, 146.

17
MOLIÈRE (baptized Jan. 15, 1622–1673)

Selected Plays

Molière's real name was Jean-Baptiste Poquelin. The son of a prosperous Parisian upholsterer, he received a good Jesuit education, read for the law, and at twenty-one renounced security and upholstery for the chancy and unrespectable life of the stage. His company failed in Paris. He spent many years, perhaps thirteen, knocking about in provincial inn-yards, mounting farces, learning from the ground up the business both of the theater and of human nature. In 1658 his company reestablished itself in Paris under the patronage of the brother of Louis XIV. It was successful and so was Molière, operating as actor, manager, and writer of whatever seemed called for—farces, court entertainments, comedies.

In his personal life he was less fortunate. At forty he married Armande Béjart, who may have been the illegitimate daughter of his former mistress, and, some said, his own daughter, though there is little evidence for this contention. Half his age, Armande doubled his troubles, which were complicated by overwork, illness, and the many controversies brought on by Molière's satires on affectation, religious hypocrisy, and conventional prejudices. One night, while playing the title role in his own comedy *The Imaginary Invalid,* he hemorrhaged onstage, dying soon after.

There are at least two Molières. Unhappily they are often found in the same play. The first is the play-it-for-laughs commercial hack who knows all the tricks. Molière the gagman and knockabout farce-confector would have no trouble in Hollywood today. Indeed Hollywood, though it does not know it, is still using switches on comedy situations developed or, less often, invented by Molière.

The second Molière is the strange man who turned his own sad life into comedy: his illness into *The Imaginary Invalid;* his tragic marriage into *The School for Wives;* and, I think, his own bittersweet view of his society into *The Misanthrope.*

Molière will never be a great favorite of the English-speaking world. His characters are conceived in the French classic tradition (when they are not even simpler reincarnations of the Italian commedia dell'arte). That is, they are not individuals, as Hamlet and Falstaff are, but walking and mainly talking incorporations of single passions or ideas. From our viewpoint his plays are lacking in action. Finally he has none of the richness or unexpectedness of our Shakespeare. Molière is all logic and neatness.

Yet if we are willing to accept the French classic notion of a play as a kind of organized argument, constructed in accord with the rules of rhetoric, Molière is suddenly seen to be a master. We do not have to know much about the rules he followed (or quite often broke) to enjoy his thrusts at exaggerated conduct, his constant sense of the ridiculousness of human behavior, and the curious sadness that underlies much of his most hilarious comedy. "It's a strange business, making nice honest people laugh," says Dorante in *The Critique of the School for Wives.* Molière must have found it so.

For those who do not know French he offers only moderate enjoyment. Somehow in English he sometimes sounds what he was not—simpleminded. I rather like the translations by either Frame or Wilbur. Try: *The School for Wives, Tartuffe, The Misanthrope, The Would-Be Gentleman.* There are four other equally major plays: *The Miser, Don Juan, The Imaginary Invalid,* and *The Learned Ladies.* But none of the translations of these latter that I have come across conveys fully either the elegance or the vitality of Molière.

18
JOHANN WOLFGANG VON GOETHE
(1749–1832)

Faust (especially Part 1)

Goethe is often called "the last Universal Man." He possessed the sort of nonspecialized mind that no longer exists, and the lack of which may be leading us to disaster. This colossus lived a long and superbly favored life. He loved plurally. He wrote, brilliantly or tediously, in every possible form. Creative artist, government administrator, scientific researcher, and theorist, he was fantastically versatile. He invented German literature, and then dominated it for half a century. Like his contemporary Napoleon, he was more a force of nature than a man.

Perhaps more than either he was a process. One key to Goethe is a pair of words: change (he might have said metamorphosis) and development. Although he felt both himself and nature to be wholes, his sense of himself, as well as of nature, was evolutionary. He outgrew women, ideas, experiences, only to incorporate what they had taught him into a new, larger, ever-growing Goethe. "I am like a snake," he said. "I slough my skin and start afresh." Perhaps we should speak of Goethe as we do of some great country, like the United States. At any moment he is the sum of a complex historical past and the potentialities of an incalculable future. In his lifelong emphasis on growth, change, striving, activity, and the conquest and understanding of the world Goethe was himself what we have come to call a Faustian man, typifying a major aspect of our modern Western life-feeling.

His masterpiece grew as Goethe himself did. As a small boy in his native Frankfurt he saw a puppet show based on the old folk-character Faust. From that day to a few months before his death, when he finished Part 2, *Faust* continued to develop in his mind and on his writing table. Part 1 was started in his early twenties and completed almost thirty years later. Neither part is really a play for the stage. Both are changing visions of life, written, as Goethe's own career was conceived, in many different tonalities and styles, from the obscene to the sublime.

Part 1 is the simpler and less profound of the two, and the easier of access. It is familiar to us partly because its legend has attracted so many writers and composers. The Faust-Margaret love story inspired Gounod's famous opera.

Part 1 deals with an individual soul, the seeker Faust: his intellectual disillusionments and ambitions; the temptations put in his way by the fascinating, all-denying Mephistopheles; his seduction of Margaret; and the promise of redemption through love. Part 2 deals with the "great world," not of the individual Faust but of Western humanity. It is really a kind of historical phantasmagoria, with the legendary Helen, whom we met in Homer (1), symbolizing the classical world (see 1 through 12) and Faust himself symbolizing the modern or post-Renaissance world. Heaven, Hell, and Earth are the settings of *Faust* as they are of *The Divine Comedy* (14). But Goethe is not as clear as Dante, and many of his meanings are still being quarreled over.

In translation Goethe, like Molière, is not entirely satisfactory reading. Yet some acquaintance, however superficial, must be made with this European titan who has influenced hundreds of writers, including the greatest moderns such as Thomas Mann (44).

19

HENRIK IBSEN (1828–1906)

Selected Plays

You will note that, in addition to the Greek dramatists (7, 8, 9), the Plan suggests only eight famous writers of plays, plus T. S. Eliot, better known as a nondramatic poet. Of these eight Ibsen, though by no means the greatest or most readable, has perhaps had the widest influence on the modern theater. Single-handed he destroyed the lifeless, mechanical, "well-made play" that dominated Europe when he began his life work. He turned the theater into a forum for the discussion of often disruptive ideas. He introduced a new realism. He made plays out of people rather than situations. And, being partly responsible for Shaw (20), he is the grandfather of modern social drama.

The son of a Norwegian merchant who went bankrupt in Henrik's eighth year, Ibsen passed through a difficult boyhood and youth. In his twenties he began to write poems and romantic historical dramas, but was at first no more successful as author than he was as stage manager and theater director. In 1864 he left Norway for Rome, on a traveling scholarship. For the next twenty-seven years, except for two brief visits home, he lived abroad, mainly in Germany and Italy. During this fertile period he wrote most of the plays that astounded, shocked, or delighted Europe. Mental illness clouded the last few years of his long and probably not very happy life.

There are at least three ways of looking at Ibsen.

To H. L. Mencken and many others he is no iconoclast but "a playmaker of astounding skill," a superlative craftsman without a message, whose originality consisted in taking ideas generally accepted by intelligent people and giving them a novel setting: the stage. Mencken quotes with approval Ibsen's statement: "A dramatist's business is not to answer questions, but merely to ask them."

However, to Ibsen's disciple George Bernard Shaw, the asking of questions, if they be the right ones, can itself be a revolutionary act; and the Plato (5) who recorded or created

Socrates would agree with him. Shaw sees Ibsen's theater as the means by which the nineteenth-century middle class was enabled to free itself from false ideas of goodness, from what Shaw calls "idealism." To him Ibsen is essentially a teacher, we may even say a teacher of Shavianism. Whether or not Shaw's interpretation is accurate, it does seem fair to say that Ibsen's plays, particularly those dealing with marriage, the position of women, and the worship of convention, had a decisive effect on the ideas of his generation and the succeeding one.

There is still a third Ibsen, and that is Ibsen the poet, whom in translation we can only dimly glimpse. To Norwegians his early *Peer Gynt,* written in verse, is, though not at all nationalistic, a kind of epic, an ironic-fantastic résumé of the Norwegian character. It is possible that the so-called social plays, such as *A Doll's House, Ghosts,* and *Hedda Gabler,* will soon be forgotten; and that the more difficult, imaginative, symbolic dramas (*Peer Gynt, The Master Builder, When We Dead Awaken*) will eventually be ranked among the dramatic masterpieces of the last two centuries.

The plays here recommended are arranged in their order of composition. To my mind the finest are *Peer Gynt* and *The Wild Duck,* but there is no absolute agreement on Ibsen's best work. At any rate try: *Peer Gynt, A Doll's House, Ghosts, An Enemy of the People, The Wild Duck, Hedda Gabler, The Master Builder, When We Dead Awaken.*

20

GEORGE BERNARD SHAW (1856–1950)

Selected Plays and Prefaces

For the better part of a century GBS explained and advertised himself and his intellectual wares with dazzling wit, energy, iteration, and clarity. A man who lived to be ninety-four; who probably began thinking in his cradle if not in the womb; who left behind him, in addition to a vast library of correspondence, thirty-three massive volumes of plays, prefaces, novels, economic treatises, pamphlets, literary criticism, dramatic criticism, musical criticism, and miscellaneous journalism dealing with every major preoccupation of his time and many trivial ones; and who, like all his favorite supermen, lived forward, as it were, toward an unguessable future—such a man reduces to no formula.

Except perhaps one, and it is his own: "The intellect is also a passion." Whether or not one agrees with Shaw at any point in his long mental wayfaring is less important than the solid fact that he made intellectual passion exciting, or at least modish, for hundreds of thousands, perhaps millions, of human beings. He was a ferment, a catalyst, an enzyme. He left neither system nor school. But one cannot come fresh to any half-dozen of his best plays and prefaces without having one's mind shaken, aerated, and often changed.

At the moment, the more rarefied critics tend to pass him by, or to stress his lacks: lack of any other than intellectual passion; lack of the tragic sense we find in the Greeks or in Shakespeare; lack of what we call poetry. My own opinion is that he will be recognized as a master prose writer in the plain or unadorned style; and that, merely as a nonstop influential *personality,* he will rank with Voltaire, Tolstoy, and Doctor Johnson.

It will help us, as we read Shaw, to remember a few simple facts.

First, he was Irish—or, as he put it, "I am a typical Irishman; my family came from Yorkshire." Hence he viewed English life, his immediate world, with a detachment and an irony difficult for an Englishman.

Second, he was a Fabian (antiviolent, gradualistic) Socialist who never recovered from Karl Marx (75). Hence, in his work economic knowledge, as he says, "played as important a part as the knowledge of anatomy does in the work of Michael Angelo."

Third, he had a deep faith in the capacity of human beings to rise by effort in the scale of mental evolution. His mouthpiece Don Juan in *Man and Superman* speaks for him: "I tell you that as long as I can conceive something better than myself, I cannot be easy until I am striving to bring it into existence or clearing the way for it."

Fourth, he is probably the greatest *showman* of ideas who ever lived. He is continually using all his resources of wit, paradox, clowning, humor, surprise, invective, and satire, plus a thousand stage tricks, in order to fix firmly in the reader's or playgoer's mind ideas ordinarily found in volumes of sociology, economics, politics, and philosophy that would be inaccessible to the average intelligence. He is always preaching—but from the middle of the center ring of the circus.

You will see below the titles of eleven of Shaw's forty-seven plays. (He wrote ten more than Shakespeare, a man he considered rather inferior to himself as a dramatist—but then he lived almost twice as long.) Always read the prefaces that usually accompany the plays. As prose they are masterly. As argument they are often more comprehensive and persuasive than the plays—see, for example, the astounding Preface to *Androcles and the Lion* on the prospects of Christianity. Arranged in order of publication or production, this list suggests a little of the evolution of Shaw's mind over his most fertile quarter century, from 1894 to 1923: *Arms and the Man, Candida, The Devil's Disciple, Caesar and Cleopatra, Man and Superman, Major Barbara, Androcles and the Lion, Pygmalion, Heartbreak House, Back to Methuselah, Saint Joan.*

21

ANTON CHEKHOV (1860–1904)

Uncle Vanya, Three Sisters, The Cherry Orchard

The experience of reading Chekhov's plays is never quite satisfactory, because the reader's imagination must meet a difficult challenge. The page cries out for the stage. The words demand the actor's voice. The dialogue is not tidy and explicit, as with Shaw, but more like ordinary conversation. It is marked by breaks, pauses that make their own statements, involuntary gestures, small digressions, abrupt transitions, incomplete thoughts, careless syntax. Chekhov's apparently inconsequential talk is designed to reflect the contradictions, the confusions, the frustrations hidden deep within his characters.

Chekhov has no program. A doctor by profession, he has some of the physician's requisite detachment. He does not care about changing your mind; he cares only about telling the truth about the human heart. He wants to make you feel what lies behind the daily, the ostensibly trivial. As playwright he has no option, words are his only medium. But these words he thinks of as a mere screen. His business is to reveal holes and gaps in the screen, thus allowing us glimpses of the reality it conceals.

In these respects, as in others, Chekhov contributed something new, as did Ibsen, to the art of the playwright. Since Chekhov the serious theater has never been quite the same.

The theme of the three major plays I have suggested is human wastage. His characters, the provincial intelligentsia, the petty aristocracy, the small landowners and bureaucrats of prerevolutionary Russia, are in effect functionless. Essentially they have nothing to do except to contemplate their unsatisfactory lives. They are talkers, not doers. And they sense their own weakness. They know, as Yeliena Andryeevna puts it in *Uncle Vanya,* that "things have gone wrong in this house," and we cannot but feel that the house is Czarist Russia. In *Three Sisters* Baron Toozenbach says, "The time's come: there's a terrific thundercloud advancing upon us, a mighty storm is coming to freshen us up!" (*Three Sisters* premiered in 1901.) In the same play Olga offers the vague consolation: "Our suffering may mean happiness for the people who come after us."

But we must not think of Chekhov as a leftist, much less a revolutionary. He would not have welcomed 1917. His mind was not political, only contemplative.

That contemplation is pessimistic; perhaps melancholy is a better word. Chekhov's exposure of the provincial middle class is sad rather than indignant. And even that sadness is qualified by humor; he once wrote to a friend that *The Cherry Orchard* (which to most readers seems so downbeat) was "not a drama but a comedy: in places almost a farce."

The mood of many Chekhovian characters is one many of us have felt. It is expressed by Chebutykin in *Three Sisters:* "What difference does it make?"

Yet Chekhov is no nihilist. His own life was marked by generosity, adherence to traditional moral values, and a persuasive compassion. He has no fixed or comprehensive view of life. What interested him was detection of the almost unseizable reality of human behavior. Few dramatists have done this more successfully. To his friends he would say, "Let the things that happen on the stage be as complex and yet just as simple as they are in life."

The social world of his plays is rather restricted. To perceive the full extent of his understanding of other Russian types, including the peasant, we must go to his short stories. In this field he is one of the few great names. He helped revolutionize the short story as he helped revolutionize modern drama. The Bibliography will guide you if you care to read the best of his many tales.

22

EUGENE O'NEILL (1888–1953)

Mourning Becomes Electra, The Iceman Cometh, Long Day's Journey into Night

Despite his unquestioned position as the greatest of American dramatists, the original edition of this book omitted Eugene O'Neill. At that time (1960) I did not feel that he ranked with such figures as Shaw and Ibsen. I still hold to this opinion. During the years since his death, however, it has become clear that his appeal did not die with him. His plays continue to be revived both here and abroad. He has become a classic figure, exerting an influence far transcending his historical importance as the first truly serious dramatist ever to write for the American stage.

It is interesting that O'Neill maintains and even strengthens his position despite the fact that his plays, when read, lack certain literary qualities. He is almost entirely humorless. When he essays the lyric flight, trying for elegance or beauty of language, he sounds mawkish, even naive. Worst of all, for a playwright specializing in characters who use the vernacular, he has a tin ear for dialogue. There is something not grossly but subtly wrong, for example, with the presumably low-life phrasing of the speakers in one of his finest plays, *The Iceman Cometh*.

Yet on the stage these defects, and other literary weaknesses, are hardly noticed, so powerful is his emotional thrust, so insistent the reiteration of his bleak theses. And even on the page his power forces its way through, at least in his best work.

Much of O'Neill is, or was in its day, experimental in technique: the use of masks; the fresh employment of that old standby, the soliloquy; enormously long and multidivisional dramas; the abandonment of realism in favor of an expressionism influenced by the Swedish dramatist Strindberg; the rehandling in modern terms of plots from the classical Greek drama that we have discussed under Aeschylus (7), Sophocles (8), and Euripides (9).

The most successful example of the latter is the trilogy *Mourning Becomes Electra*. The Clytemnestra-Agamemnon-Electra-Orestes story is ingeniously transferred to a New England post–Civil War setting. O'Neill, decisively influenced by the Greeks, is trying here to write pure tragedy, a dramatic mode rather foreign to the American stage tradition. Its force, however, derives less from the fatalities implicit in the plot than from a sense the reader gets that O'Neill's own conflicts are here transmuted.

This is even truer of the other two recommended plays. To my mind they are his masterpieces, both derived from intense personal experience, both dealing not with the periphery of life, but with the most agonizing questions man can ask of the cosmos.

The Iceman Cometh is about failure, not only the failure of the whisky-sodden derelicts in Harry's Bar, but the failure of perhaps all of us. It is relentless both in its stripping away of the illusions by which we live and its bitter demonstration that without them we could not live at all.

Long Day's Journey into Night is probably the most striking example in dramatic literature of a nakedly autobiographical play. Its characters are O'Neill's family, its tragedy theirs, its hopelessness his own.

O'Neill once remarked, "I am interested only in the relation between man and God." One must not take this literally, for

O'Neill did not, as did his master Aeschylus (7), have a truly metaphysical mind. But the statement points to the underlying and intense preoccupation of O'Neill's intelligence with the deepest and most permanent concerns of humankind. It is this anguished seriousness that sets him apart from every other American dramatist.

23

SAMUEL BECKETT (1906–   )

Waiting for Godot, Endgame, Krapp's Last Tape

In *Waiting for Godot* Estragon remarks to his pal Vladimir, "We always find something, eh Didi, to give us the impression we exist?" Perhaps Beckett's entire lifework is the "something" designed to give his audience and himself the impression that they exist. However absurd or painful life may be, art somehow ratifies or vindicates it. Of his own motivation he has said, "With nothing to express, no desire to express, but with the artist's need to express."

What kind of art is Beckett's? It completely ignores the traditional conventions of the stage, among them clarity. Beckett's most famous play is *Waiting for Godot.* Asked who Godot was, Beckett replied, "If I knew, I would have said so in the play." As for form, he once wrote to his younger disciple Harold Pinter, "If you insist on finding form [for my plays] I'll describe it for you. I was in hospital once. There was a man in another ward, dying of throat cancer. In the silences I could hear his screams continually. That's the only kind of form my work has." Ever since the Greeks, physical or mental action, adding up to some kind of statement or resolution of conflict, has been a staple of drama. But early in *Godot* we have:

ESTRAGON (*giving up again*): Nothing to be done.

and the curtain lines are:

VLADIMIR: Well, shall we go?
ESTRAGON: Yes, let's go.
                        They do not move.

59

Shakespeare has accustomed us to a mixture of humor and tragedy in the same play, but the dominant tone is always clear. Beckett, however, in accord with absurdist doctrine, deliberately carries this confusion of genres to almost frightening extremes. Once, directing the Berlin production of *Endgame,* he remarked that the most important line in the play was:

NELL: Nothing is funnier than unhappiness, I grant you that.

Beckett has removed himself completely from Aristotle's mimetic theory of drama. He throws out all the play's traditional furnishings, somewhat as Virginia Woolf (40) has done for the novel and minimalist painters for art. One playlet (*Come and Go*) contains only 121 words. Another, *Breath,* lasts thirty seconds.

Interpretations of Beckett have been as endless as they are ingenious, but each reader or viewer must make up his or her own mind. Perhaps mind is the wrong word, because the meaning is the play itself, to be felt rather than understood, as with music. Beckett is trying to make us share his agonized inability to answer the two darkest questions: Who are we? Why are we? All his work is an elaboration, sometimes bleak, sometimes comic, of Hamm's statement (in *Endgame*): "You're on earth, there's no cure for that!"

So far twenty-five volumes of Beckett have been published, certainly the most comprehensive treatment in all literature of the theme of negation. Yet he is no cynic; indeed he is deeply moved by human misery, and his own life (he performed nobly during the French Resistance) evinces great purity of character. His nada, unlike Hemingway's (60), is not a response to the dislocation of our time but is deeply metaphysical, a vision of life as eternally the same and eternally incomprehensible. It is interesting that a dramatist so obscure, so nightmarish, so uncompromising, and so oblivious to what we normally expect from drama should have met with worldwide acclaim. However strange his way of saying it, he must be saying something to us.

Contemporary Drama (four volumes), edited by
E. Bradlee Watson and Benfield Pressey

How to Read a Book (VI) offers some hints for the reading of
plays. Such reading involves a specialized attitude, for readers
must do their imaginative best, not only to mutely voice the
dialogue, but to direct and even act out each play. Once one
gets the hang of it, reading a good play can be a delightful and
challenging experience.

Your reading of Ibsen (19), Shaw (20), O'Neill (22), and
Beckett (23) will introduce you to these towering figures of
modern drama. But the theater of our era is so rich, so varied,
so studded with the names of men and women of talent and
even genius that it is worthwhile to make a library study of
the field, inasmuch as few of us see many plays in the course
of our lives.

The four anthologies recommended are not completely up
to date (Harold Pinter and Eugène Ionesco, for example, are
not included) but they cover a very broad field indeed. Of the
older generation, Strindberg, Barrie, Synge, and Wilde are,
among others, included. The middle generation is represented
by such names as O'Casey, T. S. Eliot, Pirandello, Odets, Saroyan, Brecht, Wilder. Coming closer to our time we meet Tennessee Williams, Arthur Miller, Lillian Hellman, William Inge.

Each volume contains a short general Foreword and each
play is preceded by a useful introduction, a skeleton list of
important biographical dates, and a bibliography.

The complete table of contents of each of the four volumes
follows:

Contemporary Drama: 15 Plays

Henrik Ibsen: *Hedda Gabler*
Oscar Wilde: *The Importance of Being Earnest*
Anton Chekhov: *Uncle Vanya*
August Strindberg: *The Dream Play*

George Bernard Shaw: *Man and Superman*
John Millington Synge: *Riders to the Sea*
Luigi Pirandello: *Henry IV*
Eugene O'Neill: *Ah, Wilderness!*
Federico García Lorca: *Blood Wedding*
T. S. Eliot: *Murder in the Cathedral*
Sean O'Casey: *Purple Dust*
Thornton Wilder: *The Skin of Our Teeth*
William Inge: *Come Back, Little Sheba*
Arthur Miller: *The Crucible*
Ketti Frings: *Look Homeward, Angel*

Contemporary Drama: 13 Plays

Henrik Ibsen: *The Wild Duck*
Anton Chekhov: *Uncle Vanya*
August Strindberg: *Miss Julie*
Federico García Lorca: *The House of Bernarda Alba*
Jean Giraudoux: *Ondine*
Bertolt Brecht: *The Caucasian Chalk Circle*
George Bernard Shaw: *The Devil's Disciple*
Sean O'Casey: *Juno and the Paycock*
Clifford Odets: *The Country Girl*
Tennessee Williams: *The Rose Tattoo*
Arthur Miller: *A View from the Bridge*
Jean-Claude Van Itallie: *American Hurrah*
Ed Bullins: *A Son, Come Home*

Contemporary Drama: 9 Plays

Eugene O'Neill: *The Hairy Ape*
Elmer L. Rice: *Street Scene*
Robert Emmet Sherwood: *Abe Lincoln in Illinois*
Sidney Howard: *The Silver Cord*
John Galsworthy: *Justice*
J. M. Barrie: *What Every Woman Knows*
W. Somerset Maugham: *The Circle*
Karel Čapek: *R.U.R.* (*Rossum's Universal Robots*)
Edmond Rostand: *Cyrano de Bergerac*

Contemporary Drama

George Bernard Shaw: *Pygmalion*
Marc Connelly: *The Green Pastures*
Thornton Wilder: *The Happy Journey to Trenton and Camden*
Noel Coward: *Ways and Means*
William Saroyan: *Hello Out There*
Jean Anouilh: *Antigone*
Tennessee Williams: *The Glass Menagerie*
Jean Giraudoux: *The Madwoman of Chaillot*
Lillian Hellman: *Another Part of the Forest*
Arthur Miller: *Death of a Salesman*
Christopher Fry: *Venus Observed*

NARRATIVES

25

JOHN BUNYAN (1628–1688)

The Pilgrim's Progress

A hundred years ago anyone who spoke of a muckraker or a worldly-wise man or Vanity Fair or the slough of despond or the valley of humiliation would have known he or she was quoting from *The Pilgrim's Progress.* For over two centuries, starting with the publication of the first part in 1678, this book was probably more widely read among English-speaking people than any other except the Bible. It cannot, of course, speak to us as powerfully today as it did to the plain, nonconformist folk of Bunyan's time, wrestling with their conviction of sin, fearful of Hell's flames, hoping devoutly for salvation. And yet, for all its revivalist theology and its faded Dissenter's devotionalism, it is still worth reading, not alone for its historical importance, but as a work of almost unconscious art.

We marvel that Christianity could have been founded by so few men, most of them obscure and unlettered. The miracle seems a little less baffling if we consider that these men may have been like John Bunyan. Recall his life: a poor tinker and ex-soldier, almost completely unschooled—indeed he tells us that at one point he had forgotten how to read and write; converted to the Puritan creed; arrested in 1660 as "a common upholder of several unlawful meetings and conventicles"; spending, except for a few weeks, the next twelve years in Bedford jail; refusing the conditions of release—"If you let me out today, I will preach again tomorrow!"; leaving behind him a wife and four children, one of them blind; spending his imprisonment in writing as well as in memorizing the Bible and John Foxe's *Book of Martyrs;* jailed again for six months in 1675, during which time he wrote the first part of *The Pilgrim's Progress*: released once more, only to become one of the most popular preachers of his time.

Written in what is now quaint English, *The Pilgrim's Progress* is a simple allegory for simple people, offering terribly simple answers to the dread question, What shall I do to be saved? It is whole cultures remote from Augustine (13) and Dante (14), whose books it in certain respects resembles. Its faith recognizes only a black-and-white ethic. It appeals to a ferocious piety (though Bunyan himself was kind and tolerant) discoverable today only in our intellectual backwoods. And its author, with his dreams and voices and visions and his skinless conscience, was, no doubt of it, a fanatic who would offer Freud a perfect field day.

But it is a remarkable book all the same. It has swayed not only millions of God-fearing plain folk, but sophisticated intellects like Shaw (20). Its prose is that of a born, surely not made, artist—muscular, hard as nails, powerful, even witty. Has a certain kind of business morality ever been more neatly described than by the comfortable Mr. By-ends? "Yet my great-grandfather was but a water-man, looking one way and rowing another; and I got most of my estate by the same occupation." And, if we cannot respond to the theology, it is hard not to respond to the strong rhythm and naked sincerity of that triumphant climax: "When the day that he must go hence was come, many accompanied him to the river side, into which as he went, he said, 'Death, where is thy sting?' and as he went down deeper he said, 'Grave, where is thy victory?' So he passed over, and all the trumpets sounded for him on the other side."

Of the writers, listed in this Plan, who had preceded him, Bunyan had read not a line. He merely quietly joined them.

26

DANIEL DEFOE (1660–1731)

Robinson Crusoe

Robinson Crusoe is one of the most famous books in the world. Its publication, however, though successful, was a minor incident in its author's crowded, singular, and not entirely unspotted life. A butcher's son, Defoe traveled widely in his youth; was once captured by Algerian pirates; went bankrupt for seventeen thousand pounds—which he later paid off; supported William of Orange in 1688; served as pamphleteer, propagandist, and secret agent under four sovereigns; changed his allegiance without ever abandoning what we would today call a liberal political position; got into trouble through his partisan writings and was stood in the pillory, from which rather unliterary vantage point, with true middle-class enterprise, he managed to sell quite a few copies of a broadside entitled "Hymn to the Pillory"; saw the inside of a prison; wrote *Robinson Crusoe,* the first of his novels, when he was almost sixty; in all composed over four hundred books and tracts, very few of which bore his name on the title page; and, according to one account, died hiding out from his creditors. He also married and engendered seven children.

Defoe was perhaps the first truly outstanding professional journalist (or hired hack, if you prefer) in England; the father of the English novel (try his *Moll Flanders,* if you haven't read it); and a master of the trick of making an invention seem so true that to most of us Robinson Crusoe (a figment, though suggested by a real episode) is a living person.

Robinson Crusoe is supposed to be a boys' book. However, like its greater cousin *Huckleberry Finn* (57), it is a boys' book only in that it satisfies perfectly those male dreams that happen to be most vivid in boyhood but continue to lead an underground life in most men until they die. Virtually every male dreams of being completely self-sufficient, as Crusoe is; of building a private kingdom of which he can be undisputed lord; of having that deliciously lonely eminence emphasized in time by the establishment of a benevolent colonial tyranny over a single slave (Friday); of accumulating wealth and power that can never be endangered or vulgarized by competition; of enjoying success through the wholesome primitive use of muscle and practical good sense, as against the effete and troublesome exercise of the intellect; of doing all this in an exotic setting quite remote from his dull daily habitat; and finally of living in a self-made Utopia without any of the puzzling responsibilities of a wife and children. (*Robinson Crusoe* and *Moby Dick* are the two great novels that manage superbly without involving more than one sex. They have never been popular with women.)

Robinson Crusoe has no plot. Its hero, though a sturdy stick, is nonetheless a stick. On reflection, the book's smug mercantile morality seems offensive. All this matters not at all against the fact that it is a perfect daydream, a systematic and detailed wish-fulfillment. Its appeal is heightened in that the most romantic experiences are related in the baldest prose. Its utter lack of fanciness makes the daydream respectable. We believe it precisely because it is not "literature."

When we were young we could see only that it was entertaining. Now, rereading it, we can perhaps see why it is also, as books go, immortal.

27

JONATHAN SWIFT (1667–1745)

*Gulliver's Travels, A Modest Proposal,
Meditations Upon a Broomstick, Resolutions
When I Come to Be Old*

Thackaray (32) once said of Swift: "So great a man he seems to me, that thinking of him is like thinking of an empire falling." Swift's mind was not comprehensive, perhaps not even very subtle. But it was extremely powerful, it was the mirror of an extraordinary temperament, and so its frustration, decay, and final extinction do suggest the tragic dimensions of which Thackaray speaks.

Swift was an Anglo-Irishman, born in Dublin and dying

there, as Dean of St. Patrick's Cathedral. Like his fellow-countryman Shaw (20), he had a genius for exposing the vices and weaknesses of his age. Like Shaw, too, he was a master of the English language, so that today his prose can be read with pleasure even though much of what he wrote about is of interest only to scholars. But here ends the parallel. Shaw's was one of the most successfully managed careers in history; Swift's one of the least. Shaw died after bestriding his world like a colossus. Swift died much as he foresaw, "like a poisoned rat in a hole."

His century is often called the Age of Reason and he was one of its chief ornaments. He *did* worship reason: *Gulliver* may be seen as a picture of the consequences of humanity's refusal to be reasonable. The irony is that this apostle of reason should also have been a man of volcanic, baffled passions; that the terrible fits of dizziness and, later, deafness from which he suffered beginning in his twentieth year led him at last to the loss of that reason he so much admired; that some enigmatic lack apparently precluded what we think of as a normal sex life; that his split allegiance (Was he an Irishman or an Englishman?) helped to unbalance him; that his semiexile in Dublin for his last thirty-two years was a permanent cross to his spirit, even though the Irish loved him as their champion. This man should have been the intellect and conscience of England. But melancholy marked him for her own; ambition denied withered him; and so his life, whose inner secrets we shall probably never know, was what the world called, and he himself called, a failure. Pointing to a blighted tree, he once remarked that he too would die first "at the top," and so he did, a ruined monument to frustration.

He left behind him a great mass of poetry and prose. Much of it is in the form of political pamphleteering, for he was in large part a journalist and propagandist. Some of it is in the form of his strange letter-diary, addressed to his ward, and known as the *Journal to Stella.*

One small part of it is a masterpiece. When first published in 1726 *Gulliver* was an instant success "from the cabinet council to the nursery." It is one of those curious works to which we may apply Lewis Mumford's sentence: "The words are for children and the meanings are for men." In fact, however, though children have always taken to their hearts at least the first two books of *Gulliver* (Lilliput and Brobdingnag), Swift wrote it with a serious purpose—"to mend the world." *Gulliver* is so rich a book as to bear many interpretations, but I think we may say that Swift wanted to hold up a mirror that would show humanity its true and often repellent face; and by doing so to force us to abandon our illusions, forswear our lies, and more nearly approach that rationality from which his Yahoos are the terrible declension.

In addition *Gulliver* is a political allegory. Its hidden references mean less to us than they did to the Londoners of 1726. The best thing is to pay no attention to the transient satire that threads it. As readers have discovered over more than two and a half centuries, there is plenty left: irony that applies to the human race wherever and whenever found; a biting humor; delightful invention; and a prose style of utmost clarity and power.

Swift's essence you will find in the last book, describing the voyage to the land of the Houyhnhnms. Here the misanthropy flows not from meanness but from an idealism broken under the buffets of fortune. Somehow, despite his ferocity, it is impossible to think of Swift as malicious. His inner contradictions are sorrowfully hinted at in the Latin epitaph he wrote for himself. In St. Patrick's Cathedral he lies at peace at last in a place "where bitter indignation can no longer lacerate his heart."

28
LAURENCE STERNE (1713–1768)

Tristram Shandy

Sterne is a rare bird, a bit gamy, and not to everyone's appetite. You may find yourself one of the many, including the most cultivated minds, who simply do not read Sterne with pleasure. But the Lifetime Reading Plan cannot well omit his book. It is original in two senses: though indebted to Cervantes (62), Rabelais (46), and Swift (27), there is nothing quite like it; and it is the origin, or at least the foreshadowing, of much great modern fiction.

Sterne was himself something of an original. Born of an unsuccessful English army officer and an Irish mother, he was, following an irregular childhood, educated at Cambridge. He took holy orders, though of neither holiness nor orderliness did he ever possess a scrap. Family connections helped him to obtain a series of livings in Yorkshire. He settled down to the light duties of a typical worldly eighteenth-century parson, punctuated by "small, quiet attentions" to various ladies; a sentimental romance, recorded in his *Letters of Yorick to Eliza;* health-seeking trips to France and Italy, one of which produced his odd little travel book, *A Sentimental Journey;* and his death of pleurisy at fifty-five. His external life has no distinction. Everything that matters in it is to be found in *Tristram Shandy,* whose first two volumes burst upon a delighted (and also shocked) world in 1760.

If you can take *Tristram Shandy* at all, the first thing you will notice is that very little happens in it. Not till the fourth of its nine books does its hero even manage to get himself born. It seems one vast digression, pointed up by blank pages, whimsical punctuation, and a dozen other typographical tricks. Second, you will note that it is a weirdly disguised story about sexuality; in a sense it is one long smoking-room yarn. Sterne's interest in sex is not frank and vigorous, like Fielding's. It is subtle, suggestive, enormously sophisticated, and some have called it sniggering. Certainly it is sly. Third, you will find a quality more highly prized by Sterne's generation than by ours. They called it sensibility or sentiment. To us it sounds like sentimentality, the exhibition of an emotion in excess of that normally required by a given situation.

Though *Tristram Shandy* seems a completely whimsical book, it is actually one of the few great novels written in accord with a psychological theory. Sterne was much influenced by John Locke's (72) *An Essay Concerning Human Understanding,* with its doctrine of reason and knowledge as derived from sensory experience. *Tristram Shandy* dramatizes this theory, and in the course of the dramatization creates half a dozen living characters: My Uncle Toby, Mr. and Mrs. Shandy, Parson Yorick, Dr. Slop, the Widow Wadman.

Tristram Shandy, unlike most novels, is not about things that happen. As its full title, *The Life and Opinions of Tristram Shandy,* suggests, it is about thought, about the inner lives of its characters. It is a true psychological novel, perhaps the first. Hence its rejection of straight-line chronology, as well as its odd punctuation, which mirrors the wayward, associative, crisscrossing paths of our minds and memories. Thus it anticipates Joyce (39), Proust (51), Mann (44), and the modern psychological novel in general, with its flashbacks, abrupt transitions, zigzags, and serious attempts to reflect the pressures of the unconscious.

Sterne is more than a genius of the odd. He is the most modern, technically creative novelist produced by his century. If *Tristram Shandy* seems strange, it is not merely because Sterne is an eccentric, though he is, and glories in so being. It is because the book is actually nearer to the realities of mental life than a conventional novel is. And this is something that takes getting used to, because we so rarely stop to look at ourselves in the acts of thinking, feeling, and remembering. Some awareness of all this may help you to enjoy Sterne's strange masterpiece.

29
HENRY FIELDING (1707–1754)

Tom Jones

Like his fiction, Fielding was open, generous-hearted, full-blooded. Some of his character as a young man is doubtless reflected in Tom Jones himself, as perhaps the adult Fielding may be seen in the wonderful portrait of Squire Allworthy.

Well connected, well favored, well educated, Fielding led the pleasantly unrestrained life of the upper-middle-class youth of his time, getting into the proper improper scrapes with girls. For some years he supported himself by writing successful, worthless plays. The best of the lot, *Tom Thumb,* was at least good enough, it is said, to make Swift (27) laugh for the second time in his life. This career as a playwright

Fielding cheerfully abandoned when the Prime Minister, Walpole, engineered a government censorship act directed primarily at him, which incidentally stultified English drama up to the advent of Shaw. Fielding then turned to the law, journalism, and novel writing, mastering each in turn. Appointed Justice of the Peace in London, he fulfilled his duties conscientiously, even brilliantly, organizing a detective force that later developed into Scotland Yard, and being generally influential in softening the harsh justice of his day. Having abused his body hopelessly, he journeyed to Lisbon in search of health and there died at the early age of forty-seven.

One episode of his vigorous, crowded life is typical. His first wife—she is the model for Sophia Western, the heroine of *Tom Jones*—he loved to distraction. Three years after her death he married her maid, and was condemned for doing so by every snob in England. He married her, however, because she was about to bear his child, and he wished to save her from disgrace. The word for Fielding is manly.

About his best novel little need be said. It lies open for your enjoyment. It has no depths to be plumbed. Its style, though a bit long-winded by our post-Hemingway standards, is transparent. The characters are lifelike and simple—we may have forgotten that in real life there actually are simple people. At one time its plot was greatly admired; Coleridge (92) foolishly declared it one of the three perfect plots in all literature, the others being those of Ben Jonson's *Alchemist* and Sophocles' *Oedipus Rex* (8). Today the intrigue, turning on Tom's true paternity and maternity, though manipulated with masterly skill, seems rather mechanical.

What we cannot help responding to are the comic genius animating the long, crowded story; the quick-moving panorama of eighteenth-century life in town and country; the colorful procession of picaresque incidents; and especially the zest for and tolerance of human nature, which, as Fielding says, was all he had to offer on his bill of fare.

Fielding elevated the novel to the high estate it has since enjoyed. His aim, he tells us, was to write comic epic poems in prose, in which the lives of recognizable men and women of all stations would be presented without fear or favor by means of an organized, controlled narrative. He once described himself as a "great, tattered bard"; and there *is* a little of Homer in him.

Among the other attractions of *Tom Jones* are the essays that precede each section. These should not be skipped. Not only do they exhibit a mind of great charm and health and sanity, but, together with the prefatory remarks to his other three fictions, they comprise the first reasoned esthetic of the English novel.

30
JANE AUSTEN (1775–1817)

Pride and Prejudice, Emma

Jane Austen is the first woman writer so far suggested by the Plan. By common consent she is what Virginia Woolf (40) calls her: "the most perfect artist among women." It can also be said that the six novels she finished have always been more keenly relished by women than by men; that her genius for small-scale but deadly accurate domestic comedy is feminine rather than masculine; and finally that her central theme—the search for a husband—has for some time been one of the major preoccupations of women. Supremely feminine (say male critics) is the circumstance that she lived right through all of the Napoleonic wars without mentioning them in her work.

Miss Austen, as it somehow seems proper to call her, was the daughter of a rural rector and one of a large family. Though her own circumstances were always modest, she was well connected with the middling-rich landed gentry of southern England, and it is their traits and worldly interests that she reflects in her novels. Though there is some evidence of a frustrated love affair, she never married. During all the years of her brief life she lived quietly with her family, writing her novels in the midst of the domestic come-and-go, for years on end not even boasting a room of her own. Her social life was pleasant, active, genteelly restricted. While her genius generally is a sufficiently bewildering phenomenon, it is particularly hard to figure out how she could have known so much about human life when she saw so little of it.

Among other qualities, Jane Austen had one many modern novelists lack: she knew her own mind. Her novels are not (like those, let us say, of Thomas Wolfe) experiments in self-discovery and self-education. She knew precisely what interested her—"those little matters," as Emma puts it, "on which the daily happiness of private life depends." She knew that the private lives of her special world turned not on high ideals, intense ambitions, or tragic despairs, but mainly on money, marriage (sometimes but not always complicated by love), and the preservation of a comfortable division between social classes. The activities of these limited people she viewed as a comedy, more or less as a highly intelligent, observant, articulate maiden aunt might view the goings-on of a large family. Jane Austen is sensible, rational in the eighteenth-century manner, ironical, humorous. She would think little of philosophers and perhaps not much of poets.

What gives Miss Austen her high rank, despite her limited subject matter, is the exquisite rightness of her art, the graceful neat forms of her stories, the matchless epigrammatic phrasing of her unremitting wit. She has little passion, no mystery, and she prefers to avert her face in a well-bred way from the tragedy that lies on the other side of the comedy she understands so well. She was born to delight readers, not to shake their souls.

There is no agreement as to her best book. *Pride and Prejudice* has perhaps had the most readers, but *Emma*, I think, is a more searching as well as a gayer story; so I have suggested these two. If you have read them, try *Mansfield Park* or *Persuasion* or *Sense and Sensibility.* They are all pure Miss Austen, a writer so charming that it seems clumsy to call her a classic.

31

EMILY BRONTË (1818–1848)

Wuthering Heights

It is unsettling to pass from Jane Austen to Emily Brontë. They do not belong to the same world. They do not even seem to belong to the same sex. All they have in common is that they were both parsons' daughters. One is a master of perfectly controlled domestic comedy. The other is a wild demiurge of undomesticated tragedy. One excludes passion, the other is all passion. Jane Austen knew her limited, highly civilized world thoroughly; her novels grew out of needle-sharp observation as well as native power of mind. Emily Brontë knew the Yorkshire moors, her own family, and little else, and we can hardly say what her one novel grew out of.

The three Brontë sisters and their brother, Branwell, a kind of forerunner of the Beat Generation, lived most of their short lives (Emily died of tuberculosis at thirty) in their father's parsonage at Haworth in the North Riding of Yorkshire. For entertainment they depended largely on their own minds plus the stories they heard about the often violent behavior of the semiprimitive countryfolk of the neighborhood. None of the novels produced by the three sisters exhibits that solid acquaintance with real life that we feel at once in Fielding (29). In their childhood and youth the Brontës invented imaginary kingdoms of extraordinary complication. Over the years they recorded the history and characters of these fantastic countries, playing with their literary fancies as other children play with toys. Something of this daydream atmosphere is retained in *Wuthering Heights.* But the daydream has become a nightmare.

In many respects *Wuthering Heights* is an absurd book. Its plot, turning on the devilish Heathcliff's revenge on all those who stood in the way of his passion for Catherine Earnshaw, is sheer melodrama. Its story-within-a-story method of narration is confusing. Its characters use a language unconnected with normal speech. And these characters, except for Heathcliff and Catherine, are drawn with no special skill.

And yet somehow people have found the book gripping. Not as a work of art, perhaps, but as a dream is gripping. Its primary quality is intensity. Despite all the old-fashioned machinery of the intrigue, we succumb to this intensity, or at least are made uneasy by it.

Emily Brontë is an original. She had, it is true, read a few of the romantic poets and romancers of her time, but *Wuthering Heights* owes little to them. It is also true that she may have received some real-life stimulus, when composing her novel, from the crazy love affair through which Branwell was passing at the time. But at bottom the origins of this strange book are untraceable. It was spewed up out of a volcanic, untrained, uncritical, but marvelous imagination. It had no true forebears. It has had no true successors.

32

WILLIAM MAKEPEACE THACKERAY (1811–1863)

Vanity Fair

Thackeray was a broken-nosed giant of a man, standing six feet four, yet without giving the impression of strength. Unlike Dickens, he was educated as a gentleman. His novels have a sophistication Dickens's lack, though they are greatly inferior in vitality.

In 1833 Thackeray lost virtually his entire inheritance of twenty thousand pounds. Despite his natural bent for writing, were it not for this misfortune he might never have been forced into the business of grinding out novels and essays to support his family. In 1840 his wife, following the birth of their child, lost her reason, and never regained it. (There's something gruesome about the fact that she survived her husband by thirty-one years.) This tragedy contributed to the melancholy suffusing Thackeray's work, and also to his idealization of women, perhaps a mechanism by which he bought off the guilt feelings his wife's insanity would naturally arouse in him.

Thackeray might have been happier among the elegant

rakes of the preceding century. But he did not have the temperament to flout his time as Emily Brontë did. She could do so because she lived outside the great world. Thackeray was very much in it, and so are his novels.

He seems to have given the Victorians just what they wanted, a mixture that both soothed and stimulated. His best book, *Vanity Fair* (the phrase is from Bunyan [25]), is really concerned with the rise, fall, and partial rise again of a high-grade whore. At no point, however, does Thackeray make this explicit; he is a master at saving appearances. Furthermore he is careful to present in his dimwitted Amelia the standard picture of the ideal Victorian female, and to pay his respects at regular intervals to those domestic virtues Queen Victoria had substituted for sterner ones.

But *Vanity Fair* rides two horses at the same time. Even while preserving an atmosphere of respectability and senti-mentalism, it is delicately exposing human nature in its weakness, egotism, capacity for self-delusion, and mean genius for compromise. In their secret hearts his readers knew that their England, like that of the Napoleonic period Thackeray was depicting, was a Vanity Fair, with much about it that was ignoble and canting. Thackeray appealed to their critical intelligence and yet at the same time managed to support their conventional prejudices.

In *Vanity Fair* the contradiction is covered over by his art, which is a kind of sleight of hand. How well, how gracefully he tells his story and manipulates what he calls his puppets! How pleasantly conversational is his tone! How easy to take is his irony, that of the tolerant, worldly-wise clubman—and how flattering to our own picture of ourselves as precisely such a charming and superior raconteur! And so, though our conventional prejudices are quite different from those of the Victorians, though our novels are frank about sex while Thackeray is disingenuous, nevertheless we can still enjoy *Vanity Fair.*

We can enjoy the panoramic picture of high life in England and on the Continent around the time of Waterloo. We can enjoy the well-controlled plot. But mainly we can still enjoy the perfect symbol of Vanity Fair—Becky Sharp. Becky is of course the ancestress of all the beautiful, immoral female adventuresses (Scarlett O'Hara, for instance) who have since enraptured readers. Because of Becky Sharp, Thackeray's masterpiece will never completely fade. She resolves one of the simpler contradictions in our human nature. For men will always (if possible) marry good women and secretly admire bad ones. And women, knowing that one of their jobs is to keep the race going, will always come out strongly for morality, and tend to have a furtive feeling that somehow immorality seems darned attractive. Thackeray, who had little depth but much worldly wisdom, understood this division in our nature and through Becky Sharp exploited it perfectly.

33

CHARLES DICKENS (1812–1870)

One or more of the following: *Pickwick Papers, David Copperfield, Bleak House, Great Expectations, Hard Times, Our Mutual Friend, Little Dorrit*

The commentaries you have so far been reading average perhaps eight hundred words. In writing about Dickens the most economical way to use about fifty or so of those words might be as follows: The Artful Dodger, Fagin, Dick Swiveller, Flora Finching, Sairey Gamp, Mr. Micawber, Sam Weller, Uriah Heep, Mr. Dick, Bella Wilfer, Joe Gargery, Miss Havisham, Pumblechook, Wemmick, Bumble, Pecksniff, Mrs. Nickleby, The Crummleses, Quilp, Podsnap, Toots, Rosa Dartle, Chadband, Miss Flite, Inspector Bucket, the Tite Barnacles, Mme. Defarge, the Veneerings. As soon as a Dickens reader recalls any of these names a mental curtain goes up and he sees and hears living, talking human beings.

With Tolstoy (68) Dickens is perhaps one of the two novelists who have been accepted by the whole world—and Dickens with the greater joy. Santayana (87), after listing all of Dickens's defects, such as his insensibility to religion, science, politics, and art, concludes that he is "one of the best friends mankind has ever had." That is true. And possibly just because

Dickens has been so overwhelmingly popular, it is only in recent years that he has been assessed, not as a beloved household fixture, but as a novelist almost of the stature of Dostoyevsky (67), with whose passionate, troubled imagination he has much in common.

I assume that in your youth you read at least *David Copperfield* and were probably forced to read *A Tale of Two Cities,* one of his worst novels. When rereading him, I suggest you consider the following:

1. Dickens, though children love him, is not a writer only for children or the immature. He is enormously easy to read, yet is a serious artist. He is serious, even though one of his main methods of exposing life is that of high (or low) comedy. He is more than a creator of funny eccentrics. For example, see whether you can detect his constant and powerful use of symbolism, almost in the modern manner; the dust heaps in *Our Mutual Friend* furnish a good illustration.

2. Whatever the sentimentality in Dickens may have meant to his time, it is hogwash to us. An understanding of him as a whole will only be blocked if we try to be moved by his mechanical pathos, or indeed pay more than cursory attention to it. Everyone remembers Oscar Wilde's "One must have a heart of stone to read the death of little Nell without laughing."

3. If Dickens's characters are "caricatures," as some think, why do they stick in the mind and continue to move us so strongly?

4. Dickens was a passionate, unhappy man, who apparently never recovered from his miserable childhood (how many waifs and strays there are in his books!) and who failed signally as husband and father. His passion and unhappiness are subtly reflected in his novels, as is his sense of guilt. Thus as he aged his books grew in depth. Compare the lightheartedness in *Pickwick* (and yet there are those Fleet prison scenes) with the sense of suffering in *Little Dorrit* or the dark, brooding atmosphere of *The Mystery of Edwin Drood,* left unfinished at his death. The notion of Dickens as a kind of jolly literary Kriss Kringle has stopped many readers from seeing all there is in him.

5. If Dickens is merely a "popular" novelist, why is he still

read, whereas Scott, who was just as popular in his day, is not?

I am merely hinting that, as with Shakespeare, it is best to abandon most of the notions derived from our childhood and high school experience with Dickens. There's more in him than met the Victorian eye. It is there for us to find.

34

GEORGE ELIOT (1819–1880)

The Mill on the Floss, Middlemarch

It may interest only historians of literature, but there does exist a kind of shadowy stock exchange on which the reputations of established writers fluctuate, though not wildly. During the last forty years or so the stock of Shaw, Dewey, and Wordsworth may have slipped a few points. That of O'Neill, Forster, Kafka, Donne, Boswell, and Tocqueville has probably risen. With George Eliot the rise has been marked. In large part this is due to the advocacy of the formidable English critic F. R. Leavis as well as that of other scholars.

The Common Reader (the phrase comes from Virginia Woolf)—recalling the high school infliction of *Silas Marner,* or possibly merely intimidated by the memory of the author's countenance, so suggestive of a sorrowful, though brainy, horse—still shies away from her. George Eliot is one of many writers handicapped by the existence of photographers and portrait painters.

In many ways, however, she is a most interesting figure. Born Mary Ann Evans, of a middle-class commercial family in Warwickshire (her father was a carpenter who rose to be estate agent), she early evidenced the passion for learning that was to mark her career. In her teens she was deeply and narrowly pious, but wide reading, plus conversations with minds less evangelically committed, soon stripped her of dogmatic faith. Her rejection of a conventional God and of Immortality was, however, balanced by her devotion to Duty, an abstraction that seems to have taken on for her some of the attributes of the Deity.

After her father's death she moved to London, engaging successfully in highly intellectual journalism and meeting some of the best minds of her time, including Herbert Spencer and John Stuart Mill (74). In 1854 she decided the shape of her life. She formed a permanent, illegitimate but not covert connection with the learned journalist and biographer George Henry Lewes. Lewes's wife had already had two children by another man (ah, those proper Victorians), was mentally unbalanced, and was not living with Lewes at the time. The relationship between Eliot and Lewes, lasting till Lewes's death in 1878, was both happy and eminently respectable. A year and a half after Lewes died, Eliot married an American banker, John W. Cross, she being sixty to his forty. Obviously a strong-minded lady.

The strength of her mind is apparent not only in her courageous, laborious life but in her novels. To us they may seem rather prosy, supersaturated with reflection and moralizing, and, especially in *Romola,* smelling somewhat of the lamp. Yet they quietly blazed wide trails without which the modern novel would have been impeded in its evolution. D. H. Lawrence (41) summed it up: "It was really George Eliot who started it all. It was she who started putting action inside." Perhaps in this respect Sterne (28) preceded her, but the eccentricity of *Tristram Shandy* put it outside the mainstream of English fiction, whereas George Eliot navigated its very center. She depicted the interior life of human beings, and particularly their moral stresses and strains, in a way then quite new to fiction. She also deliberately departed from other conventions such as the Dickensian happy ending and the standardized conception of romance. Finally, she poured into her stories something few previous novelists had possessed— the resources of a first-class *intellect.* She included *ideas* in her view of life. She even dared to portray intellectuals—a commonplace proceeding since Joyce but one not to be found in Jane Austen or Fielding or Dickens.

If you are to read only one George Eliot novel, I suggest *The Mill on the Floss.* Its partly autobiographical early chapters recreate the special atmosphere of childhood with an insight, tenderness, and charm unsurpassed until we reach *Huckleberry Finn* (57). The minor characters, particularly

Aunts Glegg and Pullet, are so solidly conceived that the passing of the society in which they are rooted has not diminished their vitality. The struggle of poor Maggie to express her genius for love in a world that is too much for her is still poignant. And finally *The Mill on the Floss,* like all Eliot's fiction, is suffused with a moral seriousness neither prissy nor narrow, but rather the effluence of a large, powerful, pondering, humane mind. In current novels such moral seriousness is rarely found. But a few hours with George Eliot may serve to suggest that, for all her didacticism, this novel must always be one of the staples of major fiction.

Middlemarch is today considered not only her masterpiece but one centrally located in the tradition of the English novel. In an essay written as long ago as 1919 Virginia Woolf (40) called it "one of the few English novels written for grown-up people." In accord with the taste of its period it is intricately, even densely, plotted, tracing the careers of several pairs of lovers and spouses. One of its themes turns on the political and social controversy preceding the passage in 1832 of the first Reform Bill. We are more likely to respond to the broad picture of provincial society displayed on all levels, as well as to the sexual and intellectual frustrations of its heroine, Dorothea Brooke. As a study in unhappy marriage it made Victorian readers uncomfortable, and so thorough and compassionate is its psychology that it still moves us today.

Each great novel requires its own reading tempo. This one must be read slowly. It does not march. It unfolds.

35

LEWIS CARROLL   (1832–1898)

Alice's Adventures in Wonderland, Through the Looking-Glass

Some may think Lewis Carroll has strayed into this rather formidable list through some error. But he belongs here, for he proved, doubtless not quite knowing what he was doing, that the world of nonsense may have strange and complex relations with the world of sense. I do not include him because he is a juvenile classic, for in that case we should also have Grimm and Andersen and Collodi and E. B. White and a dozen others. I include him because he continues to hold as much interest for grown-ups as for children.

In fact he is more alive today than he was in the sixties and seventies of the last century, when the two *Alice* books were published. He continues to fascinate not only ordinary men and women of all countries and races, but the most sophisticated intellects: critics such as Edmund Wilson, W. H. Auden, Virginia Woolf (40); logicians and scientists such as Whitehead (III, IV), Bertrand Russell, and Eddington; and philosophers, semanticists, and psychoanalysts by the score.

His real name was Charles Lutwidge Dodgson (pronounced Dodson). The son of a rector, he had seven sisters, a circumstance that may in part account for his seemingly arrested masculinity. From age nineteen to his death he passed his life at Christ Church, Oxford, as student, mathematics master, and ordained dean. He remained, as far as we know, chaste. His life was proper, pleasant, and donnish, marked by fussy little academic controversies, many hobbies (he was a first-rate pioneer photographer and invented something very much like Scotch Tape), and the one passion of his life, an apparently innocent attraction to little girls.

He was a dull teacher, a mediocre mathematician, but a rather exceptional student of Aristotelian (6) logic—defective syllogisms are among the many slyly hidden features of *Alice*. A queer chap on the whole, kind, testy at times, prissy, shy (he even hid his hands continually within a pair of gray-and-black gloves), with a mind that seems to be quite conventional, but which in his letters and diaries flashes forth from time to time with some startling insight that it is hard not to call Freudian or Einsteinian.

Doubtless, like many Victorians, he was an internally divided man, and some of these divisions and tensions can be traced by the careful and curious reader. In *Alice* four worlds meet, worlds that he knew either consciously or intuitively. They are the worlds of childhood, dream, nonsense, and logic. They partly fuse, drift in and out of each other, undergo mutual metamorphoses. Their strange interaction gives *Alice* its complexity and, more important, its disturbing reality. The adult reader continues to delight in its fanciful humor but feels also that this is more than a child's book, that it touches again and again on half-lit areas of consciousness.

Some years ago I wrote an essay on Lewis Carroll, from which I extract this sentence: "What gives the *Alice* books their varying but permanent appeal is the strange mixture in them of this deep passion for children and the child's world, with an equally deep and less conscious passion for exploring the dream world, even the nightmare world, filled with guilts and fears, which is a major part of the child's life, and therefore a major part of our grown-up life."

36

THOMAS HARDY (1840–1928)

The Mayor of Casterbridge

Thomas Hardy came of Dorset stock and lived the larger part of his life just outside Dorchester. The beautiful, history-freighted, and rather desolate countryside around Dorchester (Hardy calls it Wessex) is in a way the main character in his novels. His formal education—he was the son of a builder—lasted only from his eighth to his sixteenth year. He was then apprenticed to a Dorchester, and later to a London, architect. At twenty-seven he started what turned out to be a quarter-century of increasingly successful novel writing. The indignation aroused by supposedly shocking situations and passages in *Jude the Obscure* (1895) made the sensitive Hardy turn back to his first love, poetry. At his death he had written over a thousand poems, not including his gigantic cosmic panorama of the Napoleonic wars, *The Dynasts*. Many rate his verse above his novels. Certainly he is one of the two dozen or so English poets you may wish to read most closely in the Auden and Pearson anthology (97).

It may be some time before the cycle of taste returns Hardy to favor, just as it has brought back Dante, Conrad, Stendhal, Melville, and Henry James. This Plan, however, is not designed to take more than casual account of fashion. It deals mainly with writers of generally acknowledged long-term influence and interest. Among these Hardy will doubtless occupy a secondary rank. But not a minor one.

He died at eighty-eight. Just as his life linked two centuries, so his work acts as a kind of bridge between Victorian and modern fiction. Bravely (for their time) his novels defied many of the sexual, religious, and philosophical taboos to which even so independent a mind as George Eliot's on occasion succumbed. Hardy, influenced by Darwin and by a generally mechanical-determinist nineteenth-century view of the universe, dared to show man as the sport of Nature. His view is sometimes bleak, sometimes merely sorrowful; and it proceeds not only from theory, but from the bias of his own brooding temperament. His humor and his remarkable sensitivity to the magic of landscape and weather prevent his novels from being merely depressing. But if you find modern fiction on the whole uncheerful, that is partly because Hardy pioneered the campaign against the unrealistic optimism of some of his contemporaries.

The Hardy novels most generally admired are *The Return of the Native, Tess of the D'Urbervilles, Jude the Obscure,* and the one suggested here. In *The Mayor of Casterbridge* I find in balance the most striking elements of Hardy's art: a complex plot, which despite some concessions to melodrama, such as the secret document, is powerfully constructed; that sense of place and of the past that gives his work such deep-rooted solidity; the sympathetic portrayal of rustic character, often compared to Shakespeare's; the ability to work out with relentless elaboration a succession of tragic fates; and finally his special atmosphere of ruminative compassion.

The opening scenes, in which a man auctions off his wife, are extraordinary in their capacity to catch our interest. That interest is sustained, page after deliberate page, as we watch Michael Henchard, "the self-alienated man," devising his own self-destruction and expiating his guilt.

The English critic Desmond MacCarthy, speaking of Hardy, says that "it is the function of tragic literature to dignify sorrow and disaster." By this criterion the creator of *The*

Mayor of Casterbridge, for all his faults of style and taste, is a true master of tragedy.

37

JOSEPH CONRAD (1857–1924)

Nostromo

The same year, 1895, in which Thomas Hardy gave up novel writing saw the publication of Joseph Conrad's first book, *Almayer's Folly.* The traditional English novel—a large, loose, free-flowing narrative, depending largely on external action and easily grasped characters—has begun to die. A new kind of fiction—original in form, full of technical devices, its tensions flowing from the exploration of mental life—is being born. Sterne, Austen, George Eliot, and Hardy had all helped to clear its path. But it is really Conrad who announces its themes and methods. At this point in our reading we will feel a greater richness if we see Conrad as helping to make possible our understanding of Henry James, D. H. Lawrence, Joyce, Mann, Proust, Faulkner, and others, such as André Gide, not included in the Plan.

Strangeness, somberness, nobility: these mark Conrad's career. He repels affection, he compels admiration. Born a Pole, of a family tragically dedicated to the desperate cause of Polish freedom, he was left an orphan at twelve. At seventeen he turned westward "as a man might get into a dream." Without ever forgetting his aristocratic Polish heritage, he committed himself to a new world. Some years of curious, almost cloak-and-dagger adventure followed, during which, for instance, he smuggled arms for the Carlist cause in Spain. Then, adopting the life of a seaman and an Englishman, he spent twenty years in the British Merchant Service, rising to the rank of master. He pursued his vocation on most of the seas of the world and particularly in the fabled Far East, the setting of many of his stories. At last came the fateful decision which had doubtless been incubating in his mind for years.

With a certain reluctance he abandoned the sea and, now a mature man, using a language not his own, and interpreting the world as a Continental writer would, this Polish sailor in the end became (this is my own opinion, though shared by many others) one of the half-dozen greatest novelists to use our magnificent tongue.

For years, stoically suffering neglect and, what is worse, misunderstanding, Conrad toiled at his desk. He tested his craft by a set of standards unfamiliar to the Victorians. He sought the perfect *form* for each of his stories. He searched human character in depth, fearless of what he might find there. He sought out wonderfully suggestive symbols (such as the silver mine in *Nostromo*) to mirror large areas of emotion. Just as Flaubert (50) did, he consciously forged a style suited to his special view of human nature under special conditions of moral stress. He thought of himself as an artist fiercely dedicated to his calling. He had no friendly relation to his public as Dickens and Thackeray had. His relation was to the vision within himself.

Nostromo is not an easy novel to read and it is best to take it slowly. It does not tell itself, as *Tom Jones* seems to. It uncoils, retraces its steps, changes its angle of attack. Into it Conrad put his most anxious effort, and if he has a masterpiece this is probably it.

But before we read *Nostromo* it is best to clear our minds of some notions about Conrad still entertained by many.

First, he is not a writer of "sea stories," much less of adventure stories. He is a psychological novelist who happens to be exploiting material he knew intimately.

Second, though he wrote many tales of the Far East, he is not an "exotic" novelist. Local color is there, of course, laid on with a painter's eye, but again this is subordinate to his interest in the roiled depths of the human heart.

Third, he is not, except superficially, a "romantic." The tests of fidelity, fortitude, and understanding to which he submits his characters are ruthlessly true to the human condition as seen by a most unsentimental eye. Conrad does not flee or evade, nor, despite his sense that life itself is a kind of dream, does he take refuge in dreams. He is far more realistic than a Sinclair Lewis.

Critics always quote one sentence from his famous Preface to *The Nigger of the Narcissus.* I will quote it too. But we must understand what Conrad means by the word *see.* He is not talking like an impressionist painter. He means the kind of seeing that has the depth, clarity, and often agony of a vision, visible only when the mind and the imagination are at full tension. Once we grasp this, the sentence may stand as a shorthand summary of Conrad's ideal relationship to the ideal reader: "My task which I am trying to achieve is, by the power of the written word, to make you hear, to make you feel—it is, above all, to make you *see.* That—and no more, and it is everything."

For additional reading in Conrad I would suggest three long short stories: "Heart of Darkness," "The End of the Tether," "Youth."

38

E. M. FORSTER (1879–1970)

A Passage to India

Compared with a Faulkner or a Hemingway, E. M. Forster has made little noise in the world. He wrote only five important novels, none of them radiating a portentous air. Of these, four are pre–First World War. The fifth, *A Passage to India,* was published in 1924. Only this title has attracted many readers (although, together with *A Room with a View,* it has become familiar through film versions). Why, then, is Forster included in our short, highly debatable list of twentieth-century novelists?

One reason is that he is considered among the finest of them by the most perceptive critics. Finest, not greatest. The latter adjective somehow seems inappropriate to Forster; he would have rejected it himself. The second reason is that, though his output is small and the publication dates seem remote, it is rich in import and as modern as you wish.

Forster's quiet power of survival springs from his special gift for treating crucial problems in human relations in a style showing not even a chemical trace of journalism, a style marked by grace, delicacy, and a pervasive sense of comedy. Comedy rather than satire. Except for a generally liberal viewpoint (which he was quite capable of mocking) he was an uncommitted writer. His values are those of civilization— not Anglo-Saxon civilization or even European civilization, but a kind of timeless civilization of the heart unlinked to any special group or creed.

In *A Passage to India* there are no heroes or villains. The Hindus, the Moslems, the English—they are all at times "right," at times "wrong." Each character, even those the author dislikes, has a certain dignity; each character, even those the author admires, has a certain absurdity. But one quality they all share: they are incapable of perfect communication. This strange and wonderful book (see whether the worn adjective wonderful does not properly apply to the scene in the Marabar Caves) is not about the claims of Indian nationalism; nor about the obtuseness of English imperialism; nor about the appeal of Hindu mysticism. All three themes are involved. But if their involvement were the book, *A Passage to India* would now, since the liberation and partition of that subcontinent, be unreadable. This novel is about separateness, about the reverse of Donne's sentence, for every man is also an island unto himself. It is about the barriers we or Fate or God throw up and that isolate us one from another. It is about that permanent tragic condition in human intercourse arising from poor connections.

If you have read *A Passage to India*, reread it. If you have reread it, try Forster's other major novel, *Howards End*. Many consider it his masterpiece.

JAMES JOYCE (1882–1941)

Ulysses

With *Ulysses* we at last reach a novel that seems impenetrable. It is best to admit that this mountain cannot be scaled with a single leap. Still, it is scaleable; and from the top you are granted a view of incomparable richness.

Here are five simple statements. They will not help you to enjoy or understand *Ulysses.* I list them merely to remove from your mind any notion that this book is a huge joke, or a huge obscenity, or the work of a demented genius, or the altar of a cult. Here is what a large majority of intelligent critics and readers have come to believe about *Ulysses* since its publication in 1922.

1. It is probably the most completely *organized,* thought-out work of literature since *The Divine Comedy.*

2. It is the most *influential* novel (call it that for lack of a better term) published in our century. The influence is indirect—through other writers.

3. It is one of the most *original* works of imagination in the language. It broke not one trail, but hundreds.

4. There is some disagreement here, but the prevailing view is that it is not "decadent" or "immoral" or "pessimistic." Like the work of most of the supreme artists listed in the Plan, it proposes a vision of life as seen by a powerful mind that has risen above the partial, the sentimental, and the self-defensive.

5. Unlike its original, the *Odyssey* (2), it is not an open book. It yields its secrets only to those willing to work, just as Beethoven's last quartets reveal new riches the longer they are studied.

These statements made, I have three suggestions for the reader:

1. Read Joyce's *A Portrait of the Artist as a Young Man.* This is fairly straightforward, as compared with its greater sequel. It will introduce you to Stephen Dedalus, who is Joyce; and to Joyce's Dublin, the scene of both novels.

2. In this one case, read a good commentary *first.* The best

short one, I think, is by Edmund Wilson, the best long ones by Stuart Gilbert and Anthony Burgess.

3. Even then *Ulysses* will be tough going. Don't try to understand every reference, broken phrase, shade of meaning, allusion to something still to come or buried in pages you've already read. Get what you can. Then put the book aside and try it a year later.

As you read it, try to keep in mind some of Joyce's purposes:

1. To trace, as completely as possible, the thoughts and doings of a number of Dubliners during the day and night of June 16, 1904.

2. To trace, virtually completely, the thoughts and doings of two of them: Stephen Dedalus, the now classic type of the modern intellectual, and his spiritual father, the more or less average man, Leopold Bloom.

3. To give his book a form paralleling (not always obviously) the events and characters of the *Odyssey* of Homer. Thus Stephen is Telemachus, Bloom Odysseus (Ulysses), Molly an unfaithful Penelope, Bella Cohen Circe.

4. To invent or develop whatever new techniques were needed for his monumental task. These included, among dozens, interior monologue, stream of consciousness, parody, dream and nightmare sequences, puns, word coinages, unconventional punctuation or none at all, and so forth. Ordinary novelists try to satisfy us with a selection from or summary of their characters' thoughts. Joyce gives you the thoughts themselves, in all their streamy, dreamy, formless flow.

Even the attempt to read *Ulysses* can be a great adventure. Good fortune to you.

The best edition to use is the 1986 Vintage Books (Random House) paperback, described as "The corrected text edited by Hans Walter Gabler with Wolfhard Steppe and Claus Melchior."

VIRGINIA WOOLF (1882–1941)

*Mrs. Dalloway, To the Lighthouse,
Orlando, The Waves*

Three names among the brilliant but over-publicized Bloomsbury group have not only survived but grown more impressive with the passage of time: the economist John Maynard
Keynes and the novelists E. M. Forster and Virginia Woolf.
Long before her death in 1941 Woolf had already begun to
influence decisively the course of the English novel. That
influence has continued to expand. We can legitimately claim
that, along with Conrad, Henry James, Proust, and Joyce
(whom she did not admire), she is truly seminal.

To put it in formula terms, she demonstrated that the
accepted realistic English novelists of the first quarter of the
century—Arnold Bennett, John Galsworthy, H. G. Wells—
suffered from an inadequate view of the resources of their art.
They dealt in surfaces, as she argued in her trail-breaking
essay "Mr. Bennett and Mrs. Brown." She proposed to get
underneath these surfaces by using devices that have become
familiar—stream of consciousness, interior monologue, the
abandonment of linear narrative, and a sensitive adaptation of
some of the techniques of poetry. At times she failed in her
endeavor; more often she succeeded.

Of the four novels here recommended, *Mrs. Dalloway* is
perhaps the most accessible. Through the central figure, a
wealthy political hostess, Woolf gives us a picture of the London upper class, of a whole society at its highest peak of
self-confidence. The great themes of love and death dominate.
But there are interesting minor ones such as snobbery (Woolf
herself was partly a snob), rebellion against privilege, and, more
faintly, lesbian attachment. Her own intervals of madness,
which were to culminate in suicide, gave her extraordinary
insight into the mind of the shell-shocked veteran Septimus
Smith, a character as firmly realized as Mrs. Dalloway herself.

In *To the Lighthouse,* as in all the novels beginning with
Mrs. Dalloway, we slip in and out of people's minds, some-

times with no warning. The personages, drawn from Woolf's own family memories, are consciousnesses rather than characters. Not chronological time but moments of epiphany determine the novel's form and structure. She writes, "... any turn in the wheel of sensation has the power to crystallize and transfix the moment."

The original of Orlando, in the book so titled, was Virginia Woolf's great friend, the aristocratic Vita Sackville-West, wife of the writer-diplomat Sir Harold Nicolson. This elaborate fantasy glancingly recapitulates parts of English history from Elizabethan times to 1928. It seems to anticipate the Latin American school of magic realism (64). An element of play enters; perhaps *Orlando* bears the same relation to Woolf's total production as Graham Greene's Entertainments bear to his.

The Waves is her most difficult novel. Six members of the privileged class, three of each sex, are carried rapidly from childhood through youth, university, and middle age. There is no movement in the usual sense, merely six souls soliloquizing in turn. As one of them, Bernard, reflects: "There is nothing one can fish up in a spoon; nothing one can call an event." Not everything the characters say or think or feel is graspable by even the most sensitive reader. The effect is of beauty without clarity. Not her most successful book, *The Waves* is nevertheless probably the most original development novel of the first half of the century.

41
D. H. LAWRENCE (1885–1930)

Sons and Lovers, Women in Love

It is hard to realize that when Lawrence died of tuberculosis he was only forty-five. From 1911, when his first novel appeared, to his death in 1930, no year passed without the appearance of at least one book. In 1930 there were six, and his posthumous works (excluding the extraordinary *Letters*) total another dozen or so. While producing so prodigiously,

Lawrence was traveling widely, meeting and influencing large numbers of people, working at various hobbies, and engaging in the unhappy controversies caused by his uncompromising ideas. This frail, thin, bearded man—novelist, poet, playwright, essayist, critic, painter, and prophet—had a central fire of energy burning inside him. He stands out as one of the most alive human beings of his time.

Lawrence was born of a Nottinghamshire coal miner and a woman greatly superior to her husband in education and sensitivity. His early life, dominated by his mother's excessive love and his excessive dependence on it, is portrayed quite frankly in the first part of *Sons and Lovers.* Lawrence excelled at school and for a few years was a schoolmaster. In 1912 he eloped with Frieda von Richthofen Weekley, a member of a patrician German family, and in 1914 married her. The latter part of his life was one of almost continuous wandering. In exotic primitives and undeveloped countries he sought the equivalent in fact of the life-feeling that blazes in his fiction.

This life-feeling attracts some readers, alienates or shocks others. You will not be able to tolerate Lawrence at all unless you understand that he was neither poseur nor hysteric, but a prophet with a message fervently believed in, a message with which he sought to change the day-to-day behavior of the human race. The message is implicit even in so early a book as *Sons and Lovers,* which is certainly the one with which to start one's reading of Lawrence. It is to be found more particularly in *The Rainbow, Women in Love* (perhaps his masterpiece), and *Lady Chatterley's Lover,* one of his poorest novels.

We must understand that Lawrence was an absolute revolutionary. His rejections were complete. He made war against the entire industrial culture of his and our time. He felt that it had devitalized us, dried up the spontaneous springs of our emotions, fragmented us, and alienated us from that life of the soil, flowers, weather, animals, to which Lawrence was preternaturally sensitive. Worst of all, he thought, it had withered our sexual lives. For Lawrence sex was not merely something to enjoy. It was the key to the only knowledge he prized— direct, immediate, nonintellectual perception of reality. As early as 1912 he was writing, "What the blood feels, and believes, and says, is always true." (To some readers this will seem pernicious nonsense.)

He hated science, conventional Christianity, the worship of reason, progress, the interfering state, planned "respectable" living, and the idolization of money and the machine. It is easy to understand therefore why he was forced to live, though bravely and even joyfully, a life of poverty, struggle, and defiance. Aldous Huxley (42), who knew him well, described him as "a being, somehow, of another order." It does at times seem that he drew his energy from some primal source most of us cannot tap. In this respect as in others he reminds us of the prophet-poet Blake (90).

His books are not constructed, as Conrad's are. They flow, eddy, flash, erupt, or sing in accordance with the electric changes in the author's own personality as he composed. Unless you are willing temporarily to accept this personality, his books may seem intolerable.

But Lawrence wants you to do more. His view of the novel was deeply moral. The novel, he passionately believed, "can help you not to be a dead man in life." He wants nothing less than to change you, to reawaken in you an intensity, a joy in life that he felt humanity was losing or had lost.

It is hard to say whether a century from now Lawrence will be thought of as a major prophet (as well as a remarkable artist) or merely as an oddity of genius.

42
ALDOUS HUXLEY (1894–1963)

Brave New World, Collected Essays

T. S. Eliot (94) and Huxley had much in common. Both were formidably intelligent, as well as formidably learned. Both summed up in their personalities a large part of the Western tradition that is the subject of this book. Both moved from a position of destructive critical irony to one of faith—Eliot to Anglo-Catholicism, Huxley toward a mysticism drawn from the East but also from such Western visionaries as Blake (90),

Eckhart, Tauler, and others. Eliot's may have been the profounder intellect, as he was certainly the greater artist. But Huxley's intellect was more adventurous, more playful, and more closely involved with insistent concrete problems of our time, particularly those pointing the way to race suicide, such as total war and murderous overpopulation.

The variety, the flexibility, the erudition, the sheer brilliance of Huxley's restless mind may be enjoyed through a reading of his essays. He leaves few of humanity's major concerns untouched. His skepticism, never cheap or easy, has a cleansing power still to be properly estimated. I know no other single English or American writer of his time who reflected with such clarity certain shifts and modulations in the Western intellect, including a shift toward the thought of the East.

Huxley was famous before he was thirty, a circumstance perhaps not entirely fortunate for him. But the book that gave him a worldwide audience was *Brave New World,* published in 1932, reissued in 1946 with an important new Preface by the author. Probably this terrible fable will lose its point and force as unconsciously we take on in reality the condition he describes in fantasy. For our period, however, it is what might be called a temporary classic. No one who really wishes to learn what is happening, not to our environment but to our souls, should remain unacquainted with this nightmare of a book.

The utopian literature of the twentieth century, unlike that of the Renaissance, is negative, dystopian. In it we hear not shouts of encouragement but cries of warning. As Berdiaeff, quoted by Huxley, puts it, our concern now is not how to attain but how to avoid Utopia. For the Utopia we are so busy preparing is, according to Huxley, Orwell (43), and dozens of other thoughtful writers, a hell of dehumanization.

Huxley's *Brave New World,* projected six hundred years into the future, is populated by animals (still known as human beings) and their managers. The managed animals have been taught to love their servitude; they are happy, or, as we proudly say, adjusted. The Constitution of the state has but three articles: Community, Identity, Stability. Religion as we know it, art, theoretical science, the family, emotions, individual strivings and differences—all have vanished.

Not a good novel, *Brave New World* should be read as a prophetic fable, differing from other prophecies in that it is the product not of intuition but of cold intelligence. Its ideas (and all its characters are ideas), first advanced more than fifty years ago, have proved prescient. All the gambits of then-current cocktail party conversation are prefigured in *Brave New World*: the conformist, the nonconformist, the relapse to primitivism, the new chartered sexuality, the organization man, the lonely crowd—they are here extended into a future that seems less remote today than it did in 1932.

I do not suggest that *Brave New World* be taken literally. It is not a textbook of the future but a purposely exaggerated satirical vision, in the tradition of *Gulliver* (27). Doubtless Huxley will rank below Swift. But not too far below. And what he has to say is perhaps more immediate, if less crushing, than Swift's total misanthropy.

43
GEORGE ORWELL   (1903–1950)

Animal Farm, Nineteen Eighty-four

Eric Blair (George Orwell is a pen name) attended Eton, passed up university, and in 1922 shipped out to Burma where for a few years he served in the Burma Imperial Police. The values of the British Establishment did not take; indeed he spent the rest of his life repudiating them. Returning to England, he immersed himself in the culture of the poor, calling himself an anarchist, later a socialist. Unlike many British intellectuals of his time, Orwell was never seduced by Communism. The Spanish Civil War, in which he was wounded while fighting on the Republican side, intensified his distrust of all totalitarian doctrines. Back in England he engaged in journalism and book writing, gradually working out for himself a libertarian-socialist political stance quite at variance with doctrinaire Labour Party socialism.

Animal Farm made Orwell famous. Like parts of *Gulliver's Travels* (27) it is a sophisticated adaptation of a simple and ancient literary form, the animal fable. Just as *Candide* (47) ranks as the classic satire on Leibnizian optimism, so *Animal Farm* has become the classic satire on Soviet Communism. Its lively movement, directness, and wit recall some of Voltaire's outstanding qualities.

The two pigs Napoleon and Snowball may make us think of Stalin and Trotsky but Orwell is not really playing *roman à clef* games. He is questioning the whole notion of the ordered state, perhaps questioning the value of any revolution that sets the ordered state as its goal. Funny as *Animal Farm* often is, it is also full of dismaying insights into the venality and hypocrisy of all power-obsessed natures. One of these insights has entered the language: All animals are equal but some animals are more equal than others.

In an article headed "Why I Write" Orwell made his purpose clear: *"Animal Farm* was the first book in which I tried, with full consciousness of what I was doing, to fuse political purpose and artistic purpose into one whole."

Nineteen Eighty-four is not only his finest work but one of the most influential books of our time. You might want to compare it with *Brave New World* (42) to feel how much blacker the world became during the seventeen years, 1932 to 1949, separating these two exercises in dystopian thought.

To avoid despair we must interpret *Nineteen Eight-four* as warning rather than prophecy. We are still some distance away from the picture of the future imagined by O'Brien, the book's most important character: "Imagine a boot stamping on a human face—forever." But Stalin's ruthlessness and the Nazi mechanized techniques of mass torture and murder, not to mention the Cambodian, Iranian, and other horrors, have to some degree changed *Nineteen Eighty-four* from a cautionary tale to a bleak commentary on our era. Newspeak, the art of the Big Lie, may have been developed by the Russians and the Germans, but it has been adopted by many quick-study leaders of the Free World. To Huxley's vision of a dehumanized future Orwell adds new dimensions of terror and torture; and of course terror and torture are now prominent features of our world's political landscape.

As a novel *Nineteen Eighty-four* hardly ranks with the greats. Yet some of its scenes—for example, the keystone

Smith-O'Brien dialogue—are almost as telling as similar ones in Dostoyevsky (67). The episode in which Winston Smith actually does begin to believe that $2 + 2 = 5$ is a remarkable translation into imaginative terms of the terrifying power of propaganda backed by force.

In addition to the two recommended books, you will find some of Orwell's essays worth reading. One realizes, viewing his work as a whole, that the style is truly the man. It is plain, honest, without a hint of striving for effect. Now that we can survey his whole career, Orwell himself seems an admirable example of the nonconformist temperament at its best, integrated and unfoolable.

More than that of any other writer of his generation, his reputation has steadily risen since his death. It is often said that the engaged writer must pay for his engagement by becoming outmoded. In Orwell's case this does not appear to be true.

44
THOMAS MANN (1875–1955)

The Magic Mountain

Some books (they can be first-rate ones, like Jane Austen's) isolate parts of human experience. Others sum up these parts. Thus the masterpieces of Dante and Homer, though they do other things as well, sum up their cultures. So does *The Magic Mountain.* The reader will get more out of it by seeing it as a synthetic, inclusive work. Mae West once remarked, in a somewhat different connection, "I like a man who takes his time." In his Foreword to *The Magic Mountain* Mann puts it thus: "Only the exhaustive is truly interesting." His great novel is exhaustive, and it is truly interesting.

It is a story about a rather simpleminded young German who comes to visit a sick friend at a Swiss tuberculosis sanitarium; finds that he is himself infected; stays on for seven years; listens, talks, thinks, suffers, loves; and is at last swept up into the holocaust of the First World War. As you read this story you will feel, slowly and almost imperceptibly, that it is more than the usual narrative of the education of a young man. In dialogue, in symbol, in fantasy and dream, in argument, in soliloquy, in philosophical discourse, Mann is trying to sum up the mental life of the West.

In the Preliminary Talk with the Reader, I pointed out that all our authors are engaged in a Great Conversation, as it has been well called. A minor proof of this is the number of these authors who have helped to form Thomas Mann and whose ideas are orchestrated in *The Magic Mountain*. I could name dozens. Here are a few acknowledged by Mann himself: Goethe (18), Nietzsche (76), Turgenev (66), Tolstoy (68), Conrad (37), Whitman (95), Ibsen (19), Freud (77). In this sense too *The Magic Mountain* is summatory.

Look at it another way. As you read, try to see the Berghof sanitarium as Europe, the Europe (which means America too) that in 1914 died violently, passing into some other culture whose form is still unclear to us. Think of its characters as being not only themselves but incarnations of powerful modes of thought and feeling: Settembrini is liberal humanism; Naphta is absolutist terror (Lenin, Stalin, Hitler, Mussolini, Khomeini, and all the others still to come); Peeperkorn we have perhaps already met, for his message is not unlike D. H. Lawrence's (41). And the patients, drawn from so many countries and social levels—what are they but the sickness of the West, which Mann understood clearly in 1924 and which in the last years of our century may reach its feverish crisis?

In this gigantic work Mann touches on a dozen themes and issues that have since come to pervade the thought of our day: psychoanalysis and spiritualism; the links connecting art, disease, and death; the relative nature of time, to which Einstein has accustomed us; the nature of Western man, and particularly of middle-class man; the relations between the artist and society; the proper education of a human being. Mann's special genius lies in his ability to combine high-level reflection with the creation of character and atmosphere.

The Magic Mountain takes place in two worlds. One is a world of ideas. The other is a world of subtle human relationships, which we can sense all the more clearly because they are cut off from the confusing contingencies of the "flatland," the clock-bound "healthy" world you and I inhabit.

Now that we have read Conrad, Lawrence, Joyce, and Mann (with Proust and Henry James still awaiting us) we are borne on the full tide of the modern novel. We can begin to see its character. It is marked by enormous self-consciousness, profound delvings into the human spirit, technical innovations of bewildering variety. Its main difference from the simpler fictions of the English authors of the eighteenth and early nineteenth centuries lies in its receptive openness to the whole creative life of humanity. It intellectualizes without dehumanizing. Its entire drift is perhaps most clearly exemplified in Thomas Mann's masterpiece, one of the most magnificent works of art produced in our unhappy century.

45

FRANZ KAFKA   (1883–1924)

The Trial, The Castle, Selected Short Stories

If one were to list the five creative writers of the century who have most influenced other twentieth-century writers, Franz Kafka's name would probably be among them. He would be classed with Joyce, Proust, Yeats, and T. S. Eliot. About two decades after Kafka's death the poet W. H. Auden wrote: "Had one to name the author who comes nearest to bearing the same kind of relation to our age as Dante, Shakespeare and Goethe have to theirs, Kafka is the first one would think of." Even less restrained praise was accorded him by the great French poet and dramatist Paul Claudel: "Besides Racine, who is for me the greatest writer, there is one other—Franz Kafka."

These judgments were expressed at perhaps the peak of the Kafka boom. I say boom because his reputation is in part cult-inspired. But it remains true that the dark anomie and spiritual hunger of our unhappy epoch are both classically reflected in the dreams and nightmares of Kafka's fictions.

None of this was apparent during his brief lifetime. His enormous reputation is almost entirely posthumous. It is based, furthermore, on very little actual production: three not-quite-finished novels, a dozen short stories, and a scattering of brief parables, plus some correspondence. It may in part be explained, as in the cases of Stendhal (48) and Tocqueville (82), by Kafka's powers of prophecy. He died in 1924. But his symbolic visions seem to us to foretell our own period, marked by the German near-imposition of a state of total terror; by the bureaucratic maze that is the essential structure of all modern governments; by a sense that, as spiritual beings, we have lost our way and must rediscover it; by the invasion of our very souls by the machine; by a pervading feeling, hard to pin down, of universal guilt; by dehumanization. Borges (63) speaks of "the Kafka of somber myths and atrocious institutions."

Kafka's external life, though not notably happy, was sheltered, reasonably rich in interesting friendships, and untouched by war. (His three sisters, however, were murdered by the Nazis; he would not have been surprised.) His personality was intensely neurotic. This neurosis he put to creative use in his disturbing fictions. He suffered all his life from an obsessive sense of domination by his materialistic father, a Jew who acted more like a Prussian. This obsession reflected itself in his two major works, *The Trial* and *The Castle,* though their symbolism is so intricate and multileveled that biographical interpretation becomes hazardous. Yet it is clear that these novels turn on feelings of guilt and inferiority. *The Trial* tells the story of a man who feels guilty but is never able to discover just what he is accused of. *The Castle* is about a similar figure enmeshed in a bureaucratic system with which he can never make contact but which nevertheless represents some kind of redeeming authority.

Kafka is not difficult to read, because he employs a style of the utmost calm, lucidity, and simplicity. The surface narrative, however, is deceptive. He is trying to suggest, using familiar images and seemingly commonplace episodes, the disturbed condition of modern man. We may put it this way: there is, for Kafka, a Goal. But is there a Way? Kafka, though he belonged to no sect and was devoid of any trace of mysticism, was a deeply religious man. He thought of his writing, not as a profession, but as a form of prayer to a God who continually eluded him. His heroes suffer from lostness, alienation, an inability to identify themselves. It is a feeling many of us have had. But at the same time they are seeking some redemptive grace (the Castle perhaps symbolizes this), which they vaguely sense. They have no place in the universal order; yet surely there must be one. In this sense Kafka may be said to be a metaphysical novelist, in some respects akin to the less agonized Borges.

In some of his shorter works—especially *The Metamorphosis* and *In the Penal Colony*—Kafka seems to foresee the dehumanization, the terror, and the bureaucratic tyranny of our epoch. They are chilling stories, recounted in quiet prose, parables of guilt and punishment, that strike to the very heart of our age of anxiety.

Though he died over sixty years ago, Kafka is contemporary. A neurotic genius, he was perfectly equipped to create a visionary world that reminds us of our real one.

46
FRANÇOIS RABELAIS (ca. 1483–1553)

Gargantua and Pantagruel

I have listed this book under Narratives because I don't know where else to put it. It contains plenty of narrative, but it has no plot, is virtually formless, and eludes classification. It takes its place near the beginning of French literature but the French novel does not descend from it. Nothing descends from it. Though it has had imitators, it stands by itself. It is a wild, sane, wonderful, exasperating, sometimes tedious extravaganza. Open to a dozen interpretations, one thing at least can be said of it: it is the work of a supreme genius of language whose vitality and power of verbal invention are matched only by Shakespeare and Joyce.

About Rabelais's life we know little. He was a monk, a doctor, personal physician to the important Cardinal du Bellay, an editor, and of course a writer. At various times his books got him into trouble with the authorities. The more bigoted Catholics of his time attacked him; so did the

Calvinists, whose bigotry one cannot qualify in any way. Still, despite his satiric view of the churchly obscurantism of his period, there is nothing to prove he was not a good, though hardly straitlaced, Catholic. Anatole France said that Rabelais "believed in God five days out of seven, which is a good deal." Fair enough.

The five books of *Gargantua and Pantagruel* (the fifth may not be entirely genuine) deal with two giants. The first book tells us about Gargantua, his birth, education, farcical war adventures, and the Abbey of Thélème he helped to build, whose only rule was: Do as you wish. The other four books are concerned with Gargantua's son, Pantagruel, that son's boon companion, the rascally, earthy, Falstaffian Panurge, and their wars, travels, quests for wisdom.

The tone varies. It is serious (we have still to catch up with Rabelais's ideas on education), mock-serious, satirical, fantastic, always exuberant. However, even at his wildest, Rabelais evidences two well-blended strains: one proceeding from his humanist conviction that all men desire knowledge and that all knowledge is a joyous and attainable thing (the book is, among other things, an encyclopedia); the other flowing from his personal conviction that "laughter is the essence of mankind."

Of all the writers we have met or shall meet he is the one most unreservedly in love with life. Even when attacking the abuses of his day, he does so in high, almost manic spirits. He would not know a neurosis if he saw one, and most of our gloomy modern novels he would destroy with a guffaw. He is a kind of happy Swift, or perhaps a Whitman with an intellect. His characteristic gesture is the embrace. He can love both God and drunkenness. His laughter is so free and healthy that only the prudish will be offended by his vast coarseness, his delight in the eternal comedy of the human body.

Pantagruelism he defines as "a certain jollity of mind, pickled in the scorn of fortune." To enjoy him you must be a bit of a Pantagruelist yourself. His is a book you must give, or at least lend, yourself to, not bothering to ponder every morsel of his gargantuan erudition, and perhaps not trying to read more than a dozen pages at a time.

One final suggestion: read any good *modern* translation—

Cohen's or Putnam's or Le Clercq's. Avoid the famous Urquhart-Motteux version—a classic, but not Rabelais.

47

VOLTAIRE (1694–1778)

Candide and Other Works

Voltaire died at eighty-four, the uncrowned king of intellectual Europe, the undisputed leader of the Age of Enlightenment, the most destructive of the many sappers of the foundations of the Old Regime destroyed by the French Revolution. As dramatist, poet, historian, tale teller, wit, correspondent, controversialist, and coruscating personality, he had achieved a formidable reputation. His productivity is unbelievable; he left behind him over fourteen thousand known letters and over two thousand books and pamphlets. Yet he is most easily remembered for an extended little bittersweet joke that he wrote in three days. All his tens of thousands of ironies fade before the irony of this one circumstance.

Voltaire—his name was possibly an anagram for his probable real name, François-Marie Arouet—handled his career, including his business affairs, with the capacity of a Shaw. But he made one error. He wrote *Candide*. By doing so he obscured the remainder of his vast production. So much else is brilliant and well worth reading—the *Philosophical Dictionary, Zadig, Micromégas, The Age of Louis XIV,* the *Letters Concerning the English Nation.* Yet *Candide* is what we read, for it is perfection.

Also it is so lucid as to need little commentary. It was partly inspired by one of the events it chronicles, the devastating Lisbon earthquake of 1755. Voltaire uses this—as well as all the other misfortunes of poor Candide, Dr. Pangloss, and their companions—to make fun of what he conceived to be the smug optimism of the famous philosopher Leibniz, caricatured in the figure of Pangloss. As philosophy *Candide* is oversimplified, indeed shallow, for Voltaire's intelligence was quick and comprehensive rather than deep. But as lightning narrative, flashing with wit, as a pitiless yet funny indictment of the follies and cruelties of mankind, it has not yet been surpassed.

Its form is a favorite one of Voltaire's century, that of the philosophical romance—*Gulliver's Travels* (27) belongs to this category, and a good modern example is Thornton Wilder's *The Bridge of San Luis Rey*. It anticipates also another of the forms later fiction was to take, that of the development novel, tracing the education of a young man. We have already seen this form extended and deepened in *The Magic Mountain* (44) and we will meet it again when we discuss *The Red and the Black* (48). Candide's education of course was of a uniquely violent nature, so violent that one can hardly help sympathizing with his rather mournful conclusion that, in this far from the best of all possible worlds, the most sensible thing we can do is to "cultivate our garden."

The reader, however, must not be misled by this jewel of wicked irony into thinking that Voltaire was no more than a genius of mockery. Like Shaw he could not help being witty; and like Shaw he was a very serious, courageous, and humane fighter for the liberation of the human mind.

48

STENDHAL (1783–1842)

The Red and the Black

One hundred years ago Stendhal (one of his more than 150 pseudonyms, his real name being Marie-Henri Beyle) would not have been listed among the major novelists of Europe. Fifty years later the situation would have changed: he would have been named among the first half-dozen novelists of France. Today the shift is even greater: many rank him among the foremost novelists of any time and place. Stendhal lived partially in the future, and so he would have foreseen all this. Indeed he did foresee it. "I have drawn a lottery ticket," he wrote, "whose winning number is: to be read in 1935."

So, though most of Stendhal's stories are laid in Napoleonic and post-Napoleonic Europe, we would expect his feeling for life and his way of expressing it to be modern. And that is roughly what we do find. Some qualifications should be made, however. His plots seem to us to smack of opera. His dialogue is more formal than that our phonographic realists have accustomed us to. And, in the case of his masterpiece *The Red and the Black,* the title refers to forces no longer operative, the Red standing for the uniform of Napoleon's soldiers, the Black for the cassock of the clergy. The hero, Julien Sorel, wears the black because in his day a poor youth with his special talents could advance himself only through the church, whereas Julien's heart and imagination belong to the Napoleonic era he thinks of as more glorious than his own. However, the deeper tensions in Julien are not peculiar to the France of his generation. They are part of our modern consciousness.

Stendhal's genius lay partly in prevision. His novels, particularly this one, anticipate many of the motifs and devices we are used to in contemporary fiction. That is one reason why he can be called the novelist's novelist. *The Red and the Black,* for example, is the first classic expression of the young-man-from-the-provinces theme—a theme on which all the books of Thomas Wolfe and dozens of other novels merely ring changes. Also it heads a long line of narratives whose subject is the dissatisfaction of the heroine with an empty society—see Carol Kennicott in Sinclair Lewis's *Main Street* and of course Emma Bovary (50). Though George Eliot (34), as we noted, dared to portray an intellectual, it is in *The Red and the Black* that we first get the type fully and closely studied. And so we can keep on identifying in Stendhal other anticipations of twentieth-century fiction: his systematic rather than intuitive use of psychology, even Freudian psychology; his understanding of what is now called ambivalence; his extraordinary detachment from his characters; and especially his major preoccupation, which is with the outsider, the "being apart," who cannot become reconciled with an inferior or materialistic or merely boring society.

The reader will perceive all this only *after* reading *The Red and the Black.* While reading it you will be caught up in a fascinating love story, which somehow seems far more adult than any encountered in the Victorian novelists. Furthermore you will experience the sensation only the finest psychological novelists can give—that of actually, for a dozen hours or so, living inside the passionately intense, complex minds of a few invented persons who become realer to you than your own neighbors.

Final note: many good judges rank *The Charterhouse of Parma* as equal to *The Red and the Black*. Try it.

49

HONORÉ DE BALZAC (1799–1850)

Père Goriot, Eugénie Grandet

Unlike Stendhal (48), of whom he was one of the few to show any early appreciation, Balzac is not widely read by Americans today. Everyone admits his achievement but no one is quite sure what it is. Does he rank among the greatest of novelists? The answer is not clear. Faults stand out that were not so apparent during his century: faults of taste especially; a weakness for melodrama, almost for detective-story melodrama; an incapacity to portray character as changing and developing; and, most important, certain defects of intelligence. Another trouble is that he never wrote a masterpiece. I recommend two titles, among his best known, but they do not represent him properly. Nor would any other two titles. To be overcome by Balzac (he *can* overwhelm you, though he may not move you) you should read fifty or sixty of his novels; and life is too short.

Balzac was a Stendhalian Young Man from the Provinces. There is a famous scene at the end of *Père Goriot:* the ambitious young Rastignac looks down on the lights of Paris and cries, "Between us henceforth the battle is joined." There was plenty of Rastignac in Balzac. Perhaps that was his central flaw: he did not think and feel like an artist, but like a conqueror. Once as a young man he seized a pencil and, under a picture of the Little Corporal, wrote: "What Napoleon could not achieve with his sword I shall accomplish with my pen."

With this ideal of conquest always before him, Balzac lived like a madman and died exhausted at fifty-one, perhaps, as has been said, as the result of drinking fifty thousand cups of coffee. He engaged in frenzied financial operations for which he had no talent. He wasted time on one of the most absurd love affairs in literary history. He piled up huge debts. And always he wrote, wrote, wrote, through the night, incessantly for twenty years and more, sometimes from fourteen to eighteen hours a day. Only the scholars know exactly how many books he turned out, perhaps over 350 in all, with perhaps 100 making up what he called his "Human Comedy." Here is his description of this manic, comprehensive design: "The immeasurable scope of a plan which embraces not only a history and criticism of society, but also an analysis of its evils and an exposition of its principles, justifies me, so I believe, in giving my work the title . . . The Human Comedy." The implied comparison is, of course, with a man he resembled in virtually no way—Dante.

Balzac did not live to complete his vast picture of the French society of his day. *Père Goriot* and *Eugénie Grandet* are merely two bricks of this unfinished edifice. The first is a study in irrational passion, the unrequited love of a father for his two daughters, a kind of middle-class *Lear* minus Cordelia. The second is a study in avarice. Both deal with monomanias, as do so many of Balzac's fictions. He had little of Stendhal's sense of the ambivalent and ambiguous in human character.

These two novels, one drawn from the worldly life of Paris, the other a picture of provincial manners, have what is found in all his work—force, vivid detail, a talent that makes him the father of a certain school of modern realism. Finally, they both expose Balzac's major obsession, which was money. He lived in a period, like our own, of money making, money losing, money loving; a period in which the greatest sin was not treachery but bankruptcy. No other novelist before him understood the world of money as Balzac did. Thus he may be considered the ancestor of all our contemporary novelists of business and finance.

These are not inconsiderable qualities. To them we must

add a demonic power of static characterization. Mme. Marneffe, Grandet, Gobseck, Goriot, César Birotteau—if not complex creations, these are solid ones. And when one looks at the mere formidable bulk of his work, so firm in its grasp of reality, so loaded with hard, vivid detail, so close to so many kinds of life, it is difficult not to take off one's hat to this flawed titan.

50

GUSTAVE FLAUBERT (1821–1880)

Madame Bovary

Before commenting on this novel, I wish to recommend the one translation that does it justice—that by Francis Steegmuller. It will serve to convince the reader that good reasons exist for its author's high reputation.

When *Madame Bovary* was first published, in serial form, Flaubert had to defend himself before the public prosecutor against charges that it was offensive to morality and religion. He won the case. But the excitement over *Madame Bovary,* though transferred from the moral to the literary plane, has never since quite died down. The novel has continued to agitate many readers, including other novelists and critics. I must at once admit that, while I admire it as an unquestioned masterpiece, I nevertheless find it cold and depressing. That, however, is not the general verdict.

Unlike Balzac, Flaubert was the classic type of the pure and dedicated artist. The son of a Rouen surgeon, he pursued law studies in Paris briefly and unhappily; in 1844 suffered a nervous attack; then withdrew to a life of study and writing varied by intervals of travel and erotic experience. He was not by nature a happy man. His native melancholy was further underlined by the loss of loved ones, by the misunderstanding with which the world greeted much of his work, and by the self-torture that followed from his literary perfectionism.

"The Idea," he wrote, "exists only by virtue of its form." Form to Flaubert meant more than a frame or a pattern. It was a complex affair. A few of its many elements were: "the perfect word," cunningly contrived and varied rhythms, assonance, reverberant or echoing sequences of symbols, and a genuine architectural structure. Over *Madame Bovary* he spent five laborious years. Before his time, no novels in French had been so carefully written. Which is why I suggest Steegmuller's translation: the emotional tone and weight of *Madame Bovary* are created by the use of a special language, requiring the most careful carry-over into English.

Flaubert believed that the artist hovered somewhere above the moral universe, that he should not judge, explain, or teach but merely understand and perfectly record. Insofar as this novel is devoid of sentimentality, as it is of pity, Flaubert succeeded in his aim. Yet it conveys a message, if only a negative one; and that message we have already received in the pages of *Gulliver's Travels* (27). Flaubert did not love the human race. *Madame Bovary,* for all its seeming detachment, seems to me a beautifully organized confession of misanthropy.

Whether or not this is true, no one can deny the influence of the work. Most of the later novels that turn on the discrepancy between our ideal lives and the actual gray ones that we live owe much to Flaubert. Madame Bovary is the first Walter Mitty. She has given a name, *Bovarysme,* to her disease, a morbid passion for believing oneself other and better than one is. It is even possible that thousands of young men and women have rebelled against their environment, in daydream or in reality, not because they were spontaneous rebels, but because *Madame Bovary* infected them—just as young men committed suicide as a consequence of reading Goethe's *Sorrows of Werther,* or in our time turned Beat because of Kerouac.

There are other sides to Flaubert than those revealed in what is by most critics considered his masterpiece. I recommend particularly a reading of *Three Tales,* of which one, "A Simple Heart," discloses an almost Christian compassion not elsewhere to be found in this great, unhappy writer.

51

MARCEL PROUST (1871–1922)

Remembrance of Things Past

This is the longest first-rate novel ever written. Its difficulties, like its rewards, are vast. If you respond to it at all (many do not) you may feel quite justified in spending what time you can spare over the next five or ten years in making it a part of your interior world.

Though it shares some features with *Ulysses* (39) and in a minor way with *Tristram Shandy* (28), it is basically unlike any novel we have so far discussed. It has a story, of course, and characters, and a clear setting in time and place—and all are most interesting indeed. But Proust is less concerned with these matters than in dramatizing a metaphysical system. Metaphysics tries to answer the question, What is the fundamental nature of reality? Proust devoted his life to answering the question in the form of a work of art. Of course he answered only part of the question. He tells us what reality means to Proust. But the answer has enormous scope and range.

He never had to work for a living. His family was moderately wealthy and from an early age the brilliant boy had access to the worlds of fashionable and intellectual Paris, as it was before World War I. His attachment to his Jewish mother, a sensitive woman of fine character, was powerful and neurotic. Though Proust loved women as well as men, there is little doubt that his later homosexuality was caused partly by his relationship to his mother. Her death in 1905, together with his own physical weaknesses (particularly asthma), determined the shape of his life. He withdrew to the seclusion of a dark, vapor-filled cork-lined room. There, sleeping by day, working by night, with occasional sorties into the outer world (with which he also kept in touch through a huge correspondence), he slowly, painfully elaborated his masterpiece.

The hero of *Ulysses* is a place, Dublin. The hero of *Remembrance* is Time. To project in art the very "form of Time" was Proust's passion, his answer to the question, What is it to be? He jettisoned completely the methods of the conventional novelist. For him, being is not a chronological succession of events. Being is the complete past, "that past which already extended so far down and which I was bearing so painfully within me."

How shall we grasp this past, this reality? Quantum theory tells us that in a sense reality is unseizable because observation itself changes the thing observed. Proust understood this. He therefore gave us the past as well as he could, by a series of approximations, by presenting it to us in a thousand aspects, by showing it for what it really is—not a smooth flow of discrete events, but an ever-changing continuum. Parts of our past are continually erupting in us. These parts are felt differently at different times, by different people, under different circumstances. Proust evades none of these difficulties; he triumphs over them.

The past is evocable, we say, by memory. But this memory is not under our control. The taste of a small cake dipped in tea, the outline of some towers against the sky—such small events reawaken in Proust a stream of memories and half-forgotten experiences, which color his whole life. We cannot understand ourselves at any given moment, nor are we merely the static sum of all the moments we have lived—because we are continually reliving them, and so the sum is always changing. Only through a complete evocation of the past can the content of any moment be even approximated. Because this is so, reality, as we say, eludes us, and life seems sad, evanescent, and puzzling. Only art, Proust's religion, by imposing on life's mutations an orderly form, can give us consolation.

Proust's method, even the structure of his interminable sentences, flows from this conception of time, from this enthronement of subjectivism. In his book, time turns and twists upon itself like a snake, past and present merge, motifs and themes are recalled and redeveloped and answer each other in echo and counterpoint. Every critic has pointed out that the book is less like a narrative than like a symphony.

But had Proust done nothing more than incorporate a metaphysic he would not be as interesting as he is. In addition to his peculiar, neurotic sensibility and his phenomenal memory, he possessed most of the gifts of any first-rate novelist. His book, for example, is a social panorama of unprecedented depth (though not of range): compare his Vanity Fair with Thackeray's (32). He describes the agonies and death of a whole aristocratic and upper-middle-class society. He analyzes, sometimes with intolerable exhaustiveness, the baffling and to him frustrating nature of love, and particularly of homosexual love. He creates at least a half-dozen characters comparable to the most living in the literature of the novel. And he invents a prose, often opaque, but always, in its slow sinuosities and plangent rhythms, proper to his difficult theme. His realism is unlike that of any novelist we have so far met. It is the realism of the symbolist, not the naturalist. When he wishes, he can describe to perfection. But he omits all details that do not reinforce his conviction that our only reality is the aspect of things remembered. This partial reality is not all we need to know, but it is all we do know; and that limitation is the cause of the tragedy of life.

For some this is the greatest novel in the world. For others it is unreadable. For still others it is, as one good critic wrote, "mammoth but minor." You must pass your own judgment. I will, however, in conclusion quote the considered estimate of the finest American critic of his time, Edmund Wilson: "We must recognize in Proust, it seems to me, one of the great minds and imaginations of our day, absolutely comparable in our own time, by reason both of his powers and his influence, to the Nietzsches, the Tolstois, the Wagners and the Ibsens of a previous generation. He has recreated the world of the novel from the point of view of relativity: he has supplied for the first time in literature an equivalent on the full scale for the new theory of modern physics."

52
ANDRÉ MALRAUX (1901–1975)

Man's Fate

The biography and work of André Malraux are in a class by themselves.

As a man of action Malraux was involved, often responsibly, in several insurrections, revolutions, and wars: China in 1925–27; the Spanish Civil War (sixty-five flights over enemy territory, two wounds); the Resistance (wounded, captured, escaped, rising to a colonelcy, decorated). As a political figure he held Kuomintang office, was a cabinet minister in De Gaulle's provisional government, and reorganized the French theater as Minister of State for Information. As an adventurer-explorer-archaeologist he tracked down virtually unknown works of art in the jungles of Indo-China and flew over what may have been (considerable doubt here) the fabled capital city of the Queen of Sheba. As esthetician and philosopher of art he revolutionized, in *The Voices of Silence*, our way of looking at the art monuments of the world. He was an orator and conversationalist of major proportions. His erudition was apparently endless. His political evolution, from Popular Frontism to Gaullism, though bizarre, had no trace in it of either the hysterical or the opportunistic. In a country where the production of intelligence is virtually a major industry, he was conceded to be one of the most intelligent Frenchmen of his time.

To add to all this, he was a stunning novelist.

Man's Fate, translated into sixteen languages, is probably his masterpiece. Its setting is Shanghai and its ostensible subject the aborted Shanghai insurrection of 1927. What Malraux said of an earlier novel, *The Conquerors,* is true of *Man's Fate:* "The principal emphasis is on the relation between individuals and a collective action, not in collective action alone.... The book is first of all a representation of the human condition."

La condition humaine ... the phrase, now trite, found in Pascal and others, is the French title of *Man's Fate.* It deals with revolution, which Malraux sees as the key tragic experience of our century. But it is not a revolutionary novel in the Marxist sense. It is a study, which should have been illustrated by El Greco, of the paroxysms of violence, tension, eroticism, sadism, and courage which convulse men engaged in revolutionary action. It is about as far from the proletarian novel as are the fictions of Dostoyevsky (67), who was Malraux's master, if so original a writer may be said to have one.

In another of his novels, *Man's Hope,* a character asks and answers a question: "What can a man best do in his life? Translate into consciousness the largest possible experience." In Malraux's universe of emotion the deepest possible experience is the foretaste of death. (Compare Hemingway [60].) Against this inevitability he marshals all the resources of his tragic but indomitable nature. At their richest these resources produce art, which Malraux sees as "a revolt against man's fate," as "an attempt to give men a consciousness of their own hidden powers." Thus his novels, though their content is often horrifying, are not negative or depressing. True, they do not reveal us to ourselves in our more normal, our quieter aspects. But for Malraux our century has already dedicated itself to a mode of experience in which quietude and normality are overborne by the increasing domination of catastrophic change, by terror, by recurrent situations in which the human will is tested on the rack of history, sometimes to be broken, sometimes to be exalted.

53

ALBERT CAMUS (1913–1960)

The Plague, The Stranger

Like many of his generation, Camus was much preoccupied by man's incomprehensible situation within a seemingly absurd universe. Appropriately enough, he was killed at the age of forty-six in an automobile accident. For the world of the mind, though perhaps not for the absurdist, this was a major tragedy. With unmatched eloquence and moral seriousness Camus spoke for his disillusioned postwar contemporaries. Because his underlying theme was the permanent human condition, he speaks to us today.

He was born in Algeria of impoverished parents, and the countryside and cityscapes of that sun-dried land are reflected with joyful intensity in many of his narratives. From the start he was a brilliant student, specializing in philosophy. Surviving a brief infection of Marxism, he retained for the rest of his life a sense of community with the poor and oppressed. As a journalist he was among the first to document the injustices from which the Algerians suffered and which were to spark the independence movement. During the German occupation of France and for part of the post-Liberation period he edited the Resistance paper *Combat.* During the forties and fifties he achieved his major work. In 1957 it was recognized by the award of the Nobel Prize. He was only forty-four. Three years later he was dead.

Camus is distinguished as journalist, polemicist, memoirist, and philosopher. He also contributed, as playwright and worker in the theater, to the tropical growth in the forties of the theater of the absurd. But his most enduring work lies in his handful of novels and especially in his major effort, *The Plague.* He once wrote: "We only think in images. If you want to be a philosopher, write novels." For him this was true; his novels (as also his plays) dramatize involved moral and metaphysical problems.

While it is useful to have some acquaintance with his specifically politico-philosophical works, such as *The Myth of Sisyphus* and *The Rebel,* one can, I think, effect entrance into Camus's beautiful mind through a reading of his short novel *The Stranger* and his full-length effort *The Plague. The Stranger,* concerned with an act of seemingly gratuitous murder, is one of many studies of the rootless nonconformist sensibility so symptomatic of our time. The gesture of violence that delivers the hero up to society's power to punish also measures the gap separating him from the values that society takes for granted, but which are open to troubling questions. In an absurd universe, how may evil and good be distinguished or perhaps even identified?

His masterpiece, *The Plague,* may be interpreted (but there is no single interpretation) as Camus's resolution of the problem. In his Preface to *The Myth of Sisyphus* he writes: "Even within the limits of nihilism it is possible to find the means to proceed beyond nihilism." Just because the universe seems absurd man must rebel against that very absurdity, guiding his actions by the twin lights of truth and justice. It is precisely in a world of apparently meaningless disaster that some develop, almost unconsciously, the power to recognize and act by truth, justice, and compassion.

This sounds very moralistic and old-fashioned, does it not? But *The Plague,* you will find, is neither one nor the other.

Sometime in the forties, Camus imagines, bubonic plague strikes the Algerian city of Oran. Quietly, coolly, Camus records in detail the differing ways in which men, women, and children react to agony, isolation, and death. Our eyes are never allowed to wander from a definite city, identifiable people, specific fates, and the particular character of the pestilence. And yet, as we read, we become deeply aware that this study of the effects of plague is also a study of the isolated condition of man in an uncaring universe and his attempts to transcend that condition. Camus prefaces his novel with a quotation from Defoe (26): "It is as reasonable to represent one kind of imprisonment by another, as it is to represent anything that really exists by that which exists not." At no time does Camus offer us a parable or allegory. The narrative is rigorously realistic. Yet reading it, we feel that, as Dorothy Canfield wrote in her review of *The Plague,* it "casts a light on all catastrophes which shut men and women up in misery together." Life itself is such a catastrophe, Camus seems to be saying. But the catastrophe is not total; such men as Dr. Rieux and Tarrou, such women as Dr. Rieux's mother, can compel, by the force of their moral character, community to emerge from isolation and a qualified freedom from human bondage.

54
EDGAR ALLAN POE (1809–1849)

Short Stories and Other Works

Poe may not rank among the greatest writers, but he ranks among the unhappiest. He has become a symbol of unappreciated genius.

His life was made up of misfortunes, some caused by lack of understanding on the part of his contemporaries, and many caused by his own disastrous inheritance and weaknesses. The child of wandering actors, he was brought up as the ward of a prosperous merchant with whom he quarreled as soon as possible. His education, at the University of Virginia and West Point, was interrupted by his talent for delinquency. He married his thirteen-year-old cousin, and her early death may have been the deciding factor in his ruin. His first volumes of poems were not noticed. He was a capable journalist but mismanaged what might have turned into a successful career. He engaged in desperate, immature, incomplete love affairs. Drugs, alcohol, overwork, poverty became the staples of his life. He died in utter wretchedness. Of all the writers we have met or shall meet, surely he was the most miserable. Even the bitter Swift for a time enjoyed the company and praise of his equals. Poe never did.

Poe's verse has always been popular and in France it was for a time much more than that. Probably all that is worthwhile can be read in half an hour. The rest sounds thin and affected today, though Poe was better than "the jingle man" Emerson (83) called him.

But his tales, monologues, and some of his critical essays, despite infuriating faults of style, retain their interest. His mind was neither powerful nor balanced—but it *was* original, running creatively counter to the rather insipid thought of most of his American contemporaries. James Russell Lowell's famous estimate may not be too far from the truth: "Three fifths of him genius and two fifths sheer fudge."

What is most notable in Poe is that he either pioneered or originated half a dozen fields. With his three tales "The

Murders in the Rue Morgue," "The Purloined Letter," and "The Gold Bug," he not only invented the detective story but practically exhausted its possibilities. The critic Howard Haycraft credits him with laying the form's complete foundation and then goes on to name ten elements of the modern detective story, all to be found in Poe. Similarly Poe blazed the trail leading to what is now called science fiction. His theories of "pure poetry" influenced the important French symbolist movement of the latter part of the nineteenth century, and so affected the great modern poet Yeats (93). Poe defined and illustrated the tale of single effect. In his strange and morbid stories we find many anticipations of modern psychology, including the motif of the death wish and that of the split personality (see his remarkable "William Wilson"). Poe's prevailing moods of desolation and isolation set the tone for much writing of our own century. Finally, for all his faults, he was our country's first important literary critic, generally making his judgments on a broad base of first principles.

Many of today's critics see in American writing two major strains that sometimes intermingle. The first is optimistic, practical, democratic. The second is pessimistic, guilt-laden, aristocratic, and deeply involved with the heart's darker concerns. The latter tradition found its first notable figure in Poe, and that is why he is more than a mere writer of gruesome romantic tales.

55

NATHANIEL HAWTHORNE (1804–1864)

The Scarlet Letter, Selected Tales

In any well-considered list of the dozen greatest American novels *The Scarlet Letter* would almost certainly appear. Yet one may wonder at first why this should be so. Its background is seventeenth-century Puritan New England. When Hawthorne wrote about it, the scene was already beginning to appear remote; today it is very far away indeed. Furthermore we are not quite sure that Hawthorne's picture of a sin-obsessed, guilt-ridden society offers even the interest attaching to historical accuracy. Most recent researches tend to show that the Puritans were a far more relaxed people than their brooding descendant conceived them to be. Finally, Hester's and Dimmesdale's adultery and expiation appear to have a forceful meaning only within the framework of a dogmatic Christian morality. Many of us, living in a post-Freud world, may read this book for the first time only to exclaim, "What's he making all the fuss about?"

And yet, though we may smile away the Puritan ethic that suffuses it, we somehow cannot smile away the book itself. Its power to move us persists, even though we may admire it for qualities different from those that originally won Hawthorne his reputation. For us this is only incidentally a story of the bitter fruits of adultery. It is even more incidentally a historical picture of a bygone society. What we now seem to be reading is a profound parable of the human heart. It happens to be expressed in symbols that were particularly meaningful to Hawthorne and his time. But they *are* only symbols, and flexible ones at that, applicable to the human condition as it exists everywhere and at all times.

Take that moral which Hawthorne, toward the end of his dark and beautiful romance, puts in a sentence: "Be true! Be true! Be true! Show freely to the world, if not your worst, yet some trait whereby the worst may be inferred!" Though couched in didactic phrases, is this not an indictment of repression, a plea for that purification of our souls that comes only from facing, not deceiving, ourselves? In the same way we feel that Chillingworth's dissolution is inevitable in any man in any society who tries to live by life-denying emotions. We feel also, as Hawthorne explicitly says, that love and hate begin to resemble each other when both depend too exclusively, too passionately on the possession of the loved or hated object.

In other words, we no longer read this as a book about how two young people were punished for committing adultery. We read it as the work of a moral psychologist who knows as much about our own hidden guilts and fears as he did about those of his tortured Puritans. I suggest that if we approach

The Scarlet Letter in this light it ceases to be the faded classic suggested by its old-fashioned style and its, to us, excessive moralizing. We begin to see what the critic Mark Van Doren means when he tells us that Hawthorne's "one deathless virtue is that rare thing in any literature, an utterly serious imagination."

Hawthorne once wrote of his workroom: "This deserves to be called a haunted chamber, for thousands and thousands of visions have appeared to me in it." Much of our life we pass in the prosaic light of day. But a part of it even the most normal of us pass in a haunted chamber. Of this haunted chamber Hawthorne is a classic historian.

I should add that it will repay you to read or reread, in addition to *The Scarlet Letter,* a few of Hawthorne's somber allegorical shorter tales, particularly "Young Goodman Brown," "The Minister's Black Veil," "The Birthmark," and "Rappaccini's Daughter."

56

HERMAN MELVILLE (1819–1891)

Moby Dick, Bartleby the Scrivener

At twenty-five Melville had already had most of the experiences that were to supply him with the raw materials for his books. As a seaman he had served aboard the trader *St. Lawrence,* the whaler *Acushnet,* the Australian bark *Lucy Ann,* and the frigate *United States.* He had sailed both the Atlantic and the South Seas. He had undergone "an indulgent captivity" of some four weeks with a cannibal tribe in the Marquesas. His adventures had been preceded by an aimless, sketchy education and were to be followed by a little formal travel in Europe and the Holy Land. These external events—plus a brooding, powerful, and original genius—were enough to produce not only *Moby Dick* but almost a score of other works in prose and verse. One of these, *Billy Budd, Foretopman,* was published many years after his death, and is well worth reading.

HERMAN MELVILLE

He wrote *Typee,* an account of his stay with the cannibals, when he was twenty-five. It had considerable success. Nothing he wrote thereafter received much popular welcome, and the latter half of his life was spent in obscurity and loneliness. *Moby Dick* (1851) was not precisely unnoticed, it is true, but it was not understood. Not until the twenties of our century, about thirty years after Melville's death, was it resurrected by a few devoted scholars. Then Melville's reputation skyrocketed, and it has never since greatly diminished. *Moby Dick* is recognized everywhere as one of the world's great novels.

"I have written a wicked book and feel as spotless as the lamb," wrote Melville to his good friend Hawthorne (55). An interesting sentence. Partly it is light irony. Partly it is a recognition of the fact that *Moby Dick*'s metaphysical and religious defiances would hardly please Melville's straitlaced family. And partly it is a fair description of the book. For, though the intention is of course not wicked, the novel *is* about evil, and it is hardly Christian in tone.

We have already noted at least two narrative prose works of the imagination that can be read on two or more planes—*Gulliver's Travels* (27) and *Alice's Adventures in Wonderland* (35). We have still to meet two others of which this may be said—*Huckleberry Finn* (57) and *Don Quixote* (62). *Moby Dick* belongs with them.

With a little judicious skipping, boys and girls can enjoy it as a thrilling sea story about a vengeful old man with an ivory leg pursuing his enemy, the White Whale, to their common death. Grown-ups of various degrees of sophistication can read it as a tempestuous work of art, filled with the deepest questionings and embodying a tragic sense of life that places it with the masterpieces of Dostoyevsky and even, some think, Shakespeare. And no one at all sensitive to our language can help being moved by its magnificent prose, like an organ with all the stops out.

Moby Dick is not a hard book. But it is not a transparent one either. We all feel that Ahab and the whale (and the other characters) mean more than themselves, but we may well differ over what those meanings may be. For some, Moby Dick symbolizes the malignancy of the whole universe, the baffling inexorability of Nature, that Nature from which we, if we are sensitive and energetic of mind, somehow feel ourselves estranged. That dark Nature is always in Ahab's consciousness. Indeed Moby Dick may be thought of, not only as a real whale, but as a monster thrashing about in the vast Pacific of Ahab's brain, to be exorcised only by his own self-destruction. *Moby Dick* is not a gloomy or morbid book, but you can hardly call it an argument for optimism.

Many years ago, writing about *Moby Dick*, I tried to summarize my sense of it. Now, rereading it for perhaps the fifth time, I find no reason to change my opinion: *"Moby Dick* is America's most unparochial great book, less delivered over to a time and place than the work of even our freest minds, Emerson and Whitman. It is conceived on a vast scale, it shakes hands with prairie seas and great distances, it invades with its conquistador prose 'the remotest secret drawers and lockers of the world.' It has towering faults of taste, it is often willful and obscure, but it will remain America's unarguable contribution to world literature, so many-leveled is it, so wide-ranging in that nether world which is the defiant but secretly terror-stricken soul of man, alone, and appalled by his aloneness."

The long short story "Bartleby," published in a magazine two years after *Moby Dick*, could have been written only by the creator of that book. Even today, in a time more receptive to its dark atmosphere, perhaps Samuel Beckett (23) alone might find in Bartleby's inveterate passivity something congenial to his talent. But in 1853 (Poe died in 1849) no American writer but Melville could have even imagined the tale's subject. Indeed it does not seem to have been understood at the time; several commentators thought it a humorous work.

With his quiet "I would prefer not to," Bartleby—"pallidly neat, pitiably respectable, incurably forlorn"—counters all attempts at human contact. Problem: how to spin fifty pages out of pure negation? Somehow Melville builds a haunting narrative around a being, otherwise sane and well conducted, who confronts life with an Everlasting Nay—and this at a period when all his countrymen were constructing a great nation with unprecedented energy and a positive passion for experience.

Using the modish phrase of our own day we may interpret

"Bartleby" as a study, some generations before Freud (77), of the death wish. Or perhaps it belongs, like Conrad's masterly "The Secret Sharer," to the rich literature of the doppelgänger—for are not poor Bartleby and his highly normal narrator eerily bound together? Or it may be a private allegory, hiding and revealing Melville's own loneliness, his remoteness from the roaring materialism of his day.

In any case, a story to trouble one's dreams.

57
MARK TWAIN   (1835–1910)

Huckleberry Finn

Many of us who read *Huckleberry Finn* in our youth still think of it as a "boys' book"—which of course it is, and a very good one too. Against this view place Ernest Hemingway's (60) famous statement: "All modern American literature comes from one book by Mark Twain called *Huckleberry Finn*." Somewhere between these two judgments lies the truth. But it lies much closer to the second judgment than to the first.

Mark Twain (real name: Samuel Langhorne Clemens) had a good deal of trouble writing *Huckleberry Finn*. It's doubtful that he knew, when he had finished, that it might turn out to be, along with Thoreau's *Walden,* one of the two central and generative books of the American nineteenth century. In a way he wrote it out of his unconscious, through which the great river that had nourished his early imagination still rolled and flooded. Into it he put his youth—but also, perhaps without quite knowing it, the youth of the Republic. He did more. The division in Huck's mind between his natural social genius (for Huck is a genius as well as a boy; indeed this boy is a great man) and his distaste for "sivilization" mirrored a split in our national soul. We too as a people have been torn and are still being torn between a desire, based on our frontier heritage, to "light out for the territory," and our apparently stronger desire to convert that territory into one great productive mill. Furthermore, Huck reflects the tensions still vibrating in the national conscience; reread the chapter in which Huck debates whether or not he will turn in Jim, who is that criminal thing, an escaped slave, but who also happens to be a friend.

In this book there is no sentimentality. The preindustrial "natural" America it depicts is one of violence, murder, feuds, greed, and danger. The river is supremely wonderful but also, as this ex-pilot author knew, supremely treacherous and even sinister. Nevertheless, no grown-up American who loves this country, its present no less than its past, can read *Huckleberry Finn* without a poignant sense that it is a kind of epic celebration of a lost paradise. We all feel, North and South, that with Appomattox a certain innocence, a certain fresh and youthful freedom left us forever, possibly to be replaced by something better. The sophisticated Periclean Greek, reading his Homer, must have felt somewhat the same way. *Huckleberry Finn* is our *Odyssey*.

Mark Twain, referring to the greatly inferior *Tom Sawyer*, called it "simply a hymn, put into prose form to give it a worldly air." That is quite true of *Huckleberry Finn*. It is a hymn to the strange, puzzled, disorderly, but still rather beautiful youth of our nation.

Hemingway implied all this in his statement. But he also meant something more precise. He meant that Mark Twain was the first great American writer to use the vernacular (indeed a dozen vernaculars) creatively. *Huckleberry Finn* deliberately destroyed the conventional English literary sentence. It introduced a new rhythm that actually followed the twists and turns of our ordinary speech, without trying for phonographic accuracy. It showed us what can be done with a de-academicized language.

For all his later worldliness and big-city culture, Mark Twain was one of those "powerful, uneducated persons" saluted by Walt Whitman. This does not make him any the less a great writer. But it makes him a great writer who heads a tradition radically different from that headed by his contemporary Henry James (58). They reflect two powerful forces in our literature and our thought. The first is native, humorous, and in the best sense popular. The second is Anglo-European-American, deeply analytic, and in the best sense aristocratic.

58

HENRY JAMES (1843–1916)

The Ambassadors

During his seventy-two years, nothing much happened to Henry James, brother of the great American philosopher-psychologist William James (85). He never married. Indeed, so far as we know, he had few passionate relations with men or women. The one decisive external event of his long, industrious life was his decision in 1876 to live permanently in England. There, varying his desk labors with trips to his native country and Europe, plus much dining out, James spent the rest of his days.

It seems a bit passive. Yet on balance James probably lived one of the most active lives of the century. Nothing happened to him except everything—everything he could observe, feel, discriminate, ponder, and finally cast into his elaborately wrought stories. He made everything pay artistic dividends. His books are his real biography.

Conrad (37) called him "the historian of fine consciences," an excellent phrase if we extend the last word so as to include the idea of consciousness. James excels in the careful tracing of subtle relationships among subtle characters. He exhausts all the psychological possibilities of any given situation; and the situations he chooses, at least in his major novels, are dense with meaning. His mastery flows in part from his perfect recognition of his own immense powers. These depend on sensibility and high intelligence, and the ability to find and mold the exactly right form for his ideas and themes. As pure artist he is the most extraordinary figure in the history of the American novel.

James himself thought *The Ambassadors* his finest book. Though written in his late period it does not suffer from the overelaboration of which many readers complain. (One well-known witticism thus describes James's three phases: James I, James II, and the Old Pretender.) All his powers are here held in beautiful balance and suspension. He handles one of his major themes—the impact of Continental moral realism on the rigid and sometimes naive ethical outlook of Americans—on the level of the highest comedy. That last word should not make you think *The Ambassadors* is not a serious work. For all its grace and wit, it is weighty enough, with its grave and reiterated plea for more life, for more perception, for the claims of the intelligence as an instrument for seizing and interpreting experience. "Live all you can," cries Lambert Strether to Little Bilham, "live, live!" In Strether, who is superbly equipped to react to the new experience that comes to him, alas too late, I think James felt he had created a peculiarly American type.

As with most of James's work, *The Ambassadors* must be read slowly. Every line tells. All is measured for its possible effect. There is no trace in it of what the author called "the baseness of the arbitrary stroke." It may take you ten times as long to read *The Ambassadors* as to read *Tom Jones*—but for some readers there will be ten times as much in it.

One of the most voluminous of great writers, James cannot be known through any single book. He worked brilliantly in the fields of the novel, the long and short story, the memoir, the biography, the critical essay, and the travel sketch, as well as unsuccessfully in the theater.

59

WILLIAM FAULKNER (1897–1962)

The Sound and the Fury, As I Lay Dying

William Faulkner has been hailed (except by a few uninfluential dissenters) as the greatest American novelist of his generation. Some critics rank him among the greatest of all time. In 1949 the award of the Nobel Prize marked the official peak of an extraordinary career.

Most of his novels and short stories are laid in Yoknapatawpha County, Mississippi. This invented region has now become hallowed literary ground, like Hardy's Wessex. The novels' time span covers almost a century and a half, beginning in 1820. They form a connected series, something like Zola's

Rougon-Macquart family chronicle or Balzac's more loosely linked "Human Comedy." Through accounts of the fortunes of a number of related families, Faulkner exposes, in a style of great complication and variety, the tragedy, and some of the comedy, of his violent, haunted, guilt-ridden Deep South. Mainly represented are three worlds: that of the black; that of the degenerate aristocracy, typified by the Compsons in *The Sound and the Fury;* and that of the even more degenerate emergent commercial class, whose emblem is the horrifying Lem Snopes.

The two novels recommended above are considered by most critics among Faulkner's finest; they are certainly among his most violent in theme and trail-blazing in technique. His champions also single out for high praise *Light in August* and *Absalom, Absalom!* as well as the Snopes trilogy (*The Hamlet, The Town, The Mansion*).

Faulkner is a serious, difficult, and daring writer. He is also, to some, a shocking writer. And finally, to a few, he is a writer only intermittently readable. The latter do not have the key to his mind, which may well be their loss. To this class I belong. If you need guidance through Faulkner's special inferno, the only fair thing for me to do is to refer you to any of the books and essays listed in the Suggestions for Further Reading. To my mind the best of these commentaries is Malcolm Cowley's Introduction to his *Portable Faulkner,* a brilliant exercise in sympathetic clarification.

60
ERNEST HEMINGWAY (1899–1961)

Short Stories

In perspective it is Hemingway's short stories, rather than his more ambitious fiction, that stand out. In them the defects of his attitudes have neither time nor space in which to expose themselves. The bellicosity, the conscious virility, the exaltation of violence and toughness, the bravado, the conception of women as romantic receptacles—these are all muted in his marvelous tales. By the same token the famous style, perfectly suited to the illumination of intense moments or isolated situations, gains a power in the short story it does not always possess in the longer works. It seems fair to say that, by virtue of his reverence for truth, the originality of his prose, the bone-bare exactness of his dialogue, and the charge of his emotion, Hemingway ranks among the first half-dozen of the world's masters of the short story.

Though he seems to grapple with ultimates, such as death, passion, and the defeat or persistence of human hopes, Hemingway's total world is actually not a large one. In even the lesser novelists we have already met more and wider gateways to human nature. To match him with the greatest is probably pointless. Beside Stendhal he seems young; beside Henry James, primitive; beside Tolstoy, simply minor. Yet his achievement is solid. Building on a foundation laid down by Mark Twain (57), he quite literally remodeled the English sentence. He forced it to reveal, without waste motion, the exact truth of a moment, an insight, an experience. This contribution to literature is not merely technical. It is moral. Hemingway taught language honesty.

His greater tales (with which we must class the novella *The Old Man and the Sea*) are now as much a part of our American heritage as "Rip Van Winkle" or "The Fall of the House of Usher." "The Snows of Kilimanjaro," "The Undefeated," "My Old Man," "The Killers," "Fifty Grand," and dozens of others compel us, no matter how often we reread them, to relive the experience the creator once felt so deeply. Whether or not we accept Hemingway's view of life, we cannot reject these tales of the veld, the bull ring, the barroom, the ski slope, the racetrack, the prize ring, the Michigan woods. For they pass beyond the novel settings and beyond the once novel style. Emotion and the control of emotion are here held in exquisite poise. An artist who is also an honest man succeeds in telling the truth.

Note: The 1987 *Complete Short Stories of Ernest Hemingway,* the so-called Finca Vigía edition, is the only exhaustive collection.

61

SAUL BELLOW (1915–   )

The Adventures of Augie March, Herzog, Humboldt's Gift

Saul Bellow may be the most intelligent imaginative writer now at work in our country. He also seems to me to exemplify beautifully the whole cultural tradition reflected in this volume. The moral dilemmas at the heart of his fiction are not constructs; they evolve from the very nature of his characters. He is penetrating rather than merely observant, wise rather than merely shrewd. A noble word currently derided in some quarters applies to him. He is a humanist.

Bellow was born in Lachine, Quebec, of Canadian-Jewish parents but has lived most of his life in Chicago, generally the setting of his fiction. He received an excellent college and university education, has taught at Princeton, Bard, and the University of Minnesota, and is, I believe, still connected with the University of Chicago as a member of the Committee on Social Thought. He is not ashamed of being an intellectual or of presenting in his work evolved rather than semibarbarian minds.

Many of his characters are Jewish, but he hardly belongs to any ethnic school. While his creations are pure urban-American, his general temper often suggests the mainstream of European fiction. Perhaps his harmonious fusion of these traditions influenced the Nobel Committee when they conferred on him the prize in literature for 1976.

Though any of his books will reward you, I have recommended three. *The Adventures of Augie March* (1953) is a modern picaresque with scenes laid in Chicago, Mexico, and Paris. The form is well suited to Bellow's sense of the free flow of big-city life. In it he exhibits masterfully a style peculiarly his own. The street vernacular of the period merges with more classical and elegant uses of the language. Two of his outstanding qualities—energy and a sense of comedy—here assert themselves as, under great control, they will in all of his work to follow.

Most of his major characters have trouble with women, as is the case with Charlie Citrine, the writer whose memories generate the structure of *Humboldt's Gift* (1975). The title derives from Citrine's friend Von Humboldt Fleischer whose sad life is said to be based on that of Delmore Schwartz, a remarkable poet and critic who died in sordid circumstances in 1966.

Many readers and critics feel that Bellow's finest work is *Herzog* (1964), perfect in its fugal form, impressive in its insight into our troubled time, and enormously skillful in the portrayal of a suffering human being whose irony is continually exercised on himself and the American scene against which he is limned. Moses Herzog is a forty-seven-year-old intellectual, a womanizer without being a libertine. He spends about a week in a crazy zigzag flight, searching for self-understanding, stability, comprehension of his country and his period. Part of the time is occupied in writing letters (unmailed) to those who have figured in his life, as well as to Adlai Stevenson, Eisenhower, and the eminent dead. He recollects his miserable childhood ("a great schooling in grief"); tries to connect his surplus store of book learning with the baffling requirements of real life; meditates on history; passes from "the dream of existence" to "the dream of intellect." He achieves almost archetypal dimensions, doing for the American intellectual what Babbitt did for the American businessman. Like many of Bellow's characters, he is an emotionally displaced person, but even those readers who consider themselves well adjusted will recognize in the comic-pathetic-heroic Herzog not a stranger but a part of their very selves.

"The soul requires intensity," thinks Herzog. We smile, but we cannot laugh off the sentence. It suggests what is perhaps Bellow's major distinction: the high charge of feeling and thought that vibrates in all his work but most notably in this novel. At the center of his preoccupations lies a concern, often tinged with irony, with the impingement of the long humanist tradition on a "posthistorical" culture.

62

MIGUEL DE CERVANTES SAAVEDRA (1547–1616)

Don Quixote

Don Quixote is perhaps the only book (but see also Tolstoy) on our list that may profitably be read in an abridged (but, please, not a bowdlerized or children's) version. Walter Starkie has done a good job along this line. However, if you use, as I suggest, a complete translation, do some skipping. Whenever (or almost whenever) you come to a goatherd or a shepherdess, some drivel lies ahead. Skip all the interpolated pastoral yarns that pleased Cervantes's audience but bore us stiff. Skip every bit of verse you meet; Cervantes is one of the world's worst poets. Finally, use *only* a modern translation—Cohen's or Starkie's or, best of all, Putnam's. Avoid Motteux's like the plague. Post-finally, do not be put off by an occasional tedious passage or chapter in Part 1. Persist to Part 2. It is by far the greater. Even the finest writers sometimes have to educate themselves through the medium of their own creation, and apparently that is what happened to this poor, maimed ex-soldier Cervantes. From writing about Don Quixote and Sancho Panza he learned how great they really were. Ten years elapsed between the publication of the two parts, and those ten years made a difference in Cervantes's genius.

These warnings are needed because, like *Paradise Lost* and *The Divine Comedy*, *Don Quixote* is one of those books more reverenced than read, more lauded than enjoyed. It has had its ups and downs. Perhaps it reached its peak of popularity in the eighteenth century—we have mentioned how much it meant to Sterne (28), for example. It is not so widely read in our time. Still, the fact remains that, after the Bible, it is one of the half-dozen books in the world most widely translated and studied. And for this there must be good reasons.

There are.

Of these reasons Cervantes himself suggests the simplest. He remarks, in the second chapter of Part 2, "No sooner do [people] see any lean hack than they cry out: 'There goes Rosinante.'" In other words, his book is crowded with immediately recognizable human types, and in this case a nonhuman type. The whole world understands at once what we mean when we call someone quixotic or say that he tilts at windmills. There are really only a few literary characters we think of as permanently alive. Hamlet is one, Don Quixote surely another.

The second reason is no less simple. *Don Quixote,* once you allow for its leisurely tempo, is one of the best adventure stories ever written, perhaps the best after the *Odyssey.* That is what makes it a classic for the young. When you reread it years later you perceive that it is also a great adventure story of the mind, for some of its most exciting events occur during the conversations between the knight and his loquacious squire, two of the best talkers who ever used their vocal cords creatively.

The third reason sounds simple but is not so. *Don Quixote* is a supremely humorous novel. Some readers laugh aloud, others grin, some smile externally, others internally. And some read it with a curious emotion mingling delight and sorrow. Cervantes's humor is hard to define because it is not a "character trait" in him; it is the man himself, hence a mystery. The best clue to his humor is Walter Starkie's remark. He calls Cervantes a humorist, "which meant that he could see more than one thing at a time."

This brings us to the deepest of all the reasons for *Don Quixote*'s greatness—the fact that, though it is not obscure, its meanings seem to change with each generation, indeed with each reader, and none of these meanings are trivial.

We all know that Cervantes started out to write a satire on chivalric romances. Or so he seems to say. Don Quixote himself, the lean, grizzled Knight of the Sorrowful Countenance, began his life as a figure of fun. So did his earthy, stocky, proverb-crammed squire, Sancho Panza. Yet, by the end of the book, both have become something else, as well as more like each other, as the critic Salvador de Madariaga remarks. Together they seem to sum up, roughly, the warring elements in all of us: our defiance of society and our acceptance of it; our love of the heroic and our suspicion of it; our passion for creating worlds of the imagination and our rueful compromise with the *status quo.*

And so we come to the Don Quixote "problem," as fascinating as the Hamlet "problem." Is this book a burlesque of chivalry? Or is it the most persuasive of pleas for the chivalric attitude, apart from any specific time or institution? Is it a satire on dreamers? Or is it a defense of dreaming? Is it a symbol of the tragic soul and history of Spain? If so, why does it speak so clearly to men of all nations and races? Is it the author's spiritual autobiography? A study of insanity? Or of a higher sanity? Or is it, couched in terms of picaresque incident, a dramatized treatise on illusion and reality, akin to the plays of Pirandello? Finally—just to indicate how complex interpretation may become—is Don Quixote, as Mark Van Doren thinks, a kind of actor, who chooses his role because by so doing he can absorb life and reflect on it in a way denied to the single, unvarying personality?

I leave you to the golden book that Macaulay thought "the best novel in the world, beyond comparison."

63
JORGE LUIS BORGES (1899–1986)

Labyrinths, Dreamtigers

Since this book's first appearance, Latin American writers have been looming larger on our literary horizon. The Plan recognizes this fact by adding Borges (as well as García Márquez) to its original list.

Borges, scion of an intellectual middle-class family, was born in Buenos Aires, where most of his life was lived. His ancestry was Spanish and English, with a small infusion of Portuguese-Jewish blood. Like Nabokov, he learned English prior to his native tongue. He was strongly influenced by English writers from Caedmon to Chesterton and H. G. Wells.

Following his partially European education Borges began his career as a poet. His father's death and a near-fatal illness made 1938 a year of crisis for him. From this year dates the finest of his "fictions," a form peculiarly his own in which his genius is most clearly reflected. Slow in growth, his reputation became international with the publication in 1944 of his collection *Ficciones*. It was more formally recognized in 1961 when Borges shared with Samuel Beckett the coveted international Formentor Prize.

Though hardly a political man, Borges opposed the Perón dictatorship and as a result was demoted from his post of librarian to that of poultry and rabbits inspector. After Perón's fall in 1955 he was named director of the National Library of Argentina. By that time his always defective eyesight had worsened; from the age of fifty-six he was totally blind, this man who described himself as one "who imagined Paradise in the shape of a library."

Borges's vast and esoteric learning, which pervades his stories, makes his range of allusion somewhat forbidding to many readers and on occasion imparts to his work a bookish flavor. But these seeming hindrances are little more than a facade of irony. Behind it works a mind of almost dismaying subtlety in which a metaphysician, a logician, and a visionary (but not a mystic) occupy continually shifting positions. His constant theme, whether he offers us science fiction, detective stories, tales of violence, or logical nightmares, is the "hallucinatory nature of the world." For him the universe is not something made. Rather it is dreamt. Or perhaps it is a great Book, whose tone is that of "irreality, one of art's requisites."

Certain metaphors recur: images of infinite regression, of cyclic reappearance, the maze, the mirror, the double, tigers, libraries, time itself. "I have some understanding of labyrinths," says his narrator in "The Garden of Forking Paths." For Borges "ambiguity is richness." Thus his endless series of possible worlds differs essentially from the alternate world of a Tolkien, unambiguous, solid, roughly referable point by point to our familiar one. Borges plays with ideas like a magician with his props, but the magic is more than legerdemain. His Library of Babel is also a universe and an emblem of infinity; his science fiction tales are not arbitrary fantasies but serious attempts to refute ordinary notions of time; and his many stories of betrayal and frustration penetrate the dream life that floats, dense, shifting, troubling, below the consciousness threshold of all of us.

As you read Borges you may feel his affinities with other

writers discussed in his book: with Cervantes (62), about whose masterpiece he has written the most coolly outrageous story one can well imagine; with Lewis Carroll (35), Kafka (45), surely García Márquez (64), and perhaps Nabokov (69). But the Borges voice is unique. He has influenced many, but his magic is his own.

I have suggested you try two of his books. *Labyrinths* contains his finest fictions, essays, and parables, as well as a useful bibliography for those who wish to know him better. *Dreamtigers* contains more parables and a fair selection of his verse, conscientiously translated.

64
GABRIEL GARCÍA MÁRQUEZ (1928–   )

One Hundred Years of Solitude

García Márquez and Borges are usually considered the two world-famous Latin American writers of our time. The term *magic realism* is often applied to their work and to that of others of the same school, such as the Cuban Alejo Carpentier, the Mexican Carlos Fuentes, the Argentinian Julio Cortázar, and the Peruvian Mario Vargas Llosa. The rather tired critical cliché does suggest their slant on the world, which diverges sharply from the mainstream tradition of English and American fiction.

"Magic realism" was first used back in 1925 to describe a group of German painters who used precise literal techniques to image fantastic events flowering in the unconscious. These artists addressed the nonlogical element deeply buried in all of us; and so do the contemporary novelists of magic realism.

García Márquez speaks somewhere of "the mistaken and absurd world of rational creatures." The phrase would seem perfectly acceptable to many South American and Central American writers. They have all been affected, to the point of obsession, by the disorderly, often nightmarish history of their native lands. Thus, though their magic realism was also influenced by French symbolism and surrealism (and in

García Márquez's case by Faulkner [59]), it developed as a special technology of the imagination, designed to cope with the abnormal experience of a whole people.

One Hundred Years of Solitude traces the rise, decline, and fall of Macondo, presumably the author's home town of Aracataca, Colombia. The era is marked by civil strife, frightful violence, political corruption, and the abuse of power. Five—perhaps seven—generations of the Buendía family compose the materials with which the narrative is constructed. Over the years, first names (Aureliano, José Arcadio) recur, identities blur, family traits reassert themselves, making us feel that Macondo's life is cyclical, without forward movement, devoid of a goal. While the outside world of industry and progress at times touches them, essentially the Buendías remain immured in their sad and sometimes mad solitude.

Winner of the 1982 Nobel Prize in literature, García Márquez has spent much of his life as a working journalist. Thus he has a keen nose for fact; much of *One Hundred Years* is realistic enough. But the story is also full of ghosts, visions, monsters, prescient dreams, happenings contrary to nature (such as mass insomnia), a man two hundred years old, another returned from the dead, others who levitate.

The book is a kind of allegory of Latin American history, as much hallucination as family chronicle. Macondo is "the city of mirrors (or mirages)." Past and present fuse. One historian of the Buendía family, the author tells us, "had not put events in the order of conventional time, but had concentrated a century of daily episodes in such a way that they co-existed in one instant." José Arcadio Buendía, we learn, "was the only one who had enough lucidity to sense the truth of the fact that time also stumbled and had accidents and could therefore splinter and leave an eternalized fragment in a room."

In its energy, its humor (for it has a kind of grim humor), its conscious exaggeration, its distortions of language, and its drive to transform human experience into myth, *One Hundred Years* recalls *Gargantua and Pantagruel* (46) as much as any title suggested in this volume.

One is tempted to say that *One Hundred Years* has a certain claim to be called the Great Latin American Novel. At any rate, for all its concentration on the sufferings, madnesses, delusions, incestuous loves, and outsize passions of a single family, it seems to evoke the tragic real life and dream life of a whole continent.

65

NIKOLAI VASILIEVICH GOGOL (1809–1852)

Dead Souls

This does not seem like a particularly appealing title. Actually the term refers, as you will discover, to Russian serfs who had died but were still carried, until the next census, on the tax rolls. The book is not as morbid as it sounds.

Gogol is not a particularly appealing figure either. His family heritage was a poor one, he had an unbalanced youth, he failed at the law, as a government clerk, as an actor, as a teacher. To the end of his short life he remained a virgin, and in his latter years religious mania clouded his mind. As a writer he enjoyed a number of triumphs, but at bottom he was appalled by the electrifying reaction to his books and plays. He wandered aimlessly over Europe and made a pointless pilgrimage to the Holy Land. During his last days he burned his manuscripts, so that we possess only a fragment of the second part of *Dead Souls,* which when completed was to show good victorious over evil. He died in what seems to have been delirium.

Yet this queer duck, who surely cannot be said to possess a powerful mind, virtually founded Russian prose and gave Russia a masterpiece that became a part of world literature. Speaking of Gogol's most famous short story, Dostoyevsky said, "We all come out of 'The Overcoat.'" One recalls Hemingway's remark about *Huckleberry Finn.* Gogol's untraditional genius apparently led him to break with the formalism and rigidity that marked much previous Russian writing, just as Mark Twain did in our own country. The giants who followed him benefited from this liberation.

I once wrote an Introduction to *Dead Souls* that the brilliant author of *Lolita* termed "ridiculous." I think Nabokov must have felt queasy over my notion (shared by many) that *Dead Souls* is a great comic novel. He must surely have objected also to my other notion (also not uniquely held) that Gogol in one of his moods—for he did not have a coherent system even of prejudices—was in this book expressing a certain dissatisfaction with the Russian feudal system. But it is also true—this is Nabokov's emphasis—that *Dead Souls* is a demonic book, as well as a funny one. It does have a nightmare, almost a surrealist, tone. Usually likened to Dickens (33), Gogol is even more akin to Poe (54). That *Dead Souls* can please me as well as Nabokov may have exasperated Nabokov, but furnishes at least some slight evidence of the variety of Gogol's appeal.

At any rate, this is a fascinating, almost madly vivid, loosely composed yarn about a great, bland rogue and his travels through what seems, to a mere American, a real, if heavily caricatured, early-nineteenth-century Russia. Its laughter is mingled with melancholy—the poet Pushkin, after listening to Gogol's reading of the first chapter, sighed, "Lord, how sad is our Russia."

I cannot command the original, but nonetheless dare to recommend one translation, and one only. It is by Bernard Guilbert Guerney. It just sounds right. The others have a stiffness foreign, I am told, to Gogol's spirit.

66
IVAN SERGEYEVICH TURGENEV (1818–1883)

Fathers and Sons

Of the four great nineteenth-century Russian novelists, Turgenev seems to wear the least well. Perhaps that is because, as authorities tell us, his style is of such delicacy and evocativeness that no translation does it justice. Or it may be that some of his themes have lost their attractive power: the "superfluous men," the charming but effete Russian gentry of the 1840s and 1850s; the struggle, if the term is not too strong, between the dominating female and the weaker male; the pale beauty of early love, of frustrated love, of remembered love; and his recurrent motif, the mutations of failure.

Turgenev's mother was a witch out of a dreadful fairy tale. The terror and despair she inspired in her son never left his mind and crept into much of his work. His lifelong passion for the famous, ugly, but apparently fascinating singer Pauline Viardot-García, offered no compensation for his bruised spirit. He followed her about Europe like a dog, enjoyed (if he did) her ultimate favors only briefly, and obtained what happiness he could by living near her or at times with her and her husband. There is no doubt that she distorted his view of women; he seems either to fear them or to sentimentalize them.

Turgenev shuttled between his Russian estates and Western Europe for many years, and spent the last twenty or so mainly in Paris and Baden. He was an expatriate, rather like Joyce. Like Joyce, he widened his own country's perspective by throwing open to it a view of cosmopolitan culture. Also like Joyce, this "Westernizer" continued to draw his central inspiration from his native land, no matter how distanced his external life became. Turgenev's political position, throughout the century that was preparing for 1917, was that of the unengaged, liberal, enlightened, humane skeptic. Hence his books, while at once winning the admiration of the cultivated, often failed to please either the reactionaries or the radicals.

Some of his shorter works (particularly many of the *Sportsman's Sketches*) are indeed beautiful. But probably his reputation will continue to rest mainly on *Fathers and Sons*, also translated as *Fathers and Children*. As its title suggests, it was intended to be a study of the conflict between the generations. The theme, in my opinion, has been more powerfully treated by other novelists, including Samuel Butler in *The Way of All Flesh*.

To us, however, *Fathers and Sons* appears more interesting as the first classic presentation of that element in the Russian character which has surfaced in our time and now challenges the entire world. Turgenev lacks Dostoyevsky's intuitive, indeed terrifying grasp of the revolutionary-terrorist temperament. Yet in Bazarov, the center of his masterpiece, he does give us a clear, almost Olympian picture of the mid-nineteenth-century *nihilist* (the word is Turgenev's invention). In Russia, as the years went by, the nihilist type was to assume a number of different forms: the terrorist, the anarchist, the atheist-materialist, the science worshiper, and at last the dedicated Communist. Though the book exhibits in relief most of Turgenev's other admirable qualities—particularly his economy and his un-Russian clarity of form—it will stand or fall, I think, with Bazarov.

67

FEODOR MIKHAILOVICH DOSTOYEVSKY
(1821–1881)

Crime and Punishment, The Brothers Karamazov

Dostoyevsky's life and work are of a piece. Suffering, violence, emotional crises, and extravagance of conduct mark both. The terrible sincerity of his novels flows in part from the anxieties that clouded the author's whole career. It is well for the reader to know this. To read Dostoyevsky is to descend into an inferno.

Like Flaubert he was the son of a physician. Again like Flaubert he was when young introduced to scenes of suffering, disease, and death, and never forgot them. In his fifteenth year his gentle mother died, and not long afterward, in 1839, his father was either murdered by his own serfs or, more probably, died of apoplexy. Dostoyevsky was left desolate and defenseless. Perhaps from this period stems the epileptic tendency that was to overshadow his whole life, if also perhaps to give him a certain visionary inspiration. In 1849 his connection with a group of dreamy young radicals caused his arrest. He was sentenced to death, but just before the firing squad was about to do its work, his punishment was commuted. This experience marked him deeply. He then spent four years in a Siberian convict camp, enduring inhumanities partially described in his *Memoirs from the House of the Dead.* Another four years were spent in military service at a remote Asiatic outpost.

FEODOR MIKHAILOVICH DOSTOYEVSKY

His first marriage was to a hysteric, his second to his secretary, who seems to have understood his manias and rages. The utopian radicalism of his youth gave way to a religious conversion. Dostoyevsky became orthodox, reactionary, Slavophile. Yet none of these labels is fair to him, for his temperament was a contradictory one in which Christ and Satan struggled continually for mastery. At times he seems to talk almost like a good European—but a very Russian one. The latter part of his life was not much happier than the first part had been, though his supremacy as a novelist and interpreter of the Russian temperament was generally acknowledged. His epilepsy continued to threaten him; debts worried him; for a time he was a compulsive gambler; and there can be little doubt that his sexual nature was unbalanced.

This is the man who wrote some of the most extraordinary novels of all time. They anticipated many of the ideas of Nietzsche (76) and Freud (77); they influenced such non-Russian writers as Mann (44), Camus (53), and Faulkner (59); and they dramatized the terrorist theory and practice that we associate with Lenin, Stalin, and Hitler. Indeed it may be said that Dostoyevsky had an intuitive sense of what the twentieth century would have to endure; and this sense plays its part in the fascination of his work.

It is hard to pin this strange man down. His central obsession was God. The search for God, or the attempt to prove God's existence, dominates his stories. Thus tormented, Dostoyevsky seems to approach a vision of love and peace only after long journeying through universes of pain and evil. In his novels the worlds of crime, abnormal psychology, and religious mysticism meet and mingle in a manner difficult to define. He is thought of as an apostle of compassion, but of the true saintly qualities he seems to possess few.

The Brothers Karamazov is generally considered his most profound work. However, if you are going to limit yourself to only one novel, there is something to be said for *Crime and Punishment.* For one thing, *The Brothers Karamazov,* though it does not leave you up in the air, is nevertheless an unfinished book. *Crime and Punishment* is a simpler, more unified one, with a strong detective-story plot of great interest. It can be read as a straight thriller. It can be read as a vision.

It can be read on planes in between these two. From its murky, gripping, intolerably vivid pages you emerge with the feeling that you have lived and suffered a lifetime. Its action takes nine days.

68

LEO NIKOLAYEVICH TOLSTOY (1828–1910)

War and Peace

War and Peace, more frequently than any other work of fiction, has been called "the greatest novel ever written." This need not scare us. However its greatness may be defined, it is not connected with obscurity, with difficulty, or even with profundity. Once a few minor hazards are braved, this vast chronicle of Napoleonic times seems to become an open book, as if it had been written in the sunlight. Just as Dostoyevsky is the dramatist of the unconscious and what is called the abnormal, so Tolstoy is the epic narrator of the conscious and the normal. His tone is one of almost loving serenity, and his characters, though their names are odd and their time is remote, are our brothers and sisters.

Most beginning readers experience three difficulties:

1. The novel is enormously long. As with *Don Quixote* (though less cogently) some sort of case may be made for an abridged version. There are several available. I prefer, if you are unwilling to tackle the complete *War and Peace,* Manuel Komroff's abridgement in the Bantam Books edition. In this curtailment you will not get the full range of Tolstoy's mind. But you will get the essential *novelist* in Tolstoy. And you may find him so interesting that you will be encouraged to try the longer version.

2. It's hard to follow both the relationships and the movements of the (to us) strangely named, complex cast of characters. All I can say is that if you persist in your reading, the characters will sooner or later sort themselves out.

3. It's hard to separate the story from the digressions. Many critics have thought this a weakness in an otherwise great

novel. Tolstoy was not a formalist, as Turgenev was. He sprawls. He tells you what's on his mind. You must take him as you find him. If you read slowly enough (and you should; the book sets its own leisurely tempo) you will probably discover that the digressions are no harder to take than were the essays scattered through *Tom Jones.*

When I first wrote about *War and Peace* many years ago, I singled out for special praise three qualities: its inclusiveness, its naturalness, its timelessness. Rereading it fifteen years later, I discovered other qualities, particularly Tolstoy's ability to reveal one to oneself. Now, reading it once more, I am impressed with a virtue that may be simple to the point of banality. Tolstoy once said, "The one thing necessary, in life as in art, is to tell the truth." When your canvas is narrow enough, this may not seem so difficult—Hemingway tells the truth about bull-fighting. But your task is overwhelming when you take human life for your subject, and human life is the real subject of *War and Peace.*

Tolstoy meets his own test. In this gigantic story of the impact of Napoleon's invasion on a whole country, he never fakes, he never evades, he grasps life at the middle, he conveys the essence of a character by seizing upon precisely the true, the revelatory gesture or phrase. That is why, though it deals in part with war and destruction, it seems one of the sanest novels ever written. And its sanity flows from Tolstoy's love for his characters, his love for the "procession of the generations," his love for the spectacle of life itself.

69

VLADIMIR NABOKOV (1899–1977)

Lolita; Pale Fire; Speak, Memory

One (but only one) way of viewing modern novelists is to divide them into two classes: the engaged and the unengaged. The engaged have something they want to tell us, often something about the state of our society. They are not necessarily propagandists or message bearers, but they have something on their minds, some special view of the world they are anxious to pass on to us. We may recognize engaged writers in such figures as Swift, Huxley, Solzhenitsyn, and Camus, different as they are in other respects. The unengaged are less interested in getting something off their own minds than in revealing the configurations, the patterns of other minds. They do not care greatly about altering our view of life. They do care greatly about displaying symbolic structures we may admire or vibrate to. Both the engaged and the unengaged may produce first-rate works of art, but the engaged writer tends to operate on our intelligence, the unengaged on our esthetic sensibility. Borges is such an unengaged writer; and, preeminently, Nabokov.

Nabokov's Slavic background, his aristocratic stance, his checkered career, his mastery of two national cultures, and his keen interest in formal literary problems—all connect him with another towering innovator in modern fiction, Joseph Conrad (37). Born in what was then St. Petersburg, Nabokov was the scion of an aristocratic family that lost its fortune in the Revolution. Educated at Trinity College, Cambridge, he spent formative years (1922–40) in Germany and France as a struggling and largely unrecognized writer. From 1948 to 1958 he taught Russian and European literature at Cornell, continuing also his extensive researches in entomology. He became a recognized authority on butterflies, as well as a remarkable chess player, and these themes from time to time reflect themselves in his novels.

The worldwide success of *Lolita* (1955) gave him financial independence, though he never at any time wrote seriously for any reason except to please himself. He spent his last years living quietly in a Swiss hotel, dying in 1977.

Complete familiarity with the Nabokovian universe is a major adventure of the mind and imagination. To accomplish this it would be necessary to read all of his novels, plays, stories, and criticism—including a brilliant, cantankerous study of Gogol (65) and such marvelous fiction as the sad-hilarious *Pnin,* the metaphysical-sexual time-fantasy *Ada,* and the tragic *The Defense,* the best piece of fiction ever written about the passion for chess. But the three books here suggested will supply a first acquaintance with the greatest stylist of our period, who wrote equally well in English and Russian, and whose elegant, allusive, and witty prose sets him apart.

Lolita, which deals with Humbert Humbert's passion for nymphets, is of course a recognized classic. Completely original, it is an examination of love that is funny, shocking to some, sad, and sophisticated in a manner quite remote from our American notion of sophistication. *Pale Fire* is partly a one-thousand-line poem in heroic couplets, partly a commentary on them by a mad exiled king—or perhaps a king only in his fantasy. It is a literary joke of enormous intricacy and at the same time, in the opinion of good critics, an addition to world literature. *Speak, Memory* is autobiographical, a unique recollection of Nabokov's childhood and youth, mainly in pre-Revolutionary Russia.

The mad Kinbote, in *Pale Fire,* describes himself in terms that might apply to his creator: "I can do what only a true artist can do—pounce upon the forgotten butterfly of revelation, wean myself abruptly from the habit of things. . . ."

The critic Gilbert Highet, reviewing the remarkable thriller *King, Queen, Knave,* summed up Nabokov as "the most original, the most tantalizing, the most unpredictable author alive." Nabokov's genius is so unbound by mere chronology that the judgment, though the man is gone, will stand.

70

ALEKSANDR ISAYEVICH SOLZHENITSYN
(1918–   )

The First Circle, Cancer Ward

If we exclude Nabokov, who was at least fractionally an American novelist, Solzhenitsyn emerges as the greatest modern Russian writer. This is not in itself high praise: Soviet authors, though doubtless excellent employees, are not greatly esteemed by the rest of the world. But Solzhenitsyn is major, even when compared with the towering Russians we have already met: Gogol, Turgenev, Dostoyevsky, Tolstoy,

Chekhov. He ranks not too far below them, both as an artist and as a human being passionately concerned with the welfare of Russia and with the idea of freedom—though doubtless he attaches to this shapeless concept meanings not entirely identical with our own.

Descended from an intellectual Cossack family, Solzhenitsyn was educated as a mathematician, fought bravely in World War II, was arrested in 1945 for a letter criticizing Stalin ("the man with the mustache"), was imprisoned for eight years, placed in a detention camp for another three years, began to write after his "rehabilitation," and electrified thinking Russia when in 1962 Khrushchev permitted him to publish *One Day in the Life of Ivan Denisovich,* a labor-camp novel that dared to tell the truth.

In 1963 he ran into trouble with the bureaucracy and none of his succeeding books has ever been published in his native land. In 1970 he won the Nobel Prize, but was not allowed to go to Stockholm to receive it. In 1973 he publicly indicted the Soviet system, was denounced, and left for the West. At this writing he is a resident of Vermont.

He has made himself the voice, heard worldwide, of the Russian conscience, as Dickens and Zola were for their countries. His notion of democracy, though it breaks absolutely with Soviet totalitarianism, is infused with an old-Russian mysticism and theocracy that would perhaps bewilder Jefferson, Lincoln, and the ordinary American citizen. But of his courage and high moral character there can be no question. Whatever his final place in the hierarchy of literature, he is a great man.

I suggest that you try his two finest novels, *The First Circle* and *Cancer Ward.* These are more accessible than either *August 1914* (published 1971), the first of a series, Tolstoyan in scope, dealing with World War I; or *The Gulag Archipelago,* a nonfictional picture of the entire Soviet prison system.

The First Circle narrates four days in the life of a mathematician (clearly a self-portrait) who is enclosed in a scientific institution outside Moscow, along with others who have committed "crimes against the state." What is described is a whole world, certainly the whole world of Soviet Russia, for the institution is a microcosm of Russian life and characters.

Equally powerful is *Cancer Ward.* Solzhenitsyn himself was treated for cancer, so far successfully, in the midfifties. In this beautiful and by no means morbid study he achieves for Russian literature—though on a lower level—something like what Mann with his *Magic Mountain* (44) did for German literature. *Cancer Ward,* like all his work, is really about a prison, all Russia being so conceived. "A man sprouts a tumor and dies—how then can a country live that has sprouted camp and exile?" For all its external atmosphere of the clinic, *Cancer Ward* is basically a celebration of human life, as is Camus's *The Plague* (53).

Solzhenitsyn requires close attention. He lacks elegance, mastery of form, and his humor may seem to us flavorless. But he has enormous drive, compassion, and the capacity to create hundreds of characters. The poet Yevtushenko has dared to call him "our only living Russian classic." That would appear to be the case.

PHILOSOPHY
PSYCHOLOGY
POLITICS
ESSAYS

THOMAS HOBBES (1588–1679)

Leviathan

We read the philosophers not only because they are in themselves interesting, but because their ideas have consequences. The quarrel between the individual and the state as to the proper division of power is central to our time. Hobbes is important because he presents the first modern reasoned case for the state as the exclusive holder of power, so long as that state can offer protection to its citizens. Thus all of today's authoritarian regimes, whether Marxist or non-Marxist, may claim Hobbes as one of their earliest and greatest advocates.

Hobbes received a good classical education at Oxford. He later used his scholarship to prepare a translation of Thucydides (4) in whose work he saw a demonstration of the evils of democracy. For some time he made a living as a tutor in a noble family. In his middle years, apparently as a consequence of reading a proof in Euclid, he turned from the classics to science and philosophy. His political sympathies during the great English Parliamentary struggle were Royalist; for a short period he taught mathematics in Paris to the future Charles II. But his deeper loyalty was to power irrespective of party. Hence, after Cromwell's victory, he made submission to the Protector. During the Restoration, though attacked as an atheist, he managed to survive successfully enough to reach the age of ninety-one.

His fame rests on the *Leviathan*. Published in 1651, it was merely a systematic development of ideas he was already holding some years before the Civil War came to a head.

Hobbes's absolutist theory of the state rests on his antiheroic conception of man's nature. He is a thoroughgoing mechanistic materialist. He does not deny God. But God is irrelevant to his thought. He believes in a proposition by no means self-evident—that all men are primarily interested in self-preservation. In a natural, lawless state this passion results in anarchy, and the life of man, in his most famous phrase, is "solitary, poor, nasty, brutish, and short."

To escape such an existence, man institutes a commonwealth or government, the great artificial construct Hobbes calls Leviathan. To secure peace, or, as we say today, "security," we must relinquish our right of private judgment as to what is good or evil, placing that right in the hands of a sovereign or assembly. Hobbes prefers a monarchy, but his logic would suggest no basic objection to a committee or party, as in the Communist Leviathan. In such a state, morality would flow from law rather than law from morality.

Most so-called realistic theories of politics find their source partly in Hobbes. Our own democratic doctrine is anti-Hobbesian in its view of human nature. It rests on the notion of a division of powers (Hobbes thought the Civil War came about because power was divided among the king, the lords, and the House of Commons); on a system of checks and balances; and on a vague but so far workable theory of the general will expressed in representative form. To understand what really separates us from all authoritarian regimes, a reading of the *Leviathan* is most helpful.

Despite his iron doctrine, Hobbes himself seems to have been a pleasant and rather timid fellow.

He writes a crabbed, difficult prose. Save him for your more insistently intellectual moods. Read the Introduction and Parts 1 and 2 entire, if possible; Chapters 32, 33, 42, and 46 of Parts 3 and 4, in which he argues against the power claims of all established churches; and finally his Review and Conclusion.

JOHN LOCKE (1632–1704)

Second Treatise of Government (full title: *An Essay Concerning the True Original Extent and Aim of Civil Government*)

With the Restoration (1660) Locke's father, a Cromwell man, lost much of his fortune. This may have inclined his Oxford-trained son to balance his wide intellectual interests with various governmental and semigovernmental activities. As he had, among other things, studied medicine he was able to serve as household physician, as well as personal secretary, to the first earl of Shaftesbury, With the latter's fall from power in 1675, Locke removed to France for four years; returned to England under Shaftesbury again; following the latter's exile and death, sought refuge in Holland; and in 1689 was back in England, favorably received by the new regime of William and Mary. During these years he worked on his *Essay Concerning Human Understanding*, which appeared, together with the two *Treatises of Civil Government*, in 1690. The latter, however, had been written twelve years before and are not, as has been thought, a defense of the Revolution of 1688, except by anticipation.

During the whole of the eighteenth century Locke's influence was marked. Through Voltaire (47) and Rousseau (100) he provided some of the ideas that sparked the French Revolution. Through Jefferson and other Founding Fathers (99) he determined to a considerable extent the ideas that went into the Declaration of Independence and the Constitution. His views on religious toleration, education, and politics, though not in every instance original, did much to establish the mental climate of the Industrial Revolution and to promote the advance of democratic government.

His major work, the *Essay Concerning Human Understanding*, is generally supposed to have founded the British empirical school of philosophy. This school rejects the doctrine that ideas are innate and derives them rather from experience. If you have a special interest in the fascinating history of theories of knowledge, you might tackle the famous *Essay.*

For the rest of us it is useful to have at least a rough idea of Locke's *Second Treatise of Government.* Like Hobbes (71), he addresses himself to the central question, What is the basis of legitimate power? His answer, though on many points open to criticism, clears the way for the development of representative government, just as Hobbes's answer does for authoritarian government. Hobbes's idea of a "contract" centers in the relinquishment of an individual's power to an absolute or almost absolute sovereign or assembly. Locke's "social contract" is made between equals (that is, property-holding male equals) who "join in and make one society." Government is not divinely instituted; it is not absolute; and its authority is limited by notions familiar to us: the separation of powers, checks and balances, and the permanent retention by the individual of certain "inalienable rights." For Locke these latter include life, liberty, and property. Against a government that does not guarantee such rights, rebellion is legitimate.

While Locke's specific political doctrines are of great historical importance to us, it is perhaps the general tenor of his thought that, through the Founding Fathers, has continued to influence the American conception of government. Locke is optimistic, as we are. He is relatively undogmatic. He hates bigotry and absolutism. He conceives of society as open and experimental. He believes the state should aim to further the happiness of all its citizens. These may seem tame ideas today, but they were inflammatory in his time. And, though few people read Locke, his views continue to exert influence.

DAVID HUME (1711–1776)

An Enquiry Concerning Human Understanding

In proportion to its population Scotland has probably produced more first-rate minds than any country in the world except ancient Greece. Of these minds David Hume is surely one.

Intended by nature for abstract reflection, Hume, after short tries, sensibly rejected both the law and a business career. He spent three years in France, wrote his *Treatise of Human Nature* (of whose first part the *Enquiry* is a development), and watched it fall "dead-born from the press." The first volume of his *Essays* (1741) brought him greater success. Following their publication he occupied a number of official posts and one unofficial one, that of tutor to a certified lunatic, who was however a peer. One foreign service job netted him almost a thousand pounds, and he increased this small fortune with the profits from his triumphant and highly partisan *History of England.* In 1769, a rich man, he retired to his new house in Edinburgh and became a sort of Dr. Johnson to that brilliant little capital.

In his interesting *Autobiography* he describes himself as "a man of mild dispositions, of command of temper, and of an open, social, and cheerful humour, capable of attachment, but little susceptible of enmity; and of great moderation in all my passions. Even my love of literary fame, my ruling passion, never soured my temper, notwithstanding my frequent disappointments."

Hume developed Locke's antimetaphysical position and so helped to clear the way for British utilitarianism in the nineteenth century (see 74). His *Enquiry,* clear but not easy reading, deals with the original sensations he calls *impressions.* "All probable reasoning is nothing but a species of sensation." He is, as the quotation would indicate, a skeptic. He sees no rational connection between cause and effect, causation in his system being equal to mere sequence.

This central skepticism he applies to the self, which he

deems unknowable; to morality, which he separates from religion; and to religion, coming "from the incessant hopes and fears which actuate the human mind."

Hume's balance and commonsensical temperament would have rejected the great romantics of the century following his. Yet they might well justify their position by appealing to Hume's total skepticism with respect to the existence of rational belief.

His skepticism was not mere academic theory. He philosophized, he admitted, not because he was certain of establishing the truth, but because it gave him pleasure. Few philosophers have been so honest.

74
JOHN STUART MILL (1806–1873)

On Liberty

Mill is the classic instance of the child prodigy who, despite an abnormal education, manages to live a good and useful life. You will find his story in his sober but extremely interesting *Autobiography*.

The elder Mill was a follower of Jeremy Bentham. Bentham's name is linked with utilitarianism, an unimaginative if well-intentioned doctrine that stressed utility and reason, two terms it never strictly defined. It taught that the object of social action was to bring about the greatest happiness for the greatest number, and tended to ignore the temperamental and psychic differences among human beings. Young John was brought up in the shadow of this doctrine, caricatured by Dickens (33) in his Gradgrind.

Educated entirely by his logic-factory of a father, Mill was reading Greek at three and starting a history of Roman government at eleven. At thirteen he was about as well educated as an English university graduate. This educational force-feeding saved him at least ten of the years most first-rate minds are compelled to waste in our own school system. But it had its drawbacks: "I never was a boy," confessed Mill. The morbid emphasis on reason produced a mental crisis in his twentieth year, from which he was saved partly by the youthful resilience of his own fine mind and partly by his reading. Wordsworth (91) in particular revealed to him the existence of a life of feeling.

His crisis, together with the influence of Mrs. Harriet Taylor, whom he met in 1830 and married twenty-one years later, led Mill to recognize the weaknesses of his father's iron calculus of pleasures and pains. He was to spend much of his life, as writer, Member of Parliament, and social reformer, in liberalizing and humanizing utilitarianism. Thus, working with other "philosophical radicals," he helped to create a climate of opinion that led to many of the reform movements of the last hundred years, from woman suffrage to the New Deal.

Mill thought that except for his *Logic* his essay *On Liberty* would outlast his other works. In its own unemotional, English way it is a masterpiece of lucid persuasion and humane feeling. Probably no finer plea has ever been written for the claims of the individual against the state. Mill stresses the need for creating a great diversity of temperaments. He urges the protection of minorities. He advocates the utmost possible freedom of thought and expression. He comes out for the encouragement of nonconformist, even eccentric thinkers. His central principle is still far from realization in our state-dominated era, and still worth realizing: "The sole end for which mankind are warranted, individually or collectively, in interfering with the liberty of action of any of their number, is self-protection."

Mill should be read as the representative of the purest liberal English thought of his century. His American brothers are Thoreau (84) and Emerson (83), though he lacks the radical daring of the first and the eloquence of the second.

75
KARL MARX   (1818–1883)
FRIEDRICH ENGELS   (1820–1895)

The Communist Manifesto

We began this section with the obvious statement that ideas have consequences. In no case can this be more clearly shown than in that of Karl Marx. He would perhaps have denied it. He would have said that, the victory of the proletariat being inevitable, his life and work were devoted merely to clarifying the issues and perhaps slightly accelerating the outcome of the struggle. Nevertheless, the history of the entire world since 1917 seems to have confirmed the judgment expressed in the first sentence of Isaiah Berlin's *Karl Marx: His Life and Environment:* "No thinker in the nineteenth century has had so direct, deliberate and powerful an influence upon mankind as Karl Marx." It is for that reason alone that a reading of *The Manifesto of the Communist Party* (for which his co-worker Engels is partly responsible) is here suggested. Marx was a highly unpleasant person and most of us reject his doctrines, but to have no acquaintance with him or them is to remain forever partially blind.

Up to 1849 Karl Marx, a German-Jewish middle-class intellectual, had spent most of his mature years in subversive journalism in Cologne, Paris, and Brussels. Forced to leave Prussian territory, he emigrated to England. The last thirty-four years of his life were spent there, mainly in the British Museum, which may claim to be the physical incubator of the Communist Revolution. Marx's life was uneventful; it has become eventful posthumously.

His major work is of course *Capital.* There is no sense in recommending that you read it, unless you are a very earnest student indeed. In addition to its impenetrable German style, its difficulties are formidable; and much of it has been rendered utter nonsense by the passage of time and the movement of Marx's revered history. But you should read a good, calm summary of its doctrine. Suggestions for Further Reading lists a number of helpful books.

The *Communist Manifesto,* however, is quite readable. Indeed one might wish it had been less so. It is not a work of literature or even an example of ordered thought. It is propaganda, but epochal propaganda. Its original function was to supply a platform in 1847 for the Communist League, as it was then called. Its continuing function has been to supply propaganda for the entire communist movement, particularly as it developed after 1917. In clear, if deliberately rhetorical terms, it presents the main theses of classical communism: that any epoch as a whole is explainable only in terms of its modes of production and exchange; that the history of civilization is a history of class struggle; that now the stage has been reached in which the proletariat must emancipate itself from the bourgeoisie by means of a total overturn of society, and not merely a political revolution.

The *Manifesto* begins with one of the most famous sentences ever written: "A spectre is haunting Europe—the spectre of Communism." It concludes with three sentences no less famous: "The proletarians have nothing to lose but their chains. They have a world to win. Workingmen of all countries, unite."

The history of the capitalist and the communist worlds may seem to have demonstrated that Marx's concluding sentences are untrue. But the influence of the *Manifesto* remains one of the iron realities of our time.

76

FRIEDRICH WILHELM NIETZSCHE (1844–1900)

Thus Spake Zarathustra, Selected Other Works

The rhapsodic singer of the strong, triumphant, joyful superman led a life of failure, loneliness, obscurity, and physical pain. Son of a Lutheran pastor in Saxony, he was brought up by pious female relatives. A brilliant student, he specialised in classical philosophy. At twenty-five he was professor of Greek at Basel University. He resigned ten years later, in 1879, because of poor health. One of the major influences in his life at this time was Wagner, whom he at first adored. (Bertrand Russell remarks: "Nietzsche's superman is very like Siegfried, except that he knows Greek.") Gradually, however, as Wagner succumbed to philistinism, anti-Semitism, German racism, and the sick religiosity of *Parsifal,* Nietzsche drew away from the great composer, and at last broke with him. From 1879 to 1888 he wandered about Germany, Switzerland, and Italy, living a lonely life in seedy boardinghouses. Yet during these nine years, working under the most depressing conditions, he produced most of his famous books. In December of 1888 he was found in a Turin street, weeping and embracing a horse. His mind had given way. For the remaining eleven years of his life he was insane, possibly—there is no proof—as a result of general syphilitic paresis.

Nietzsche is still a controversial figure. At times he writes like a genius. At times he writes like a fool, as if he had never been in touch with ordinary realities. (His views on women, for example, are those of a man who simply didn't know any very well.) And so, though he has been dead for almost a century and has been the subject of countless commentaries and interpretations, there is still no generally agreed-upon judgment of this extraordinary man. Those naturally inclined to moderation, decent intellectual manners, rationality, or plain common sense, find him ridiculous or even hateful. Others see in him a prophetic figure, a constructive destroyer of false moral values, an intuitive psychologist who anticipates Freud (77). And positions in between these extremes have been set up all along the line.

One general misconception is worth mentioning. The Nazis and Fascists in general did exploit, often by falsifying, Nietzsche's celebration of the virtues of war, ruthlessness, blood-thinking, and an elite class—or his presumed celebration, for his admirers translate his words rather differently. But Nietzsche would have despised Hitler and all the little Hitlers. He was not anti-Semitic and he condemned German nationalism. "Every great crime against culture for the last four hundred years lies on their conscience" is his summing up of the Germans. Nietzsche in one of his aspects was a good European, a defender of the culture the Nazis hated. It cannot be denied that his political influence has been deplorable. But this is not the same as saying that he was a proto-Fascist.

Yet, good European that he may have thought himself, Nietzsche in a certain sense stands outside the Western tradition to which this book is devoted. He is a total revolutionary, more total, if that is possible, than Lawrence (41) or Marx (75). At times he seems to reserve his admiration for only a few: the pre-Socratics, Socrates himself, and a few "artist-tyrants," such as Frederick II of Sicily. He indicts Christianity as a "slave morality." He rejects the traditional virtues of compassion, tolerance, mutual accommodation, in favor of the "will to power," a phrase variously interpreted. He detests the liberal democratic humanitarianism of Mill (74), whom he called, with typical courtesy, "that blockhead." He exalts the heroic, the "Dionysian," and, it would seem, the irrational and intuitive elements in the human mind. He has no interest in the ordinary conception of progress, substituting for it a somewhat misty doctrine of eternal cyclical recurrence, and stressing the positive power of heroic suffering, exultant pessimism, and tragic experience. On the whole, not a comfortable chap.

No one can deny his extraordinary, though uncontrolled, gift for language; his command of invective and irony; the variety of his poetical images; and the torrential, paradoxical inventiveness of his tortured mind. If taken in large, uncritical doses he can be not only antipathetic but dangerous; the God he denied seems to have formed him to attract the lunatic fringe. On the other hand it is true that, like Ibsen (19) and Shaw (20), he helped to point out to his century and ours many of our shams, cowardices, and hypocrisies.

Suggestion: use the edition called *The Portable Nietzsche,* published by the Viking Press. The translations are intelligent, the notes and other apparatus helpful. You might read the whole of *Zarathustra,* uneven as that strange work is; the selections from *Beyond Good and Evil, Toward a Genealogy of Morals,* and *Ecce Homo;* and perhaps *The Antichrist.*

77

SIGMUND FREUD (1856–1939)

Selected Works

Freud died September 23, 1939. In his memory W. H. Auden wrote a superb poem from which I quote:

> To us he is no more a person
> Now but a whole climate of opinion.

That is the heart of it. To the discomfiture or horror of many, Freud is one of the major components of our mental world. There is hardly an area of thought, and there are few of conduct, untouched by him, his disciples, his ex-disciples, or his opponents. You will have to determine for yourself whether this is a good thing, a bad, or a mixture of both.

When we talked about Shakespeare it was suggested that most of us think we know him when what we really know is some handed-down opinion of him. That is true of Freud. Many of us still vaguely believe that his doctrines encourage sexual license, or that "he sees sex in everything," or that he did little beyond shifting the confessional from the grating to the couch. A reading of his major works will clear up these and dozens of other vulgar misconceptions.

Freud began his training in medicine, specializing in clinical neurology. In 1884 he became interested in some work done by Breuer, with whom he later worked. Breuer had with some success treated a female hysteric by encouraging her to "talk out" her past under hypnosis. The case is classic; it marked the birth of psychoanalysis, whose actual origin Freud, himself no humble type, always credited to Breuer. By replacing hypnosis with "free association" Freud found the key that unlocked his system. By 1896 he had named it psychoanalysis. The rest of his life was devoted to the widest possible development of the new conception of mental processes. Against misunderstanding, abuse, and moralistic prejudice he worked unceasingly, deepening his insights as he extended his experience. In 1938 his books were burned by the Nazis. As he was already suffering torture from cancer of the mouth, they waived their usual methods of dealing with the weak, the good, the great, and the non-Aryan. In return for a large ransom they permitted Freud to remove to England, where he passed the last months of his phenomenally productive life.

Psychoanalysis claims to be two things: a science (at least to its adherents) and a method. It is a theory of mental life and a specific technique for the cure of neuroses. Both theory and technique are based on a few fundamental concepts. They seem trite to us now, but they were not so nearly a century ago. Among them are: the unconscious; the mechanism of repression; the formative power of infantile sexuality (Freud did not invent the Oedipus complex, he observed it); the dream life as the disguised expression of fears and desires; and, more generally, the frightening power of the irrational in determining human behavior.

Sometimes with insufficient caution, Freud and his followers applied their novel insights to fields seemingly remote from mental disease: religion, morality, war, history, death, humor, mythology, anthropology, philosophy, art, and literature. Particularly in literature Freud has had a pronounced influence, not always for the good.

With respect to your choice of reading, two difficulties present themselves. The first is the vast volume of Freud's work. The second is the change and development of his thought, which means that an early (yet still valuable) book may be in part superseded by a later one. I list herewith seven titles. Experts will quarrel over all of them, and doubtless champion others. The first four books, arranged chronologically, contain much of the general theory. The last three, similarly arranged, are more specialized or exemplify Freud's thinking on a philosophical level.

The Origin and Development of Psychoanalysis
The Interpretation of Dreams
A General Introduction to Psychoanalysis
New Introductory Lectures on Psychoanalysis
Beyond the Pleasure Principle
The Ego and the Id
Civilization and Its Discontents

Rickman's *A General Selection from the Works of Sigmund Freud* offers a sound but necessarily brief "epitome" of the development of Freud's thought. It consists largely of well-chosen excerpts and does not claim to be a substitute for reading the major works.

78
NICCOLÒ MACHIAVELLI (1469–1527)

The Prince

Machiavelli is commonly linked with Hobbes (71) as one of the two great early modern "realistic" theorists of political power. They would have understood each other, yet they diverge in some ways. Hobbes is by far the greater theorist. Indeed Machiavelli is hardly a theorist at all; he is an observer, an analyst, and an instructor. Hobbes lays down a doctrine of "legitimacy"; Machiavelli is interested only in expediency. Finally Hobbes is an absolutist. But Machiavelli (in his *Discourses on Livy,* a profounder but less influential book than *The Prince*) prefers republicanism, and anticipates several of the devices of modern parliamentary democracy. Yet the two may profitably be read in association. Together they help to explain the careers of such antimoralists as Richelieu, Napoleon, Lenin, Mussolini, Hitler, Stalin. Also they help to explain the continuous though prettily disguised power struggle that goes on in all democracies, including our own.

Machiavelli was a practical politician. Under the Florentine Republic he held office for fourteen years, serving efficiently as diplomat and army organizer. In *The Prince* he incorporated the concrete insights he had gained during his observation of the Italian city-states and the emergent nations of Western Europe, particularly France. When in 1512 the Medicis regained power in Florence, Machiavelli lost his. Unjustly imprisoned and even tortured, he was exiled, and retired to his farm. There—compare Thucydides (4)—he employed his time in writing. He achieved some reputation as historian, playwright, and all-round humanist man of letters. But it is as the author of *The Prince*, by which he hoped to regain political favor, that he is best known.

His reputation, an odd one, has given us the adjective *machiavellian*. During the Elizabethan era *Old Nick* was a term referring as much to his first name as to the Devil. Iago and a dozen other Italianate Elizabethan villains are in part the consequence of a popular misconception of Machiavelli. He became known as a godless and cynical defender of force and fraud in statecraft.

All Machiavelli did was to cry out that the emperor had no clothes on. He told the truth about power as he saw it in actual operation, and if the truth was not pretty, he is hardly to be blamed for that. He himself seems to have been a reasonably virtuous man, no hater of humanity, neither devilish nor neurotic.

Also it should be remembered that *The Prince* is a description of political means, not political ends. What Machiavelli seems really to have wanted (see his Chapter 26) was a united Italy, free of Spanish and French domination. Cavour and the nineteenth-century unifiers of Italy owe much to him; from a certain aspect he may even be considered a liberal. Yet there is no denying that his ideal Prince (he admired the ineffable Cesare Borgia) must separate himself from all considerations of morality, unless those considerations are themselves expedient. As for his view of the relationship between religion and the state: "All armed prophets have conquered and unarmed ones failed." The Ayatollah Khomeini would grin approvingly.

The Prince is a manual. It tells the ambitious leader how to gain, maintain, and centralize power. Once this power is established there is nothing, in Machiavelli's view, to prevent the state from developing just and free institutions. What is involved here, of course, is the whole question of means and ends, and Machiavelli does not resolve the problem.

Because the politics of European nationalism have been in part guided by this icy, terrifyingly intelligent book of instruction, it is well worth reading.

79

MICHEL EYQUEM DE MONTAIGNE (1533–1592)

Selected Essays

Many names on our list are far greater than Montaigne's. But the view of life he represents is so deeply rooted in many of us that, when more powerful minds retain interest only for scholars, he may still be read. He appeals to that part of us more fascinated by the questions than by the answers.

Montaigne, one of the pioneers of modern French prose, was of good merchant-family stock. On his mother's side he was partly Jewish. Apparently there was sufficient money in the family to permit him on his thirty-eighth birthday to semiretire to his round tower on the family property. In a period when educational experimentation was generally popular, his own education was unusual. Until he was six he spoke only Latin. He tells us that he was awakened each morning by "the sound of a musical instrument," an anticipation of our clock radios. He studied law, occupied a magistrate's seat in the Bordeaux parliament, served in various capacities under three French kings, and during his later years wasted some of his genius on a job, the mayoralty of Bordeaux, fit only for mediocrity. His real life is preserved in his *Essays.* Of these there are 107, if we include the book-length *Apology for Raymond Sebond.* As far as we can determine, they were written, and rewritten, from his thirty-ninth year, after he had withdrawn to a life of tranquil study and contemplation, to the year of his death.

As he says in his preliminary word to the reader, they were composed not for fame, favor, or fortune, but merely to portray himself, in all candor and indiscretion. For this purpose he invented a new form of literature, as important in its way as the internal combustion engine, and far more pleasant. The French word *essai* means literally a trial or attempt. Each essay is a trial of the content of his mind, an attempt to find out what is there, so that, though he may know nothing else, he may at least know himself.

Montaigne's essays are not like those we find in our better

magazines today. They are formless, they rarely stick to the announced subject, and they are chock-full of classical quotations, for Montaigne, in addition to being a man of practical affairs, was a learned humanist. The modern reader may at first find these obstacles irritating.

However, if the evidence of four centuries of survival is any indication, you will eventually be won over by Montaigne's charm, wisdom, humor, style, and mental slant. He began as a Stoic (see Marcus Aurelius [12]) but soon developed a generally skeptical, though never cynical or negative, view of mankind. He was interested in everything, convinced of nothing. His motto was "What do I know?" His emblem was a pair of balances. He remained a good Catholic, because he was born one, and died in the odor of sanctity. But the tendency of his extremely influential writings has been to encourage the growth of free thought. In his characteristic gesture of suspended judgment, dogmatists will find little pleasure.

Montaigne's charm inheres in his style, that of the frankest, freest conversation, "simple and unaffected, the same in writing as on the tongue." He is particularly candid on matters of sex, and those of us who are used to the naive obsessions of some modern novelists may find it interesting to see what a grown-up man has to say on the subject. Montaigne is not only the first informal essayist but incomparably the best. His art is always concealed. The man he gives you is never an improved version submitted for public approval, but always and forever himself. He writes as if he were continually enjoying himself, his weaknesses and oddities and stupidities no less than his virtues.

You may wander about almost at will in Montaigne. He should be read as he wrote, unsystematically. However, time has winnowed out certain of the essays as superior or more important. For the nearest thing to a reasoned defense of his skeptical position, see the rather long-drawn-out *Apology for Raymond Sebond.* In addition you might tick off the following, whose very titles will give you a good foretaste of Montaigne.

From Book 1: That intention is judge of our actions; Of idleness; Of liars; That the taste of good and evil depends in large part on the opinion we have of them; That to philosophize is to learn to die; Of the power of the imagination; Of custom, and not easily changing an accepted law; Of the education of children; Of friendship; Of moderation; Of cannibals; Of solitude; Of the inequality that is between us; Of ancient customs; Of Democritus and Heraclitus; Of vain subtleties; Of age.

From Book 2: Of the inconsistency of our actions; Of drunkenness; Of practice; Of the affection of fathers for their children; Of books; Of presumption; Of a monstrous child; Of the resemblance of children to fathers.

From Book 3: Of the useful and the honorable; Of three kinds of association; On some verses of Virgil; Of the art of discussion; Of vanity; Of experience.

Try to get a modern translation, either Trechmann's or, best of all, Donald Frame's. Avoid Cotton's version; it is an antique.

80
RENÉ DESCARTES (1596–1650)

Discourse on Method

Descartes is often termed "the father of modern philosophy." Even if this were not so, he would still be well worth reading for the elegant precision of his prose and the mathematical clarity of his reasoning. These two qualities, more than his specific doctrines, have deeply influenced the French character.

Descartes's family was of the minor nobility and he never had to support himself. This was as it should be; we shall never know how much genius has been lost to the world by reason of the need to make a living. We willingly provide free board and lodging for lunatics, but recoil before the idea of doing so for first-class minds.

Descartes received a good Jesuit education. As his health was poor, his masters, intelligent men, allowed him to stay late in bed instead of compelling him to play the seventeenth-century equivalent of basketball. This slugabed habit he retained all his life. It was responsible for much calm, ordered thought.

Even as a young man Descartes had begun to distrust the foundations of everything he had been taught, except mathematics. This skepticism (which did not conflict, it appears, with conventional piety) was reinforced during his Paris and Poitiers years (1614–18) when he read Montaigne (79). He finally abandoned study and set off on a career of mild military adventure and travel. He was resolved, he says, "no longer to seek any other science than the knowledge of myself, or of the great book of the world."

His great creative years, from 1629 to 1649, were spent mainly in Holland, at that time a general asylum for intelligence. His fame grew to such proportions that Queen Christina of Sweden invited (that is, commanded) him to visit her and teach her philosophy. In Sweden Descartes was forced to rise at 5:00 A.M. in cold weather in order to converse with the queen. A few months of such barbarism were enough to kill him. Had not this arrogant monarch caused his death just as directly as if she had shot him, the world might have had another twenty years of Descartes's mind.

However, he managed to do pretty well. Though the two talents were inextricably connected, Descartes was an even greater mathematician than philosopher. One morning, while lying in bed, the idea of coordinate geometry, which married algebra to geometry, came to him. On this point see Whitehead (IV). He also worked in physics, though with less distinction.

Descartes's doctrines, dualistic and materialist in tendency, are both interesting and influential. But it is as the creator of a new, or at any rate fresh, method of thought that his position was secured. He threw aside much, though not all, of scholastic reasoning and, as it were, started from scratch. He began by doubting everything. The progression of doubt, however, ended at the point where he found that he could not doubt the existence of his own thought. "I think, therefore I am" is the famous formula with which he begins. (In a somewhat different form, it is found in Augustine too, but Descartes made it do work and Augustine didn't.) He then proceeds to build a system of thought, using four main principles you will find described in his *Discourse on Method.* "Cartesian doubt," however, describes not only a method but an attitude of mind, and this attitude was to influence profoundly post-Cartesian speculation, whether scientific or philosophical.

We read Descartes, then, as the first supremely great mind to receive his stimulus from the new physics and astronomy of Copernicus, Galileo, and others. He incorporates the outlook of the tremendous renaissance of science, partly contemporary with him, that was to reach a high point with Newton.

81
BLAISE PASCAL (1623–1662)

Thoughts (Pensées)

Pascal is a seeming oddity, for he possessed in the highest degree a number of traits not usually linked in a single personality. First and foremost, he is a scientific and mathematical genius. Second, he is a master of prose style; indeed he is often thought of as the norm of classic French prose. Third, he is an acute though unsystematic psychologist. Fourth, he is a God-thirsty, tormented soul, a kind of failed saint. To a freethinker such as Eric T. Bell, author of the fascinating *Men of Mathematics,* Pascal ruined his life by his preoccupation with religious controversy: "On the mathematical side Pascal is the greatest might-have-been in history." It is hard to make a sensible judgment. Pascal was Pascal. The man who in love and terror cried out for God, and the man who thought of the omnibus and invented the syringe are somehow indivisible.

At twelve, before he had been taught any mathematics, Pascal was proving Euclid for himself. At sixteen he had written a trail-blazing work on conic sections, of which we possess only fragmentary indications. At eighteen, he had invented the first calculating machine. At twenty-four he had demonstrated the barometer. He did classic work in hydrostatics, and most of us remember Pascal's Law from high school, provided we were lucky enough to attend a high school that offered physics. In mathematics he is famous, among other matters, for having discovered and shown the properties of a notable curve called the cycloid. For its beauty and also for its power to excite controversy, this has been termed the Helen of geometry.

His major contribution, not merely to science but to thought in general, is perhaps his work in the theory of probability, the glory of which he shares with another mathematician, Fermat. It is interesting to recall that the ascetic Pascal was stimulated to his great mathematical discoveries by a gamblers' dispute involving the throw of dice. The ramifications of probability theory, writes Bell, "are everywhere, from the quantum theory to epistemology."

As mathematician and physicist Pascal will rank higher than he will as moralist and religious controversialist. Yet in these latter fields his influence has been considerable. Just as Montaigne (79), who both fascinated and repelled Pascal, stands for one mood of mankind, so Pascal stands for another. Montaigne lived at ease with skepticism; Pascal's heart and mind cried out for certainties. Montaigne contemplated the sad condition of man with interest, humor, and tolerance. Pascal, who had brilliant wit but no humor, regarded it with terror and despair, from which he was saved only by throwing himself on the breast of revealed religion.

His finest, but to us not most interesting prose, is contained in his *Provincial Letters,* which you will find in most editions that print the *Pensées.* These are masterpieces of polemic, directed against certain tendencies of the Jesuit order of Pascal's day, tendencies he and his associates of the Jansenist movement considered too tolerant of man's moral frailties. (Jansenism was a kind of puritanical sect within Catholicism, stressing predestination and asceticism, but also inspiring new and brilliant techniques in the education of children.) This controversy, which made Pascal a best-seller, is today of interest mainly to theologians and historians of religion.

The *Thoughts,* or *Pensées,* are in a somewhat different category. They consist of a series of scrappy, often unfinished notes, originally intended to serve as parts of a grand design, a reasoned defense of the Christian religion against the assaults or the lethargy of freethinkers. Into them Pascal put his painful sense of the inadequacy, even the absurdity of man, as measured against the immensity of the universe, the endless flow of eternity, and the omniscience and omnipotence of God. A great deal of modern antihumanist pessimism flows from Pascal. Those who reject man as the center of the universe, whether they are religionists or nihilists, find the *Pensées* to their taste. He represents one profound mood of mankind, that which finds man glorious in his powers yet in the end pitiful and incomprehensible to himself.

The nonscientific Pascal is preserved by his style and by his emotional intensity. As a psychologist of the soul his genius is measured by the fact that he can still move many who are quite unable to sympathize with his sometimes noble, sometimes merely frantic devotionalism. Two Pascalian sentences, or cries from the heart, are frequently quoted. The first is: "The eternal silence of these infinite spaces terrifies me." The second is: "Man is but a reed, the weakest thing in nature; but he is a thinking reed." Between them these two statements suggest moods common to all Western men and women, whether they be Christian, agnostic, atheist, or of some other creed.

82
ALEXIS DE TOCQUEVILLE (1805–1859)

Democracy in America

Had this Lifetime Reading Plan been compiled seventy-five years ago, Tocqueville probably would not have been represented. From the appearance of the first part of his masterpiece in 1835 he has never ceased to be read and studied. But it has taken considerably more than a century to disclose him in his true proportions, as one of the few supreme sociological and political observers and theorists of the American experiment.

Tocqueville's family was of the lesser French nobility. Thus he preserved all his life a deep attachment to the virtues of conservatism and aristocracy. The inexorable logic of his mind compelled him to discern in democracy the wave of the future, while his roots in tradition helped him to measure the origins and dimensions of that wave with a certain useful and lucid detachment.

On May 11, 1831, the young Tocqueville, accompanied by a brilliant colleague named Beaumont, reached our shores. Their avowed purpose was to observe and report on the American penal system. The pair traveled seven thousand miles in our country and Canada. They sailed home on February 20, 1832. In the course of these pregnant nine months Tocqueville saw us during one of our most interesting and critical periods, that of the earlier phase of the Jacksonian Revolution. The outcome was the publication, 1835 and 1840, of the two parts of his monumental work, *Democracy in America*. This, together with his briefer but no less seminal *The Old Régime and the French Revolution,* embodies the enduring Tocqueville. I might add that he wasted a certain amount of time from 1839 to 1848 serving as a member of the French Chamber of Deputies, and later held brief office as minister for foreign affairs.

Tocqueville may be described, very roughly, as a liberal aristocrat, a kind of Lafayette with brains. *Democracy in America* had a double purpose: to describe and analyze the democratic (which seems to have meant to him largely egalitarian) system in America; and to turn that observation and analysis into a guide for future political thought and action in Europe, particularly in his native land. Many good judges believe his book is still (and by far) the deepest, wisest, and most farseeing ever written about this country.

He made, of course, many errors of observation. Nor have all of his prophecies come true. Yet no thoughtful American can read his book today (and, by the way, it is a masterpiece of elegance and organization) without marveling at his sympathy, his understanding, his balance, and his prescience. Though in his day our modern capitalist structure was still only in embryo, he understood its future, its strengths, its weaknesses, and its capacities far better than did the later Marx (75). A century and a half ago he warned us against "the possible tyranny of the majority." He outlined the mass age in which we live. But he also saw how our system could mitigate and control the perils of political and social conformity, and he recognized in it one of the broad paths his century and ours would largely follow.

His basic intuition is revealed in the statement: "A new science of politics is needed for a new world." Such a new science, he felt, was developing, not always harmoniously, not without travail, in the United States. And he knew quite well what he was doing: "I have not undertaken to see differently from others, but to look further, and while they are busied for the morrow only, I have turned my thoughts to the whole future."

What probably interests us most, as we read Tocqueville, is the startling applicability of his insight to our present condition. He foresaw, while America was still largely an agricultural country, the attraction that business and industry would have for us all. He foresaw our materialism, but also our idealism. He foresaw the inequities industry would bring in its train. And, most important, he foresaw our future power and, let us hope, our future greatness. Of all his prophecies the most hair-raising is probably his quiet comparison of Czarist Russia and Jacksonian America: "There are at the present time two great nations in the world, which started from different points, but seem to tend toward the same end. I allude to the Russians and the Americans. . . . All other nations seem to have nearly reached their natural limits, and they have only to maintain their power; but these are still in the act of growth. . . . The principal instrument of America is freedom; of Russia, servitude. Their starting-point is different and their courses are not the same; yet each of them seems marked out by the will of Heaven to sway the destinies of half the globe."

These words were written in the thirties of the last century.

RALPH WALDO EMERSON   (1803–1882)

Selected Works

Thoreau's power over us has increased as his friend Emerson's has declined. Thoreau, reaping the reward of greater daring and a firmer grasp on rude fact, casts the longer shadow. Yet Emerson, for all his gassiness and repetitiousness, was, in the first place, one of the central American thinkers of his century; secondly, a formulator of certain attitudes that seem permanently American; and finally a writer, at his best, of quite wonderful force, wit, homely vividness, and freshness—surely one of the finest epigrammatists in English. For these reasons we read him. But beware of overlarge doses. At times he offers fine words in lieu of thoughts, and he never understood how to organize or compress large masses of material.

Emerson was the leader of the Concord transcendentalist school, which taught a curious hodgepodge of fashionable idealisms. After graduation from Harvard, he became a teacher, then a preacher. When he found that he "was not interested" in the rite of Communion, he left the ministry. He never ceased, however, to be both teacher and preacher, developing into a kind of benelovent pastor without portfolio, dispensing spiritual goods without benefit of theology and indeed without the support of any concrete idea of God. As itinerant lecturer and unsystematic sage he purified the moral atmosphere of his restless, expansive era more effectively than did all the ordained ministers combined.

Emerson is the first important spokesman for those elements in the national character we vaguely term optimistic, idealistic, democratic, expansive, individualistic. He preached the self-reliance on which we pride ourselves. In *The American Scholar* he issued what the elder Holmes called "our intellectual Declaration of Independence," a note we have since continually and sometimes raucously sounded. Emerson stresses the newness, the freshness of the American viewpoint; he invites his countrymen to "enjoy an original relation to the universe"; he emphasizes what up to fairly recently was one of our proudest boasts, "the infinitude of the private man," the integrity of the individual mind.

Emerson believed the universe was good. Most Americans think so too, though not always for Emerson's reasons. At any rate his emphasis on the power of the will, on inspiration, on an open-ended future, has always appealed to us. Sometimes we have vulgarized his affirmative doctrine. It is but a short series of missteps from Ralph Waldo Emerson to Billy Graham.

I suggest you read the short book called *Nature,* published in 1836, which contains most of Emerson's informal philosophy; *The American Scholar;* the essays "History" and "Self-Reliance"; the essays on Plato (5) and Montaigne (79) from *Representative Men;* the essay on Thoreau (84); and, best of all, *English Traits,* which though written for its time seems to me the most durable of all Emerson's work.

84

HENRY DAVID THOREAU (1817–1862)

Walden, Civil Disobedience

Thoreau seems to have spent much of his life talking to himself; since his death he has been talking to millions. Perhaps, indeed, hundreds of millions, for the program of Gandhi (who influenced Martin Luther King) and the politics of the British Labour Party were both profoundly affected by Thoreau's ideas. Now, more than a century after his death, it is safe to say that *Walden* (with which we may group *Civil Disobedience*) is one of the most influential books not only of its century, but of ours. Today, defying everything our industrial society lives by, it speaks to us more urgently than ever. It and *Huckleberry Finn* are probably the two *central* American statements in our literature. If I add that Thoreau's prose is as enjoyable, as crackling, as witty, as full of sap as any yet produced on this continent, I shall have listed the essential reasons for reading *Walden* and as many other of the major essays as you care to try.

Thoreau had no time to waste in making money. Early in life he decided to do not what society suggested for him, but what he himself wanted. At various times he earned his bare keep by schoolmastering, surveying, pencil-making, gardening, and manual labor. He also appointed himself to certain jobs such as inspector of snowstorms and rainstorms. He wrote tirelessly (this man was no idler—he worked harder than any fifty leading board chairmen), mainly at a vast journal, some of it still in manuscript. From his books and journalism he earned little. His first book was printed in an edition of one thousand copies, of which fewer than three hundred were sold. He remarked, "I have now a library of nearly nine hundred volumes, over seven hundred of which I wrote myself." He spent his life in occasional converse with Emerson (83) and the available Concord literati and transcendentalists; more often talking to hunters, trappers, farmers, and other plain folk who lived close to the natural world he loved; most often with himself, tramping the woods and fields around his home, noting, with two of the sharpest eyes that ever existed, the behavior of the earth, water, and air, of which our lives seemed to him extensions; and at all moments thinking.

He really lived the life Emerson so beautifully preached, of self-reliance, nonconformity, simplicity, plain living, and high thinking. Of external events there were few: a pallid, unsuccessful romance (there is no question that, though Thoreau was a great man, he was a defective male); the two crucial years at Walden Pond, where he built a house for twenty-eight dollars and fended almost completely for himself; the overnight jailing for a refusal to pay his poll tax to what he considered an immoral government; his brave public defense of John Brown.

Thoreau needs little commentary; he is an expert at explaining himself. But let there be no misunderstanding: this man is dangerous. He is not a revolutionary but something far more intense—a radical, almost in the sense that Jesus was. He does not, like Marx, want to overturn society. He would say that Marx's life-denying state is no better than any other life-denying state. He simply opposed *himself* to the whole trend of his time, as well as to that of ours, whose shape he foresaw. By withdrawal, he set his face against invention, the machine, motion, industry, progress, material things, associations, togetherness, cities, strong government. He said it all in one word: Simplify. But if that word were taken by all of us as literally as Thoreau himself took it, our civilization would be transformed overnight.

Knowing that "the mass of men lead lives of quiet desperation" (how often the phrase is quoted nowadays), he determined to live entirely by his own lights, in fact to *live* rather than to adjust, accumulate, join, reform, or compete. His rejection of our values is far more complete and, many will think, far saner than that of the one man we have met to whom he is most akin—D. H. Lawrence. His private notion of living may not appeal to those of us who lack his genius for enjoying and interpreting nature; but the force of his general doctrine of the meaning of human life does not rest on the private notion.

It is a fair guess that this queer Yankee semihermit, this genuinely rugged individualist who distrusted the state and treated July 4 like any other day, may turn out to be, oddly enough, not only the most American of all our writers, but one of the most enduring.

85

WILLIAM JAMES (1842–1910)

The Principles of Psychology (Chapters 1, 4, 7, 9, 11, 21, 26, 28), *Pragmatism and Four Essays from The Meaning of Truth* (in one volume), *The Varieties of Religious Experience*

The psychologist-philosopher William James was the slightly elder brother of the novelist Henry, whom we have already met. A warm affection linked these two very different beings. Henry's nature was fastidious; it concerned itself with the relations existing among other rarefied temperaments; and, though reflective, it was not speculative or able to handle high-order abstractions. William was, like Emerson, a natural democrat, hearty, humorous, with a deep interest in problems of science, religion, and morality. Henry was the pure artist, affecting the world by his books alone. William was a vital teacher whose personality still exerts great influence. Henry opted for upper-class and intellectual English society, occasionally the same thing. William delighted in the vigorous, growing America of his time and entered into its public life in a way that would have been difficult for his more detached brother. Whitehead (III, IV) called William "an adorable genius." The noun would also apply to Henry; the adjective (though he did have a fussy charm) hardly.

A word about the suggested reading. Very little of James is unrewarding, but these three books will give you a fair idea of both his personality and his ideas. *The Principles of Psychology,* though now partly superseded, remains James's most permanent work. Difficult in part, it succeeds wonderfully in dramatizing the life of the mind. James himself later spoke of its content as "this nasty little subject," but the world has not accepted his judgment. *Pragmatism* should be read not only because the word is so closely connected with James, but also because the idea behind the word is so closely connected with our character as a people. If you have read Mill (74) you may find it interesting to figure out why the book is dedicated to him. James's most purely *interesting* book is *The Varieties of Religious Experience.* One of the cornerstones of the literature of religious psychology, it illustrates concretely what he meant by the pragmatic test.

The pragmatic test sounds simple and to many it is at once convincing. However, it is open to philosophical objections into which it is not our present business to go. Briefly, James argues that an idea's meaning and truth depend on its practical consequences. A problem is real if its solution makes a difference in actual experience, if it performs an operation on our behavior. Thus James stresses not origins but results. In the *Varieties* he asserts that the religious states he is describing are, like all states of mind, neurally conditioned. But he goes on to say that "their significance must be tested not by their origin but by the value of their fruits." Thus religion, whether or not determinably "true," is valuable to the individual and therefore to the race. Its truth is not absolute but functional. Ideas are good only as instruments, and it is by their instrumentalism that we must judge them. To sum up, "an idea is 'true' so long as to believe it is profitable to our lives." James's moral ideals were of the highest and purest; "profitable" does not refer to the marketplace; nor is it fair to vulgarize James's pragmatism by saying that what he meant was "Anything is O.K. if it works."

There is more in James, far more, than the pragmatic idea, though it is central both to him and to our vague national philosophy, if we may be said to have one. One should understand it. But that is not the main reason for reading him. The main reason is the man himself. He is one of the most attractive figures in the history of thought—vital, alert to the whole world of experience, mentally liberating, emotionally refreshing. In addition he is master of a style of great freshness and clarity. One may disagree with the pragmatic test (believers in fixed religious and moral values are bound to do so) and still emerge from reading James feeling more alive and hopeful than before. He is the philosopher of possibility. By his own pragmatic test, he is apt to succeed with the reader. Reading him can make a difference.

86
JOHN DEWEY (1859–1952)

Human Nature and Conduct

Years ago, when I attended John Dewey's class at Columbia, I thought that he looked like an intelligent, benevolent janitor. Dewey was an unimpressive, rather dull lecturer; and to tell the truth he is, superficially, an unimpressive, rather dull writer. Compared to that of William James (85), whose pragmatism he developed and deepened, his personality is drab. Yet this quiet, drawling Vermonter has been more broadly effective than his predecessor. His mind has been felt not only in philosophy, but in law, economics, politics, esthetics, and especially in education.

If Whitehead's (III) key word is *process,* Dewey's is *society.*

His general outlook he called instrumentalism. By this he meant that the full meaning of an idea is apparent only when it is *applied,* and applied socially. Compare him with James. James stressed the individual, particularly the individual's interior emotional and religious world. As a young man James suffered an inner crisis akin to Mill's. Also, his generation was greatly troubled by the agnostic movement precipitated by Darwin and the theory of evolution. The more balanced Dewey came on the scene a little later, when the religious turmoil of the nineteenth century had partly died down, and when it was society, then in bewildering transformation, rather than the private individual, that clamored to be understood.

Of all our abstract thinkers Dewey seems the most American. That is because, despite his colorless style, he is not essentially abstract. He faced a changed world squarely. He recognized that the planet was soon to be industrialized. He asked the question, How shall we deal with a changed planet (and therefore, he thought, a changing human being) actively and intelligently? He began by initiating reforms in education, first here, then in the Near and Far East. If authoritarian instruction, learning by rote, and the separation of the school from society are not popular with us, that is John Dewey's work. The excesses of progressive education, however, should not be laid at his door. It would be fairer to say that his liberating influence has made possible the present constructive controversy as to how American children should be taught.

But in his constant endeavor "to change the world through action," Dewey advanced into a dozen other fields. Philosophy for him was not an academic exercise. He thought it "has no call to create a world of 'reality' *de novo,* nor to delve into secrets of Being hidden from common sense and science." He wished to apply to the social disciplines, as well as to such practical activities as politics and law, the methods and insights that had been so successfully used in the sciences, particularly in biology. He made philosophy go to work. All his books were meant to act as bridges between the academy and the growing, changing democratic society he saw around him, and in whose life he actively participated. He made experience the test of theory, and experiment a calculated part of experience. Thinking to him meant inquiry; and belief, as with James, was to be judged by its effects.

There are many whose temperaments cannot sympathize with Dewey's conception of a human being as essentially a social, sharing, and not a tragic animal, and who are not at all sure that the environment is there to be changed or "improved." On the whole, however, he has won more supporters than antagonists. He is now part of the American mental world.

I have suggested that you read *Human Nature and Conduct.* His profounder thought is doubtless to be found in other books but this one seemed to me on the whole to be the one most open to the general reader. Also it is typical of Dewey's activist pragmatic attitude. As a treatise on morals you may find it rather different from some we have already encountered, such as the *Meditations* of Marcus Aurelius. All conduct, for Dewey, is *interaction* between human nature and a changing environment, in our case an environment dominated by science, industry, and democracy. He mediates between the traditional doctrine of fixed moral values and that easy subjectivism which affirms that the good is merely what one happens to like. In this book, morals and human nature are again and again brought together, in a hundred different aspects, with consequences each reader will have to judge for himself or herself.

87
GEORGE SANTAYANA (1863–1952)

Skepticism and Animal Faith, Selected Other Works

Santayana was born in Spain, of Spanish parentage. From 1872 to 1912 he lived in Boston, passing twenty-three of those years mainly at Harvard. While his American period was not precisely forty years of wandering in the wilderness, there is no doubt that he was happier during the next forty, spent as an itinerant student in Europe. At eighty-nine Santayana died, quite in character, in a Roman convent, mourned by the gentle nuns whose faith he had never abjured, whose dogmas he had never accepted except as poetry.

He offers a striking contrast to his contemporary Dewey (86) and his teacher and later colleague William James (85). Though he understood Americans, particularly our weaknesses, well enough, America left few traces in him. He regarded this country with a kindly, slightly patronizing interest. He was unable to sympathize with our dominant Protestantism, optimism, restlessness, and passion for "progress." The practical philosophies of James and Dewey held no charm for him. Perhaps he thought them, as he did the poetry of Whitman (95), barbarous. His real home was not even the Europe he preferred to the United States. It lay more nearly in the classical Greece he loved; author of *The Last Puritan,* he has been called the last Greek. Perhaps even more truly, this solitary aristocrat was at home only among those timeless objects of intuition he calls *essences.* The modern world he thought of as a host to whom he happened to be paying a brief visit.

Santayana lived so long and wrote so superbly in half a dozen fields that no one book adequately reflects his complex, ironical temperament. As a philosopher he discussed metaphysics, morals, epistemology, politics, and particularly esthetics. But he also wrote first-class literary essays, philosophical dialogues, social criticism, and an interesting novel, as well as some youthful poetry still occasionally represented in the anthologies. No matter what you decide to read, however, it is well to bear in mind that of all the philosophers we have met (except perhaps Plato) he is the only one who is centrally an artist. It is not merely that he writes beautiful prose. It is that he is at all times open to concrete impressions of beauty, humor, and tragedy that are generally perceived only abstractly by such thinkers as Locke or Mill or Dewey. From this fact arises a fascinating paradox. He seems at one and the same time to be living in a timeless world of contemplation and in our own world of vivid color, loveliness, and sorrowful contingency. He is both remote and, despite his elegant snobbery, intensely human.

Basically Santayana remained a naturalist in the Greek sense. "All life," he says, echoing Aristotle (6), "is animal in its origin and spiritual in its possible fruits." He is skeptical of the exalted claims of reason, calling it "only a harmony among irrational impulses." Religion, science, and art he considers the crowns of human endeavor; yet at bottom they are not carriers of absolute truths, but only creative myths: religion is "sublimated poetry." In politics, as in other areas, he is profoundly conservative, and Deweyan liberals find him hard to stomach. No reader of Santayana will ever be spurred on to change or improve the world.

Skepticism and Animal Faith, not the easiest of his works, is probably the single volume most adequately presenting his central thought. His one novel, *The Last Puritan,* published when he was seventy-two, is not only interesting as a portrait of the New England conscience, but suggests, in highly readable form, many of Santayana's favorite doctrines. His most sheerly beautiful writing, I think, will be found in *Dialogues in Limbo* and a lecture-essay called "The Unknowable." As essayist and aphorist Santayana ranks among the finest. This aspect of his genius may be glimpsed in many of his books, particularly *Interpretations of Poetry and Religion.* If you continue to find Santayana interesting, you will want to read his three little books of autobiography, the fruit of his old age. Collectively they are called *Persons and Places.* The separate titles are: *The Background of My Life, The Middle Span,* and *My Host the World.*

POETRY

88

JOHN DONNE (1573–1631)

Selected Works

Had the Lifetime Reading Plan been compiled in 1900, Donne and Blake might have been omitted. The shift in emphasis is more than a matter of fashion, though both men do happen to be fashionable in literary circles. It is a matter of taste; but taste, when it mirrors a real change in our view of ourselves, can be a profound thing.

Neglected for some generations after his death, Donne impresses us today because he speaks to our condition, as Milton does not. In another fifty years or so this may no longer be true. At the moment, however, Donne seems to us a great writer, not merely because he has so powerfully influenced modern poetry, but because his voice is that of a modern man. It is no accident that in 1940 Hemingway (60) should have drawn the title of his novel *For Whom the Bell Tolls* from one of Donne's *Devotions,* published in 1624.

Born of a Roman Catholic family, Donne was on his mother's side related to the martyr Sir Thomas More. Some years at Oxford and Cambridge were followed by the study of law, by a period of worldly and amorous adventure in London, by foreign service, and by a marriage—injudicious from the practical viewpoint—with the highborn niece of his employer, Sir Thomas Egerton. Donne's career prospects darkened and for a decade the young couple endured discouragement and poverty. At forty-two, after much serious reflection, Donne forsook the family faith and took orders in the Anglican church. He rose until he became Dean of St. Paul's in London, and the most famous preacher of his time. The daring young spark of the earlier love poems was now a God-tormented man, assailed by visions of death and the indignities of illness. He rejected "the mistress of my youth, Poetry" in favor of "the wife of mine age, Divinity." His obsession with mortality grew with the years. Today you may visit the crypt in St. Paul's and see Donne's statue, sculpted during his lifetime, wrapped in a winding sheet. As his last hour neared he contemplated from his bedside a painting of himself in a shroud, his eyes closed as if death had already touched him.

Donne's *Devotions* and sermons are quite unlike conventional religious literature. They are works of art, combining an almost frightening spiritual intensity with cunning elaboration of rhythm and metaphor. The *Devotions* are addressed to himself. The sermons were delivered before large audiences, often before the king. No Sunday pieties, they were designed deliberately to work upon the emotions. They can still do so, with their art if not their doctrine.

Donne's poetry is at once highly sensuous (often highly sensual), uncompromisingly intellectual, and startlingly personal. By the use of metaphor, sometimes complex, sometimes brutally direct, Donne merges sense and intellect in a manner to which our own taste seems keenly receptive. At his worst his figures of speech are the ingenious conceits that annoyed the forthright Dr. Johnson (101). At his best they seem identical with the thought itself.

His love poetry bypasses not only all the Elizabethan conventions, but all the standard sentiments that had been the staple of erotic verse up to his day. "For God's sake hold your tongue, and let me love." A man who begins a poem that way is imitating no one. He is not writing exercises. He is a real man speaking, and his voice is in the room. Donne can be shocking, outrageous, tender, learned, colloquial, fantastic, passionate, reverent, despairing; and sometimes he is several of these in a single love poem. It is his awareness of the complexity of emotion that recommends him to our unsimple time. And what is true of his love poetry is also true of his devotional verse, which often seems to have an erotic tinge: it is the work of the whole man, including the physical man. Two often-quoted lines condense a great deal of John Donne:

> Love's mysteries in souls do grow,
> But yet the body is his book.

We may, very roughly, liken Donne's poetry to El Greco's painting. As El Greco distorts line, so Donne distorts language, not out of any lust for experiment, but to achieve calculated effects of emphasis, intensity, and directness obtainable in no other way. Just as El Greco's colors at first seem harsh and unnatural, so Donne's rhythms are broken, rough, the agitated reflection of emotions themselves broken and rough. The spiritual pain and tension that we feel in El Greco we feel also in Donne. His faith was not serene; it was shadowed with anxieties, perplexities, contradictions that seem to anticipate the climate of our own sorely beset time.

Donne produced much writing of interest mainly to the scholar. For the beginning reader, who may be familiar with only a few anthology pieces, I might suggest: the *Songs and Sonnets,* the *Elegies,* the *First and Second Anniversaries,* the *Holy Sonnets,* the *Devotions Upon Emergent Occasions,* and perhaps a few of the *Sermons.* At first this "angel speaking out of a cloud" may seem far-fetched and needlessly difficult. But, behind his odd metaphors (often drawn from the trades and sciences) and his seeming extravagances of style lie sound reasons. Careful reading will soon make these reasons apparent, and his personal idiom will become less and less alien as it becomes more and more fascinating.

89

JOHN MILTON (1608–1674)

Paradise Lost, Lycidas, On the Morning of Christ's Nativity, Sonnets, Areopagitica

Milton's life opened on a fair prospect and closed in darkness. At Christ's College, Cambridge, the delicate-featured boy was called, half in scorn, half in admiration, "The Lady of Christ's." He found his vocation early: poetry and classical scholarship. A period of reading and study at his father's country house

JOHN MILTON

(1632–38) was followed by a year or two of Continental travel. During this time he was a humanist not greatly different from other humanists of the Renaissance. Then came twenty years of stormy political and religious controversy. Some magnificent prose resulted, but little happiness; and many may think these years a waste of his genius. Championing the Parliamentary cause, hating "the bishops," he served as Latin secretary to Cromwell for over a decade, overlaying his original humanism with Puritan doctrine. From his forty-third year to his death he was blind; none of his three marriages turned out well; and with the Restoration all his political hopes and dreams were dashed. Nothing was left him but poetry and his personal Christianity, a kind of dissidence of dissent.

This was the man who wrote *Paradise Lost,* he and his widow receiving eighteen pounds for the effort of justifying the ways of God to men; who told us that poetry should be "simple, sensuous, and passionate," but did not always follow his own prescription; whose *Areopagitica* is the classic defense of free speech and who fiercely supported Cromwell's rigid Puritan theocracy; whose views on divorce were three hundred years ahead of his time and whose views on women were those of a dimwitted barbarian; who was a master of the language and yet may be said to have written English as if it were Latin or Greek.

The average reader, approaching this unhappy Samson, meets two obstacles. The first is Milton. The second is Miltonese.

It is hard to like John Milton. Suffering the penalty of charmlessness, of humorlessness, he has been less read than admired, less admired than merely accepted. The "God-gifted organ voice of England," as Tennyson called it, is a pretty intimidating voice as well. Milton was a man of the utmost courage; but it is not the kind of courage that kindles the imagination because it is not married to much humanity, and distills the smell of stubbornness. His pride was too magnificent for any alloy of mere conceit; yet we are made uncomfortable by his "elaborate assumption of the singing-robe," by his flat statement that he will pursue "things unattempted yet in prose or rhyme." He is a hard man to live with. Shakespeare, even Dante, had not only the uncommon but also the common touch. Milton lacked it. Making due allowance for Samuel Johnson's Toryism, it is hard not to agree with his view of Milton: "an acrimonious and surly republican."

And the style is suited to the man. It has, as Milton proudly states, "no middle flight." It can be grand; it can be windy; it can be sublime; it can be pompous. It is never charming, restful, or easy, except in the minor poems and even then infrequently. It is difficult, odd in syntax and vocabulary, uncompromising in its elevation.

Perhaps I have persuaded you to skip Milton. That was not my intention. For all the mustiness of his theology and morality, for all his mannerism (though it was no mannerism to him), for all the negative magnetism of his personality, he remains a great artist in both verse and prose. With rocklike—he would say adamantine—grandeur he continues to impose himself even on our age, which laughs at grandeur, at the noble style, and at erudition.

It is worthwhile to make a special, even a painful effort of adjustment to read Milton. If he is a museum piece, he is a rare, a precious one. If you cannot stomach his message in *Paradise Lost,* at least read it for the gorgeous sound, the elaborate imagery, the portrait of Satan, that fallen god with whom Milton himself had so much in common. No one will ever again write like this. No one will ever again conceive such perfect, rolling periods as are to be found in his most eloquent prose.

When we step inside our first great Gothic cathedral, our feelings are mixed. It seems alien, it seems too complicated, it does not seem quite human. But gradually we accustom ourselves to what the builders had in mind. Little by little the structure and sweep and decoration and color become familiar. Soon two clear emotions begin to arise in us, different in nature, yet capable of blending: awe and esthetic pleasure. Milton is a little like that. He cannot inspire these emotions all the time, nor should one be too obstinate in seeking them continually. But they are there for you, if you read him in small doses, skipping when he is too wearisome or too exalted for our commoner clay.

90
WILLIAM BLAKE (1757–1827)

Selected Works

Once, William Blake tells us, he walked to the end of the heath and touched the sky with his finger. At four he screamed upon perceiving God's head at the window. He saw angels in boughs and the prophet Ezekiel under a tree. His wife once remarked placidly, "I have very little of Mr. Blake's company. He is always in Paradise." Perhaps an exaggeration, but there is no doubt that Blake felt himself on all fours with spirits. He is the supreme type, at least in modern times, of the visionary poet.

Toward this strange, baffling man of streaky genius one has a choice of attitudes. You may put him down as a faker, though the sweetness and honesty of his whole life belie it. Some of his contemporaries, quite celebrated then, quite forgotten now, called him a harmless lunatic. A psychologist will talk of Blake's "eidetic vision," which is simply a specialized ability to project into the external world images we usually hold in our minds. Many children have this power, Joan of Arc may have had it, and rationalists cite it when trying to explain the visions of saints and even Jesus. Finally you can ponder Blake's sly and, from the viewpoint of the professional artist and poet, quite practical advice to his friends: "Work up imagination to the state of vision."

It doesn't matter. By the pragmatic test Blake is a success. His paintings, drawings, and engravings, though not of the highest order, are beautiful and moving. His finest verse, of which there is not a great deal, is original and unforgettable. His ideas, long mocked or neglected, appeal with increasing force to those who have lost faith in materialism's ability to bring happiness to the race.

Blake was that rare thing, a completely spontaneous human being. "A man without a mask," a friend called him. Living and dying in poverty, he was probably one of the most energetically joyful men of his time. He had some secret of ecstasy denied to most of us, and at times it stimulated odd behavior:

he and his wife were once discovered in their little arbor, stark naked, reading *Paradise Lost* aloud.

In his rejection of most of the institutions of his time (as well as in his crankiness) he resembles other figures we have met, such as Thoreau, Nietzsche, and Lawrence. His romanticism is a far deeper thing than that of the romantic poets who followed him—Wordsworth, Keats, Shelley. "Man is all imagination," he tells us. "God is man and exists in us and we in him." And again: "We are led to believe a lie when we see *with,* not *through,* the eye."

His scorn of what is called common sense led him to champion freedom of all kinds, in the religious, political, and sexual spheres. Calmly, in a memorable sentence, he anticipates Freud: "Sooner murder an infant in its cradle than nurse unacted desires." For him "Exuberance is Beauty." Nonconformists of all stripes love to quote "Damn braces. Bless relaxes." He hated all those virtues arising out of measure and calculation: "The tigers of wrath are wiser than the horses of instruction."

Blake has the defect of his qualities. His interior world was so vivid that he often lost touch with the exterior world. He may wrap piercing truth in a cloud of frenzy. But the cloud is there; he can be a bad communicator. His private mythology is contained in the so-called *Prophetic Books.* Scholars keep on trying to unravel them. To most of us they will seem like delirium interrupted by gorgeous eloquence.

Blake's nature mingled high natural intelligence and piercing intuition. In his aphorisms and his best verse the two elements are held in balance. His poetry is not artless—Blake was an excellent craftsman with his pen as well as with his pencil and graver. But in the best sense it is childlike—that is, pure, flowing, simple in diction, wildly imaginative. T. S. Eliot's (94) severe and just judgment is really a tribute: "Dante is a classic, and Blake only a poet of genius."

For all his extravagance and seeming mooniness, Blake must be seen as essentially a moralist, of the prophetic rather than the reflective order. His defense of imagination and instinct is religious in tone. Whether he writes about children or spirits, his concern is "to cleanse the doors of perception." His thought can be merely odd or ill-balanced: Blake shows that uncertain sense of proportion often possessed by self-educated geniuses. But just as frequently it goes straight to the heart of what is wrong with an industrial society disfigured by its "dark, Satanic mills." Yet there is no do-goodism in Blake. He is a hard-core rebel, like Shaw, and, like Shaw, a dangerous man.

Of his verse I suggest you read *Poetical Sketches, Songs of Innocence, Songs of Experience, The Everlasting Gospel,* and the *Preface to Milton.* To get some notion of the principles by which Blake lived his quietly rebellious life, see *The Marriage of Heaven and Hell, All Religions Are One,* and *There Is No Natural Religion.* His ideas on art may be understood through his divertingly ill-tempered Annotations to Sir Joshua Reynolds's Discourses.

91

WILLIAM WORDSWORTH (1770–1850)

The Prelude, Selected Shorter Poems, Preface to the *Lyrical Ballads* (1800)

In a famous parody of one of Wordsworth's sonnets, the English humorist J. K. Stephen wrote:

> Two Voices are there: one is of the deep; ...
> And one is of an old halfwitted sheep
> Which bleats articulate monotony ...
> And, Wordsworth, both are thine. ...

My Wordsworth contains 937 closely printed pages. Of these, possibly 200 are in the voice of the deep. The remainder are bleatings. Wordsworth, who never understood how to cut things short, persisted to his eightieth year. Of these years only the first half were, from posterity's viewpoint, worth living. The last forty were of great interest to Wordsworth; of considerable interest to the three female acolytes who took care of him; and of some interest to literary scholars attracted by the problem of the decay of genius.

The main influence on Wordsworth was Wordsworth. I

know of no major literary figure who was so continuously and so favorably impressed by himself. This highly successful love affair dried up in him the springs of self-criticism; and as he had no humor to start with, four-fifths of his work turned out to be a crashing bore.

Of the non-William-Wordsworthian influences the most important was the English countryside, which he may almost be said to have invented. It touched something in him deep, pure, and unselfish, releasing some of his finest verse. The second influence was the superior intelligence of Coleridge (92). Their friendship produced the epochal collaboration of the *Lyrical Ballads* (1798) and the no less epochal Preface to the edition of 1800. The third influence was Wordsworth's sister, Dorothy, a remarkable neurotic whose eyes and ears were far better than her brother's and whose alertness to the face of nature provided him with many insights for which he is usually given full credit. At this late date it would be prissy to deny that the relation between Dorothy and William was unconsciously incestuous, at least on Dorothy's part. This has no bearing whatsoever on the value of his work.

Minor influences were the French Revolution and Annette Vallon, a Frenchwoman who seems to have stimulated Wordsworth to something mildly approaching passion. At first the eager young poet was a partisan of the Revolution. Its excesses, plus his own deep quietistic bias, plus what seems to have been plain caution (compare Milton) combined to change Wordsworth into a dull reactionary. The connection with Annette Vallon, resulting in an illegitimate daughter, he did his best to hide from posterity. His whole conduct in the affair (compare Fielding) is unmanly, even callous. This again has nothing to do with the value of his work.

The odd thing is that, though Wordsworth's poetry and manifestos really did help to liberate our emotions (see Mill [74]), his own emotions were limited in number and even in depth. He wrote beautifully about nature, children, the poor, common people. Our attitudes toward all these differ today from the attitudes of the neoclassic eighteenth century against which Wordsworth courageously rebelled; and this change we owe in part to a poet most of us do not read. Yet he himself never observed nature with the particularity of a

Thoreau. He does not seem to have understood children—the sonnet "On the Beach at Calais" is supremely lovely, but there is no real child involved (even though he is writing about his own daughter), merely an abstract, Wordsworthian idea of childhood. For all his influential theories about using "the real language of men," he does not seem to have had much idea of how humble folk really talked. And, except perhaps for the Annette Vallon affair, in which he conducted himself like a poltroon, he was incapable of a strong, passionate love for a woman.

And now that I have said all this, an open confession of my dislike of Wordsworth, I must make two obvious statements far more to the point. The first is that he wrote some great verse, though I think virtually all of it is contained in his long poetical autobiography, *The Prelude,* plus "Tintern Abbey," "Ode: Intimations of Immortality," "Michael," "Resolution and Independence," "Ode to Duty," and a scattering of superb sonnets and shorter lyrics.

The second statement is that he opened the eyes of poets and ordinary human beings to the possibilities of a fresh approach to nature, to the life of feeling, and to the English language. With Coleridge, he diverted the course of English and American poetry. He helped to release it from conventionality, stock epithets, city-pent emotions. His famous definition of poetry as "the spontaneous overflow of powerful feelings" arising from "emotion recollected in tranquillity" is limited and partial. But as a corrective to the petrifactions of the eighteenth century it was badly needed. For all its excesses, the romantic protest has proved valuable to the Western tradition.

It is probable that Wordsworth will become more important as a historical event than as a poet. But he is great enough in both categories to warrant some acquaintance. After all, this humorless, mentally and emotionally straitened egomaniac in a few short years did write verse that helped to "cleanse the doors of perception."

92

SAMUEL TAYLOR COLERIDGE (1772–1834)

The Ancient Mariner, Christabel, Kubla Khan, Biographia Literaria, Writings on Shakespeare

In a moment of self-forgetfulness Wordsworth called Coleridge "the most *wonderful* man" he had ever known. Shelley hailed him as this "hooded eagle among blinking owls." His good friend the essayist Charles Lamb spoke of him as "an Archangel a little damaged" and of his "hunger for eternity." The scholar George Saintsbury ranked Coleridge, as literary critic, with Aristotle and Longinus. Mill (74) remarked, "The class of thinkers has scarcely yet arisen by whom he is to be judged," and many thoughtful students feel the statement, made over a century ago, still stands. Such judgments could be multiplied by the score.

They were made about the greatest might-have-been in English literature. For the fact is that Coleridge's reputation and influence are both far more imposing than his work. His mind, a Tuscarora for depth, a Pacific for vastness, was never quite able to pull itself together. Though the *Biographia Literaria* comes nearest to it, he wrote no single, complete prose masterpiece. Like Wordsworth's, much of his verse, though more intensely felt, is balderdash. Of the three poems by which as a poet he will live, only the *Ancient Mariner* is a finished whole. Often ranked as the finest Shakespearean critic who ever wrote, he never imposed order on his mass of essays, lectures, notes, and conversational remarks.

At no time in his incoherent life did Coleridge show any notable common sense. There are many men, often of the highest order of mind, who should be exempted from the pressures of normal living. Coleridge was one of them. He had no capacity for marriage, little for fatherhood, not much for earning his board and lodging. He tried soldiering, preaching, periodical journalism, lecturing, even foreign service under the governor of Malta. During his latter years he wasted part of what might have been productive energy in incessant and apparently uniquely brilliant monologues. ("The stimulus of conversation suspends the terror that haunts my mind.") Tortured by neuralgia and other ills, plus intense melancholy, he sought relief in laudanum and became an addict. For the last eighteen years of his life, withdrawn from his wife, he lived under the medical care of a kindly friend, James Gillman.

In a sense the "person from Porlock" who is said to have interrupted him as he was writing down the dream-dictated lines of *Kubla Khan* (modern scholarship is skeptical of this story) was a real-life reflection of his own inner disorder. He was continually interrupting himself. His mind was too active and associative for him to complete any project. His whole life is like a mass of notes, undigested, erratic, sometimes baffling, sometimes profound, rich in wonders.

The fruitful association with Wordsworth produced the *Lyrical Ballads,* to which Coleridge contributed his lone undisputed masterpiece, *The Rime of the Ancient Mariner.* Here, as also in the unfinished *Kubla Khan* and *Christabel,* he successfully compelled "that willing suspension of disbelief for the moment which constitutes poetic faith" and so contributed to the mainstream of romanticism. That magic, eerie note he never again quite sounded.

What fascinates in Coleridge is that, along with his genius for the fairy tale (these poems, though not for children, belong to the literature of the fairy tale), he possessed a speculative mind of the rarest power. He wrote on metaphysics, politics, theology. Never reducing his insights to a system, he nonetheless remains a psychologist of most original gifts. And as a literary critic of the romantic school he has no peer in the language.

When you think of Coleridge you may quite naturally think also of Poe. Neither was able to manage practical life. Both had minds that worked as well in the area of ratiocination as in that of dreams. But there the parallel more or less ends. Poe's erudition was spotty, Coleridge's incredibly vast ("I have read everything"). Poe's mind was acute, Coleridge's brooding, penetrating, and hungry for vast unities. Poe was an interesting minor failure. Coleridge was a fascinating major failure. But he was so fascinating and so major that even as a failure he bulks larger than his admired friend Wordsworth, who finished work he never should have started and ended as poet laureate, while Coleridge died in poverty.

93

WILLIAM BUTLER YEATS (1865–1939)

Collected Poems, Collected Plays, The Autobiography

Exclusive of Shakespeare and Chaucer, the Plan suggests for extended reading nine English and American poets. Among these, posterity will assign Yeats his proper rank. That he will not be at the bottom of the list we may be sure.

Yeats offers difficulties. He was a complex man and, of all the poets we have met, he is the one who offers the least satisfaction when read in anthological snatches. Also, he is more than a poet. Among his tremendous output are poems, plays, memoirs, essays, literary studies, folk and fairy tales, mystical philosophies, letters, speeches, translations from Sophocles. Like Goethe's, his long life comprised a series of evolutions. There is a vast space between the aged poet of the *Last Poems and Plays* (1940) and the young Celtic dreamer of *The Wanderings of Oisin* (1889). To bridge this space the reader must absorb a great deal of Yeats and also know something about the Ireland whose soul he tried to find and form.

That is why I suggest his *Autobiography,* a one-volume omnibus. It contains reminiscences of his life through 1902, together with extracts from a diary kept in 1909, some notes about the death in 1909 of the great Irish dramatist Synge, and an account of his reception in Sweden, which he visited in 1923 to receive the Nobel Prize.

Yeats grew and changed and deepened; his life was not simple, any more than his thought. We may identify a few influences: his early childhood in the beautiful Sligo country; his readings in the romantic English poets; the mythology and folklore of Ireland, together with the Irish literary revival that he led; theosophy, spiritualism, occultism, astrology, and

Indian philosophy; the beautiful Irish revolutionary Maud Gonne, whom he loved in vain for twenty years; the psychic powers of his mediumistic wife; and toward the end such cyclical theories of history as are to be found in Vico, Spengler, Toynbee.

The major movement of his creative life is away from the delicate, suggestive, vague but often beautiful lyricism of the early verse toward the hard, spare, condensed, intellectual, tightly passionate, often obscure poetry of his later years. The change was already apparent in a poem called "September 1913," with its plain statement: "Romantic Ireland's dead and gone." Yeats's evolution is exactly opposed to Wordsworth's: aging, he became greater as man and as artist. The growth was fed by deep conflict, not only personal but political and social, for he despised much of our world ("this filthy modern tide") and used it as nourishment for his noble rage.

The bias of his mind is aristocratic (even feudal), mystical, symbolical. Though the symbols are not as wildly private as in Blake (90), who greatly influenced Yeats, they cannot be understood without a considerable knowledge of his work and life. Unless this is frankly admitted, the reader is apt to be at first puzzled, then irritated, finally antagonistic.

Yeats often seems esoteric, remote, impersonal, wrapped up in a world of strange images drawn from antiquity or the East or his own occult thought system or Irish legend. But the more one lives with him, the more clearly one feels his unflinching closeness to reality. He may be taken in by visions; but he is not taken in by illusions. In his mature work there is a bracing tragic bitterness:

> Whatever flames upon the night
> Man's own resinous heart has fed.

His wisdom is not for children, optimists, or the comfortable:

> I must lie down where all the ladders start,
> In the foul rag-and-bone shop of the heart.

In the final lines of one of his last poems, "Under Ben Bulben," he compresses his seeming arrogance, his patrician elevation of spirit, his horror of self-pity. He is leaving instructions for his own gravestone:

No marble, no conventional phrase;
On limestone quarried near the spot
By his command these words are cut:
  Cast a cold eye
  On life, on death.
  Horseman, pass by!

94

T. S. ELIOT (1888–1965)

Collected Poems, Collected Plays

In our short list of leading twentieth-century writers the inclusion of T. S. Eliot is inescapable. Not because in 1948 he won the Nobel Prize—on balance the prize has just as often gone to mediocrities as it has to those of high talent. Nor because he was the (involuntary) leader of a highly vocal and influential school of poets and critics. Nor because he occupied a position in England held in previous eras by such literary popes as Dryden, Addison, and Samuel Johnson. Nor because he was in his time one of the most controversial figures in contemporary English letters. Nor because the klieg lights of publicity were switched on him when he declared himself "Anglo-Catholic in religion, royalist in politics, and classicist in literature"—a description fitting hundreds of thousands of virtuous and intelligent Britishers. (The fuss made over it sprang from the liberal temperament's besetting weakness, parochialism.)

Except in his lucid essays (some of which I recommend you try) Eliot is a difficult writer, though as the years pass he seems less so, for he educated us to understand him. His achievement may be stated simply. He altered, deepened, and refined the character of English and American poetry in our time. He supplied modern criticism with a set of elevated and rigorous standards useful as a counterweight to the prevailing sleazy impressionism. In so doing he retrieved for us or set in a new light a whole series of writers: the minor Elizabethans, the seventeenth-century divines, Dante (14), Dryden, Donne (88).

T. S. ELIOT

Read his poetry in chronological order. Eliot—and this is not true of all the Plan's writers—was by nature a developer. His growth was both technical and spiritual. Technically he passed from verse filled with allusions and quotations, verse often rather tricky and fantastically clever, to verse of great purity, sonority of rhythm, and symphonic form. Spiritually he moved from the dandyish irony of the Prufrock poems of 1917 through the detached, terrible despair of *The Waste Land* (1922) to the brooding metaphysical religiousness of *Four Quartets* (1943).

During the whole of this evolution he held fast to his original aim: "to digest and express new objects, new groups of objects, new feelings, new aspects." Many of these objects and feelings are unpleasant, corresponding to our modern wasteland as the traditionalist eyes of Eliot saw it. But his purpose was neither to enjoy the luxury of misery nor to shock us with the disagreeable. "The essential advantage for a poet is not to have a beautiful world with which to deal; it is to be able to see beneath both beauty and ugliness; to see the boredom, and the horror, and the glory." All three—the boredom, the horror, the glory—are woven into his verse.

Though it has forebears, Eliot's poetry is nonetheless truly revolutionary, like the fiction of Proust or Joyce or the plays of Beckett. It is exact and condensed on the one hand and rich in magical suggestion on the other. Every word or allusive echo carries its proper weight, and all is borne upon a rhythmic current whose effect becomes evident when you read the lines aloud or listen to Eliot's own recording of them. At first the language seems private, impossible to penetrate. But as one gains familiarity, it begins to emerge as a marvelously precise and evocative rendering of states of mind peculiar to sensitive Western men and women at this particular stage of our evolution or devolution. And it shares at least one quality with the greatest verse, Shakespeare's or Dante's: it is rich in lines so finally expressive that they remain in our heads forever and become part of our emotional world.

95

WALT WHITMAN (1819–1892)

Selected Poems, Democratic Vistas,
Preface to first issue of *Leaves of Grass* (1855),
A Backward Glance O'er Travel'd Roads

I hear America singing. I celebrate myself. I loaf and invite my soul. I wear my hat as I please indoors or out. I find no sweeter fat than sticks to my own bones. I am the man, I suffered, I was there. Do I contradict myself? Very well then I contradict myself. Passage to India. I sound my barbaric yawp over the roofs of the world. A woman waits for me. When I give I give myself. The long brown path before me leading wherever I choose. The never-ending audacity of elected persons. Pioneers! O Pioneers! Out of the cradle endlessly rocking. When lilacs last in the dooryard bloomed. O Captain! My Captain! Who touches this, touches a man. I think I could turn and live with animals. A great city is that which has the greatest men and women. The mania of owning things. These United States. To have great poets, there must be great audiences, too. Leaves of grass. Powerful uneducated persons.

I have omitted the quotation marks around these lines and phrases because the marks hardly exist in our minds and memories. It is Whitman's language rather than his message that exerts power. He worked with all his soul to become a national bard, the voice of "the divine average," the Muse of Democracy. But we have no national bards; the average man or woman does not feel divine, nor wants to; democracy prefers to get along without a muse. Whitman loved his country and often wrote thrillingly about it, but it is probable that he never really understood it. He has penetrated not because he is accepted by the "powerful uneducated persons" he idealizes, but because he is a poet in the original sense, a maker, a coiner of wonderful new language.

His ideas, if you can call them that, he borrowed from many sources, including Emerson (83), who was among the first to hail his genius. His rhythms echo, among other books, the Bible. Nonetheless he is a true revolutionary in poetry. His free-swinging, cadenced, wavelike verse, his fresh (even if often absurd) manipulations of language, his boldness of vocabulary—all helped to liberate American poetry, and have had a profound effect abroad. There is no doubt also that his erotic candor was useful in the revolt against the genteel tradition.

The first three issues of *Leaves of Grass* (1855, 1856, 1860) contain ninety percent of his best work. After that he tended to repeat himself or to create poses rather than poetry. Whitman was a bit of a charlatan; if you want to be fancy you can say that he wore masks.

Whitman was a homosexual. His verse, and particularly his odd notion of democracy, cannot be understood except in the light of his bias toward males.

He had an original temperament, a certain peasant shrewdness, but only a moderate amount of brains. He can excite us with his rhapsodic, prophetic note. He can move us with his musical threnodies. He can cause to pass before our eyes a series of wonderful tiny images of people and things in action. These are not small gifts. They are enough to make him the greatest of American poets, until we come to our own time.

On the other hand, he tries too hard to make a virtue of his deficiencies. He was poorly educated, his experience of life (despite the legends he busily circulated) seems to have been limited, and he depended too much on the resources of his own rich temperament and too little on the common stock of three thousand years of the Western tradition. This makes him parochial when he thinks he is being daringly American. It lends a certain hollowness to his boast that he is "non-literary and non-decorous."

Ignoring scales of values, he embraces and celebrates all creation—often with infectious passion, often absurdly. Everything in Whitman seems to be equal to everything else; everything becomes equally divine. Sometimes the reader, fatigued by so many unvarying hosannas, is inclined to agree with the poet Sidney Lanier, who said that Whitman argues "because the Mississippi is long, therefore every American is God."

All these criticisms have been made often, and more severely. Yet Whitman somehow remains. England and the

Continent, anxious to believe that his barbaric yawp is the true voice of America (it satisfies their conventional romantic notion of us), appreciate him more widely than we do. But reasonably cultivated Americans, if not Whitman's beloved workers, also acknowledge his curious and thrilling spell. It is not because his is a truly native voice—Frost is far more authentically American. It is rather because his chant is universal, almost Homeric, touching in us primitive feelings about death and nature and the gods who refuse to die in even the most civilized among us. Trail-breaking in form, Whitman seems to be preclassical, pre-Christian in feeling, though he thought of himself as the trumpeter of a new time.

In addition to the three important prose works suggested, the reader might tick off, for minimum reading, the following poems: his masterpiece, "Song of Myself"; "I Sing the Body Electric"; "Song of the Open Road"; "Crossing Brooklyn Ferry"; "Song of the Answerer"; "Song of the Broad-Axe"; "Out of the Cradle Endlessly Rocking"; "As I Ebbed with the Ocean of Life"; "When I Heard the Learn'd Astronomer"; "By the Bivouac's Fitful Flame"; "As Toilsome I Wandered Virginia's Woods"; "The Wound-Dresser"; "When Lilacs Last in the Dooryard Bloom'd"; "There Was a Child Went Forth"; "Proud Music of the Storm"; "Passage to India"; "Prayer of Columbus"; "A Noiseless Patient Spider"; "Years of the Modern."

96

ROBERT FROST (1874–1963)

Collected Poems

Though not *very* near, Frost is probably the nearest thing we have to a national poet. He is constantly anthologized. Schoolchildren are regularly exposed to his simpler work. The television screen, the lecture platform, and the college classroom made his remarkable and sometimes disquieting personality familiar to many Americans who do not think of themselves as poetry lovers. A citizen of a prize-respecting country, he won the Pulitzer Prize four times. Finally, together with other talents, he possessed that of longevity. All these factors combined to make him a kind of unofficial poet laureate. Insofar as this has helped to raise the status of poetry in a poetry-resistant age, it is a fine thing. Insofar as it has created a fuzzy or sentimentalized or incomplete image of a great writer, it is less so.

"Literature begins with geography," says Frost. The literature he created did indeed begin with the hilly, lonely, past-conserving, Yankee land north of Boston. Yet Frost is no regional poet. He may begin with geography but he advances into unmappable country. Nor is Frost, though deeply American, a representative voice; Frost is his own man. Nor is he a "poet of the people," as Sandburg may be. He writes often about farmers, hill folk, lonely small souls. But the slope of his temperament is as aristocratic as Yeats's, though more sociable, flexible, and humorous. As is often the case with him, he is half serious, half kidding in such a casual remark as: "I have given up my democratic prejudices and have willingly set the lower classes free to be completely taken care of by the upper classes." Finally, though he uses simple words and weaves into his verse the actual tones of common speech (so that it "says" itself), his technique and imagination are both extraordinarily complex. In other words, Frost is no Yankee sage, rhyming cracker-barrel philosophy, but a sophisticated mind who scorns the usual lingo of sophistication. His understatement conceals a rich growth of statement.

Frost is an uncornerable man. He will say, "I never take my own side in a quarrel." He will say, "I'm never serious except when I'm fooling." About his own art he has ideas no one else ever seems to have thought of: "Like a piece of ice on a hot stove the poem must ride on its own melting." He absorbed Thoreau and Emerson and reflected some of their independence, even their crankiness; but, that said, we have said little. Frost outwits classification, as he outwitted his own time, refusing to bow to it, refusing to be intimidated by it, using it always for his own secret, sly purposes: "I would have written of me on my stone: I had a lover's quarrel with the world."

The poems most of us know—"Mending Wall," "After Apple Picking," "The Road Not Taken," "Stopping by Woods on a Snowy Evening"—remain beautiful. But to find and wind your way into this cranky, ironic, humorous, elusive mind it is necessary to read the less familiar Frost of the later years. Aging, he grew more difficult, more philosophical, far more daring, satirical, funny, scathing. Absorb him slowly, over a long period.

97

Poets of the English Language, edited by W. H. Auden (1907–1973) and Norman Holmes Pearson (1909–1975)

We have already met many of the world's supreme poets: Homer, the Greek dramatists, Virgil, Lucretius, Dante, Chaucer, Shakespeare, Goethe. Numbers 88–96 suggest nine additional English and American poets (others might well have been chosen) for extensive and intensive reading. The anthology noted above, together with number 98, comprises a mop-up operation.

The Auden-Pearson collection is in five handy paperback volumes, titled as follows:

    I.   *Medieval and Renaissance Poets*
   II. *Elizabethan and Jacobean Poets*
  III. *Restoration and Augustan Poets*
  IV. *Romantic Poets*
   V. *Victorian and Edwardian Poets*

It ends with the opening of World War I; for post-Yeats poetry see number 98.

Each volume contains a brilliant introduction, rich in unconventional and often controversial ideas. Each also contains a useful Calendar of British and American Poetry, listing in two tables the leading events of both the poetical and the politico-socio-cultural worlds of the particular period. There are several other reader's aids. The main virtue of this anthology—beyond the fact that its editors are men of taste and learning—is that they have given themselves room in which to move around. Many long poems are printed in full;

there are no snippets; and a great many minor poets are well represented. In general, within the indicated time limits, the whole tradition of British and American verse is intelligibly and intelligently covered.

Only the heroic reader who is ruled by a systematic mind will want to start at the beginning and read this vast collection straight through, though much profit lies in doing so. You may pick and choose at random; or concentrate on a single period for a year or so; or read the verse corresponding in time with the prose work you are reading; or simply obey your mood, for poetry is a more mysterious as well as a more rigorous form of communication than prose. A poem will talk to you at one time and avert its face at another.

Two suggestions:

First, remember that a poem, if it is a good one, is good in itself. If you are reading a great deal of Voltaire it may help you to remember that he was much impressed with Newton. But if you are reading Hopkins's "The Wreck of the Deutsch-land" it will help only the tiniest bit to know the sources of his special theory of versification. Poems are only incidentally parts of history. They are essentially self-enclosed, complete messages from individual minds. In some cases, however, single poems reveal much more when read in connection with a larger body of the poet's work.

Second, if you can't or won't read this anthology entire, concentrate on the larger figures. Major poets are so called for sound reasons. In addition to our numbers 88–96, therefore, try to give attention to at least the following: Spenser, Marlowe, Jonson, Herbert, Crashaw, Vaughan, Marvell, Herrick, Dryden, Pope, Burns, Byron, Shelley, Keats, Tennyson, Browning, Arnold, Dickinson, Hopkins, Hardy, Robinson. You have plenty of time—this is a Lifetime Reading Plan.

One final word, addressed only to those of my readers who learned to dislike poetry in school and have never read a line since. Poetry is not an esoteric art, cultivated by dreamy young men in open collars and with wispy beards. Its finest masters have always been men and women of outstanding energy and great, though by no means common, sense. Poetry is the most economical way of saying certain things that cannot be said in any other way. At its most intense it expresses better than other forms of literature whatever is left of us when we are not involved in instinct-following, surviving, competing, or problem-solving. Its major property is not, as some suppose, beauty. It is power. It is the most powerful form of communication. It does the most work per syllable, operating on a vast field—that of our emotions. It gains its efficiency from the use of certain levers—rhythm, music, rhyme, metaphor, and many more—for which other forms of communication are less well adapted. Some poetry, especially modern poetry, is difficult. But just as our ears have accustomed themselves to difficult music, so our understanding, if we are willing to make the effort, can accustom itself to the most condensed and superficially strange verse. At one time poetry was as democratic an art as the novel is nowadays. It can be so again, if we are willing to make it so.

98

The Norton Anthology of Modern Poetry, edited by Richard Ellmann (1918–1987) and Robert O'Clair (1923–   )

For many of us poetry is a stumbling block, and modern poetry looms as an unascendable mountain. In most cases this is the consequence of bad teaching or of a suspicion, early forced upon us, that poetry is "something special" written by odd people for correspondingly odd readers. The fact is that a response to rhyme, rhythm, imagery, and condensed language is natural to most human beings. All small children like nursery and play rhymes. As they learn to read, they also enjoy more difficult verse, provided it is not pretentiously forced upon them. Rousseau tells us, "Man is born free and everywhere he is in chains." I think man is born a lover of poetry and is everywhere found prejudiced against it.

To overcome this prejudice (often it is fear rather than prejudice) one must first understand the nature of poetry and what it is trying to do. Then one must read it, usually more slowly than one reads prose, perhaps beginning with the simple and advancing to the more complex. Poetry is not another language (as mathematics is) but it is a more condensed, more allusive language, given to shortcuts, closely reflecting the innermost consciousness of the author. In this latter sense it is private rather than public communication. Its meaning is partly grasped by feeling as well as understanding. *How to Read a Book* (VI) offers some useful suggestions for reading poems.

Modern poetry is difficult only in the sense that it is more complex and personal than the verse (Tennyson, Longfellow) my older readers were forced to study in school. It reflects the intricacy and self-consciousness of our period, as of course it should. But its obstacles can be overcome if you will bring to it a certain receptivity—and patience.

There are many excellent anthologies of modern verse. The one here suggested is among the best. It is comprehensive, the selections are sensitively chosen, and its preface, footnotes, and brief history of modern verse comprise a splendid body of reader aids. One hundred fifty-five poets, from Whitman to James Tate (born 1943), are represented by twelve hundred poems. All employ English; no translations from foreign tongues.

HISTORY
BIOGRAPHY
AUTOBIOGRAPHY

99

Basic Documents in American History, edited by
Richard B. Morris

The Federalist Papers, edited by
Clinton Rossiter

This entry needs little commentary. Much as they have been modified, our basic political ideas are still to be found, classically expressed, in a very few documents: the Declaration, the Constitution, the Virginia Statute for Religious Freedom, the Gettysburg Address, and a few others. Many handy collections of our important state papers exist; Morris's is quite serviceable. He prints about fifty documents, from the Mayflower Compact to almost our own time. Most are of interest mainly to students of history. As examples of the use of the language they get progressively worse after Lincoln, a fact from which you may draw any conclusion you prefer.

The Federalist Papers, by Hamilton, Madison, and Jay, represents American political thought and expression at a peak of elegance and power it has never since attained. Conceived originally as journalistic letters intended to mobilize New York State public opinion in support of the proposed Federal Constitution of 1787, they are not merely historical documents but in many cases masterpieces of reasoning. In 1788 Jefferson wrote to Madison praising them as "the best commentary on the principles of government which was ever written." It is illuminating to study them in connection with your reading of Aristotle's *Politics* (6), Hobbes (71), Locke (72), Marx and Engels (75), Machiavelli (78), Tocqueville (82). Not all the Papers need to be read. A fairly thorough knowledge of this classic may be gained by a reading of numbers 1–51, 84, 85.

The particular editions I have suggested are not mandatory. There are many other equally good ones.

100

JEAN-JACQUES ROUSSEAU (1712–1778)

Confessions

Of all the great writers we have met, including Wordsworth and Milton, Rousseau is the most irritating. His whole character offends any reasonable mind. Socially awkward; sexually ill-balanced; immoral; nauseatingly sentimental; mean and quarrelsome; a liar; the victim of a large number of unpleasant ills, from persecution delusions to bladder trouble; a defender of the rights of little children who states calmly that he abandoned his five illegitimate offspring to a foundling institution: that is Rousseau, or part of him. It is simply exasperating that this absurd fellow, who died half-cracked, should also have been one of the most powerful forces of his time, the virtual ancestor of the romantic movement in literature and art, and one of the major intellectual sources of the French Revolution. Even more annoying is the fact that this vagabond-valet-music teacher, whose formal education ended at about the age of twelve, should be a writer of such persuasion that, though his arguments have been refuted by many, his rhetoric still bewitches. The whole Rousseau case is highly irregular.

We have encountered the title *Confessions* once before, with Saint Augustine (13). In one respect the two men are alike. Both had and recorded a decisive spiritual experience that changed the course of history. Saint Augustine's occurred in a garden, Rousseau's on the road to Vincennes, outside Paris. He was reading a paper as he walked along, on his way to visit the famous philosopher Diderot. He noticed an announcement. The Dijon Academy was offering a prize for the best essay on the subject: Has the progress of the arts and sciences contributed to the purification or the corruption of morals?

"All at once," says Rousseau, "I felt myself dazzled by a thousand sparkling lights; crowds of vivid ideas thronged into my head with a force and confusion that threw me into unspeakable agitation; I felt my head whirling in a giddiness like that of intoxication." Out of this trance or vision or fit came his first work, the *Discourse on the Arts and Sciences*. It won the prize, it gained him European fame, and it led to his establishment as the most revolutionary writer of his time. In it and succeeding works he attacked progress as a corrupter of man's natural goodness. He assailed private property. He inveighed against the evil influence of educational discipline on a child's mind. He pointed out the constricting power of organized religion. In his crucial *Social Contract* he cried out against those political institutions so contrived that "man is born free and everywhere he is in chains."

It is easy to say that Rousseau was a misfit, that his championship of nature and of man's innate goodness sprang from his inability to adjust to the demands of organized society. That may be true. But what he said—it was not new, merely never before so irresistibly expressed—was what his century wanted to hear. This eccentric prophet, this wild "man without a skin," as Hume called him, came at exactly the right time. And his power persists. Some of it, particularly in the field of education, has worked constructively. For Rousseau, unlike Voltaire, was a positive man; he meant his ideas to form the future.

The *Confessions* is his masterpiece. One of its opening statements arrests attention at once, and has never ceased to do so: "I am commencing an undertaking, hitherto without precedent, and which will never find an imitator. I desire to set before my fellows the likeness of a man in all the truth of nature, and that man myself. . . . If I am not better, at least I am different."

Rousseau lies, exaggerates, and often misunderstands himself. Yet, except for one thing, he makes good his boast. He was wrong in saying that his book would never find an imitator. It has found thousands. The whole literature of modern autobiography, when it is designedly confessional, stems from this one book. Renowned writings like those of Chateaubriand and Amiel stem from it; dubious self-revelations like those of Frank Harris stem from it; confessional magazines stem from it. But, in its eye-opening candor on the one hand and its remarkable free-flowing and often lyrical style on the other, it has never been equaled.

Rousseau is easy to read. You need no one's guidance to help you make up your mind about him. However, just to confuse you a little, here are two judgments. The first is Romain Rolland's: "He opened into literature the riches of the subconscious, the secret movements of being, hitherto ignored and repressed." The second judgment is by Samuel Johnson (101). To Boswell's question whether he considered Rousseau as bad a man as Voltaire, Johnson replied: "Why, Sir, it is difficult to settle the proportion of iniquity between them."

101
JAMES BOSWELL (1740–1795)

The Life of Samuel Johnson

If Rousseau's was the first modern autobiography, Boswell's may claim to be the first modern biography. His *Life* is the best in the language, perhaps the best in any language. It was published seven years after the death of its subject, in 1791. Ever since, Samuel Johnson has been the most intimately known figure in English literature. But he is more than a literary character. Many who have never read a line of his essays or his *Lives of the Poets* or his grave, rather impressive poetry nevertheless claim him as a familiar friend. He will never cease to be quoted, often by people innocent of the source of the quotation.

This is all the consequence of a meeting in Davies's London bookshop on May 16, 1763, between the literary dictator of England, then aged fifty-three, and an eager, hero-worshiping Scot, then aged twenty-two. Sensing his vocation, Boswell at once began to take notes of the great man's talk and habits and opinions. He continued this activity, with intermissions, up to Johnson's death in 1784. The result is a full-length portrait, complete with warts, of a stunning character; plus an equally lively picture of the swarming, noisy, brilliant literary and social life of the latter part of the eighteenth century, which boasted, in addition to Johnson, such colorful men as Burke, Garrick, Goldsmith, and Sir Joshua Reynolds; plus an unconscious revelation of Boswell himself, who has turned out to be possibly the most interesting of them all.

Boswell was of good Scottish family. Trained in the law, he preferred other modes of experience: good conversation, liquor, wenching, travel, some abortive meddling in politics, and the company of any great man he could contrive to meet, including Voltaire (47) and Rousseau (100). Above all, however, he was a natural writer. He possessed most of the attributes of a supremely great reporter. He wrote easily. He had a phenomenal memory. He knew how to take notes, written or mental. He wrote things down when he heard them. He had a nose for the striking, concrete detail. He loved gossip and scandal. And he always happened to be around when something new was being done or being said.

But beyond this, he knew how to *create* news. Had Boswell never existed, Johnson would still have been a great personality. But we might never have known it. Boswell *made* Johnson talk. Not that he encountered any innate reluctance, but he forced Johnson into full flower, with the aid of naive or cunning questions, by irritating or flattering him, by caressing or exacerbating his prejudices, even by demeaning himself so as to permit Johnson to enjoy a recordable triumph over him. Johnson is a creation. And that is why Boswell is more than a superb reporter. He is an artist, just as surely as Rembrandt or Hals or any other first-rate portrait painter is one.

In the last fifty years or so our view of Boswell has changed radically. Back of this shift lies what Christopher Morley called "the most exciting adventure in English letters." In 1927 Lieutenant-Colonel Ralph Isham, a rich and persuasive connoisseur, bought from the owners of Malahide Castle in Ireland some of Boswell's papers that had been lying there untouched for generations. This discovery had been preceded by others of a similar nature and was at once followed by more. Finally there was amassed an enormous collection of eighteenth-century material, by or about Boswell and other contemporaries, which has given us radically new insights into the period. Of this material numerous volumes have been published. The first, *Boswell's London Journal 1762–1763,* is the most interesting to the general reader (see Suggestions for Further Reading).

What we now see is a Boswell who is no longer merely the faithful recorder of Johnson's thunder. We have a fantastic fellow, an odd genius, with a little of Hamlet in him, a damaged soul, a divided mind, a shrewd fool, a libertine—and a far finer writer than we had ever thought him. The fact is, that though Johnson was a great man and Boswell was not, the disciple is beginning to overshadow the master. In his subtleties, his despairs, his divisions of mind, his violent alternations of emotion, he seems to make a special appeal to our time. Consequently his masterpiece gains a dimension.

102

HENRY ADAMS (1838–1918)

The Education of Henry Adams

Henry Adams was born with a complete set of sterling silver in his mouth. A scion of what is probably the first family of the United States, he was the great-grandson of John Adams, the grandson of John Quincy Adams, and the son of Charles Francis Adams, who represented us at the Court of St. James. The fascination of his life lies in the unexpectedness of what he did with his inheritance.

The family tradition of service virtually demanded that he grow up to wield high political power for his country's good. The presidency itself would not have been inconceivable. Henry Adams became a scholar, a major historian, an influential teacher, a philosopher, a marvelous letter writer, a world traveler of genius, and the author of the finest of American autobiographies. He never became a leader. His influence has been profound, but it has been indirect. At one point he remarked: "So far as [I] had a function in life, it was as stable-companion to statesmen." Acquainted with everyone of importance here and in England, he rarely departed from his role of ironic observer, the irony directed inward as well as outward.

From one standpoint (and it was also his own) he was a failure. From another, he was a success, though largely a posthumous one. His failure lay in disappointed ambitions, in his inability to live up to the family tradition. He felt—this is a major motif in the *Education*—that his eighteenth-century upbringing, with its emphasis on humane letters and strict moral accountability, had ill-equipped him for the twentieth century, with its emphasis on energy, science, and industry. His success lay in the fact that this very dissatisfaction with himself (a dissatisfaction out of which he made a virtual career) led him to probe deeply the age for which he was temperamentally unsuited. His books, particularly the *Education,* are pearls produced by irritation.

The Education of Henry Adams, written in a severely ironical third person, is an attempt to explain the author to himself and his time to the author. Adams was greatly influenced by late-nineteenth-century physics. He felt that civilizations, like matter, were subject to inexorable laws of change and degradation. In the thirteenth century (see his beautiful book of medieval studies, *Mont-Saint-Michel and Chartres*) he believed Western civilization to have achieved a state of coherence and unity, symbolized by the figure of the Virgin. Our time, symbolized by the Dynamo, he saw as one moving further and further away from unity toward multiplicity. The rate of disintegration was rapidly increasing; mankind had little to look forward to beyond a series of graver and graver catastrophes. The *Education* is remarkable for wit, elegance, wonderful on-the-scene reporting; but what gives it its sharp edge of emotion is Adams's constant cold prescience of tragedy. It makes the *Education* a work of poetry as well as truth.

The critic Paul Elmer More has decried its "sentimental nihilism," and it is true that Adams's special brand of pessimism sometimes strikes tediously on the ear. Yet, when one looks about at the world today, it is hard to find many writers who foresaw as clearly as Adams did the shape of the future. We have experienced several of the catastrophes he foretold; and it is clear that we are to experience others. Disintegration rather than coherence seems more and more to mark our era. It required a considerable depth of imagination to say in 1862, as Adams did: "Some day science may have the existence of mankind in its power, and the human race may commit suicide by blowing up the world."

Henry Adams was by nature a rather unhappy man, and his beloved wife's suicide in 1885 further predisposed him to pessimism. He was snobbish, intellectually cocky, vulgarly racist, and his self-depreciation is often spurious. Yet from these weaknesses as well as from his strengths he drew the materials that make the *Education* a great book. Being an Adams, he could not write a *Confessions.* His aim is not the revelation of a human heart but the unflinching consideration of a historical character, who happens to be the writer himself. As an intellectual analysis of a labyrinthine mind and of the changing and, as he thought, disintegrating society he knew intimately, the *Education* remains unrivaled.

103
FERNAND BRAUDEL (1902–1985)

The Mediterranean and the Mediterranean World in the Age of Philip II (two volumes); *Civilization and Capitalism, 15th–18th Century* (three volumes)

At his death in 1985 Fernand Braudel would have been ranked by many scholars as the greatest historian of our time. A typical judgment: "No one this century has done more to change the way in which history is written."

Braudel was one of the leaders of the French school of "Annales." This group was and is less concerned with events ("Events are the ephemera of history."—Braudel) than with an era's deep structure, the undercurrents that determine how people actually live.

To uncover, in Braudel's phrase, "the bedrock of history" required the most assiduous research into documents hitherto ignored. It required a new way of perceiving history in its "totality" so that we might at last identify the "structure and category behind the event." Thus Braudel demotes Carlylean heroes, treaties, wars. He emphasizes basic economic and psychological trends and facts, the influence of climate, diet, famine, disease, transportation, travel. He wishes to detect not what the textbook gives us but the basic rhythms of life at a given time and in a given environment.

In 1939 Braudel was all prepared to write his dissertation on the Mediterranean. Then came the war. It was followed by Lieutenant Braudel's service on the Maginot Line, France's surrender, and his imprisonment first in Mainz, then in Lübeck. An intellectual miracle ensued. During five years as a prisoner of war, with no notes to help him, Braudel's phenomenal memory and powers of concentration enabled him to complete his book. After the war he added notes and references. On its appearance it was at once acclaimed a "majestic monument to twentieth-century historiography."

In his later three-volume *Civilization and Capitalism* Braudel enlarges the perspective from which the age of Philip II is viewed. Economics is only its vantage point. His real object is "the entire history of the world." He quotes Novalis: "All history must necessarily be world history." Thus his approach is always global, universal. Certain words and phrases recur: "totality," "total history," "the long run." Braudel's hallmark is the harmonious merger of thousands of hard facts and a vision enabling him to use those facts in order to give history a new life.

Though master of a style of great force and elegance, he is not easy reading. To digest the five volumes here recommended you will need both determination and time. But if you like books of history, history examined closely and interpreted with startling originality, you will find your efforts well rewarded.

ANNEX

The six commentaries that follow describe eight works that are intended to help you with your reading of 1–103. They are supplements. Many more titles could have been added, but each of us has but one lifetime. As a whole they should provide some background in history, science, and art; and the last title may help you to enjoy more fully all the other titles discussed in this volume.

I

WILLIAM H. MCNEILL (1917–)

The Rise of the West

WILL (1885–1981) AND ARIEL (1898–1981) DURANT

The Story of Civilization (eleven volumes)

It is proper that in this Annex first place should go to books that, though not in themselves original communications, will help the reader understand the entire historical past out of which such communications come. No classic exists covering this vast field. Perhaps there never can be one.

The best one-volume attempt I know is Professor McNeill's work, tracing some five thousand years of Western history and paying close attention to the influence of other cultures than our own. Deeply reflective, it is the work of a master scholar for whom mere chronicling is not enough, who uses controlling ideas to make coherent and understandable his almost unmanageable subject.

But perhaps a single volume will not satisfy you. In that case there is the less profound, highly readable *Story of Civilization* in eleven stout volumes. It's expensive to buy, it's incomplete (stops with Napoleon), and scholars have objected to it on various grounds. Still, its vast scale allows the Durants to supply generous perspectives. Their work is marked by an absence of dogmatic theory, by a warm humanity, by a constant sense that the career of the human animal turns on far more than the outcome of battles and the rise and fall of kings. It moves. It is a narrative.

Volume I, *Our Oriental Heritage,* deals with the civilization of ancient Egypt and with the history of India, China, and Japan. It lies somewhat outside our scope, though the sections on Egypt, one of our ancestors, may be read with profit.

The titles of the remaining volumes—they may be bought separately—point to the content:

Each volume is conceived as a unit and may be read as such. However, that's quite a large dose of history. You may prefer, as you proceed with the Plan, to select for special attention those sections that supply background for the book you happen to be busy with. Thus your understanding of Homer (1, 2) will be increased if you preface him with the sixty-five pages of Volume II dealing with Greece up to 100 B.C.

II

SAMUEL ELIOT MORISON (1887–1976)

The Oxford History of the American People

PAGE SMITH (1917–   )

A People's History of the United States
(eight volumes)

As so many of the Plan's titles are American it is useful to have on hand a good one-volume history of our own country. I have suggested Morison's not because it is a masterpiece in its field, for it is not. But it seems to me that its 1,122 pages do as much for the reader as we have any right to expect.

Morison's chronicle covers our story from early American man to the moment when Lyndon B. Johnson took the oath of office. It is clear, fair, scholarly, readable. It has certain features, important or merely pleasing, that distinguish it from its many competitors. For example, it emphasizes what text-book histories rarely do emphasize: the ways in which we have lived as a people, our sports and pastimes, our eating and drinking habits, our fads and crazes, our sexual demeanor, etc. Furthermore (Morison was an admiral as well as a scholar) it develops with authority the theme of American sea power, which has been so potent a factor in our history. The Lifetime Plan reader will note with special appreciation the attention Morison gives to the arts and sciences. Finally, the illustrations are excellent and the citations from our songs, from a Navajo war chant to a few bars of "Camelot," further humanize this popular chronicle by a humane, even-handed, and conscientious historian.

In entry I, dealing with the history of the Western world, I suggested both a single volume and a series of volumes. So with the history of our own country: you may want to read no more than Morison, or you may want to read a far more detailed work. Page Smith has published eight lengthy volumes of what he calls a "people's history." It carries the story from our colonial beginnings through the New Deal. Somewhat diffuse and uneven, as a whole it is instructive, readable, colorful. The political stance is liberal, at times populist. I know no history of our country comparable in scope or detail.

The individual titles are:

1 and 2: *A New Age Now Begins: A People's History of the American Revolution*

3. *Shaping of America: A People's History of the Young Republic*

4. *The Nation Comes of Age: A People's History of the Ante-bellum Years*

5. *Trial by Fire: A People's History of the Civil War and Reconstruction*

6. *The Rise of Industrial America: A People's History of the Post-Reconstruction Era*

7. *America Enters the World: A People's History of the Progressive Era and World War I*

8. *Redeeming the Time: A People's History of the 1920's and the New Deal*

III

ALFRED NORTH WHITEHEAD (1861–1947)

Science and the Modern World

In the history of Western speculative thought, such men as Hobbes, Locke, Hume, and Mill have achieved classic stature. In the case of Whitehead we cannot make this statement: it is too soon. I suggest a reading of his *Science and the Modern World* because no other single volume of my acquaintance tells us more about what four hundred years of science have done to make us the men and women we are. Unless we continually correct our impressions of science by the insights of a mind like Whitehead's, there is always the danger of confusing real science with the delirious Buck Rogers phase through which some of it is now passing. (This phase is mainly an extension of ballistics, or the art of killing people, and is a minor branch of technology.)

Whitehead was the son of an English vicar. Early in life he showed mathematical genius. He became senior mathematical lecturer at Trinity College, Cambridge. With Bertrand Russell he wrote the monumental three-volume *Principia Mathematica* (1910–13), a translation of mathematical concepts into logical terms and a landmark in the important field of symbolic logic. An interval of teaching at London University was followed by his moving in 1924, when he was sixty-three, to Harvard, where he assumed a professorship in philosophy. Just as Mill had no boyhood, Whitehead had no old age. His most fertile period now began and continued to his death. His training was primarily that of a mathematician, but his mind took no account of compartments. He wrote on education, religion, metaphysics, and particularly on science in its broader aspects.

He is not easy to read, for he operates on a plane of high abstraction and uses a terminology which, though clear, is uniquely his own. Nevertheless, *Science and the Modern World* can be penetrated by any serious reader, and it will prove rewarding. Whitehead's combination of talents (he is not only a good mathematician and a powerful speculative thinker, but a beautifully trained humanist) makes him the ideal analyst of the impact of science on our age. Without some understanding of this impact we cannot understand who we are and how we got here.

The general slope of Whitehead's mind marks him off sharply from the British empirical school with which we now have some slight acquaintance. His conception of nature is opposed to the "common sense" variety. He points out again and again that our senses offer us a delusive picture of reality. He welcomes the Einsteinian physics that replaces empty space with fields of force and discrete bits of matter with energy. He is antimaterialist. More important, he is antidogmatic and an enemy of all closed systems. The words *process, organism,* and *adventure* crop up continually in his writing and serve to suggest the color of his thought, which emphasizes change and continuous evolution rather than systems and certitudes. "Philosophy begins in wonder," he writes. "And, at the end, when philosophic thought has done its work, the wonder remains." The pleasure of reading Whitehead is quite different from that of reading Locke or Mill, for he opens perspectives that enlarge the imagination and are closely akin to those of poetry. It is in this spirit that I suggest you approach him.

IV

ALFRED NORTH WHITEHEAD (1861–1947)

An Introduction to Mathematics

That our modern scientific-technological-industrial-warmaking culture rests ultimately on a mathematical base needs no demonstration. The platform of mathematics supports the physical sciences and, increasingly, the biological and even the social sciences, particularly economics. It also supports our century's major activity, wholesale killing. Nowadays a casual acquaintance with a few equations helps to satisfy our human curiosity as to just how the next war, or series of wars, hopes to kill, maim, poison, or vaporize us, as well as to deform and/or drive mad our descendants, if any.

Mathematics is not only a magnificent science and a powerful language, but a moving art. It may be contemplated in a humanistic as well as a technical spirit. An interest in mathematics is often found in writers who have won eminence in other fields. Among the artists and thinkers we have met, Plato, Lewis Carroll, Hobbes, Whitehead, Descartes, and Pascal were professional mathematicians. Artists like Leonardo, Uccello, and Dürer were informed with mathematical imagination. The thought of others, such as Dante, Voltaire, Poe, Marx, Donne, and Adams, was to a marked degree influenced by mathematical conceptions. The scientist and the humanist are not opposed types; and, should they feel themselves in opposition, they are, by that very token, inferior scientists or humanists.

If we could all read the original communications of men like Kepler or Fourier or Huygens or Newton or Archimedes, the Lifetime Reading Plan would have included them. But it is unrealistic to think that we can. The best most of us can aim at is some superficial sense of the major ideas underlying scientific and mathematical thought. Thus we may correct and balance the lopsidedness that comes of an exclusive attention to works of the imagination, as conventionally defined.

Whitehead in his own right was a mathematician of high, if not the first, order. The little book suggested above was written more than seventy years ago. It takes no account therefore of the tremendous advances made in our own time. That is for our purposes unimportant. Whitehead, writing here for the general nonmathematical public, is not concerned with the evolution of the subject, nor with its higher reaches. He proposes to give a clear explanation of its fundamental ideas and to bound its major compartments. His book runs to only 250 small pages, yet it cannot be read properly if read quickly. On the other hand, though it contains a moderate amount of mathematical symbolism, it is possible for us to grasp the basic notions without working out, or even completely understanding, every formula and equation.

If you have both time and interest, it is advisable to supplement Whitehead with one or more of the titles listed in the Suggestions for Further Reading. I hope you will find this worthwhile. You may, as I once did myself, think you are neither interested in the subject nor able to understand it. Yet (and this is true equally of that presumed bugaboo, poetry) the more intimate your acquaintance with the mathematical imagination, the more rewarding the experience becomes.

V

E. H. GOMBRICH (1909–   )

The Story of Art

There is no recognized classic in this fascinating, crowded, and controversial field. The Suggestions for Further Reading list several alternative works.

I have chosen Gombrich's book for several reasons. It is neither so short as to be superficial nor so long as to be overwhelming. The author begins his story with prehistoric and primitive peoples, carrying it through the centuries down to the experimental art of our own day. The emphasis is predominantly on European art, but there are sections on Egypt, Mesopotamia, Islam, and China. The book contains 370 intelligently chosen illustrations, a fair number in full color. No illustration is shown that is not discussed in the text, an excellent feature. The discussion itself deals only with important works of art (including architecture and sculpture) and not with eccentricities or minor examples. Gombrich stresses well-known masterpieces, a policy that pays dividends to the beginner in this field. His interest is not in rhapsodizing over "beauties" but in tracking down the artist's intention, estimating his success, and placing his work, without undue forcing, in its historical frame.

My preference for this book over many other fine histories, however, is based largely on its style. In planning and writing, the author tells us, he had in mind first and foremost "readers in their teens who had just discovered the world of art for themselves." But the result is not in the least elementary. Here is a book suitable for any adult except one whose knowledge is already considerable. The style is marked by simplicity, clarity, and candor. The approach is sensible and humane. I have learned much from it and, more to the point, enjoyed learning. As I have no expertness in the field, I feel my own experience with it may well prefigure that of many of my readers.

VI
MORTIMER J. ADLER (1902–   )
CHARLES VAN DOREN (1926–   )

How to Read a Book

For almost eighty years I have been an amateur reader and for over sixty a professional one. But I am still learning how to read. I do not mean how to decipher words. That is merely a useful trick, just slightly above the capacity of a chimpanzee. It is taught, more or less, in the schools, and suffices for the reading of most books and magazines, virtually all newspapers, and absolutely all lavatory signs. I mean the reading of books of some weight and density, into which went hard mental work and out of which comes real mental change. Such are the ones we have been considering in the Plan. Such reading involves a complex, often intense activity, not the passive reception of the author's message. And the result of such reading is not "finishing the book" but starting something in the reader's mind.

The original Plan recommended Mortimer J. Adler's *How to Read a Book* as an aid to those willing to tackle the Plan seriously. The new edition enlisting the aid of Charles Van Doren is even more helpful. Completely revised and updated, it remedies, as well as it can, a defect in the earlier version, an inability to suggest rules for reading imaginative literature comparable to those given for philosophy and the sciences. But the suggestions go beyond this. They include useful hints for making the most efficient use of reference books, current journalism, even advertising.

I speak of rules; and there are rules here, and concrete tips, and a whole course of instruction. Still, this is no manual. It is less about reading as a specific action than about a liberal education in general, about the links that connect great literature with free minds and so with free people. The ideas animating *How to Read a Book* are those animating the book you now hold in your hand; and it was from Dr. Adler, among other great teachers, that I learned them.

Its appendix lists a whole library of great books, duplicating our own in part, but laying greater stress on works of theology, philosophy, and the physical and social sciences. It also includes "exercises and tests at the four levels of reading," for really solemn disciples of the Adler method.

Bibliography

In addition to the titles suggested in the Plan, this Bibliography lists other important works, if any, by the author. Most of the titles are available in moderate-priced paperback editions, though a lesser number are available only in hardcover. For paperbacks, to save space, I list only the name of the series. The publishers of some of the better-known series are:

Airmont: Airmont Publishing Co.
Anchor: Doubleday
Bison: University of Nebraska Press
Capricorn: Putnam's
Collier: Macmillan
Compass: Viking Penguin
Evergreen: Grove
Everyman: Dutton
Gateway: Regnery
Harvest: Harcourt Brace Jovanovich
Medallion: Berkley Publishing Group
Mentor: New American Library

Meridian: New American Library
Modern Library: Random House
Penguin: Viking Penguin
Perennial: Harper & Row
Phoenix: University of Chicago Press
Pocket Books: Simon & Schuster
Riverside: Houghton Mifflin
Torchbooks: Harper & Row
Touchstone: Simon & Schuster
Vintage: Random House
Washington Square Press: Simon & Schuster

Refer also to this key when using the Suggestions for Further Reading beginning on page 253.

The publishing trade is currently in flux. Some of these series may have been discontinued by the time this book reaches you. Many titles may have gone out of print. Firms may have changed names or disappeared. Consult your bookseller or library.

THE BEGINNING

1. HOMER. *Iliad:* I prefer the translations of either Richmond Lattimore (Phoenix) or Robert Fitzgerald (Anchor). Those by W. H.

Rouse (Mentor) and E. V. Rieu (Penguin) are quite serviceable.

2. HOMER. *Odyssey:* Versions by Richmond Lattimore (Torchbooks); Robert Fitzgerald (Anchor); W. H. Rouse (Mentor). Avoid abridgements.

3. HERODOTUS. *The Histories* is sometimes entitled *The Persian Wars.* George Rawlinson's classic but rather Victorian translation is findable in *The Greek Historians* (2 vols., Random), ed. F. R. B. Godolphin; and also, introduced by Godolphin, in Modern Library. More modern and readable translations: Aubrey de Selincourt (Penguin); and especially David Grene (Univ. of Chicago Pr.)

4. THUCYDIDES. *The Peloponnesian War,* tr. Benjamin Jowett in *The Greek Historians,* ed. F. R. B. Godolphin (2 vols., Random); ed. Richard Livingstone (Oxford Univ. Pr.); tr. Rex Warner (Penguin); *Complete Writings,* tr. Richard Crawley, introd. by J. Finley, Jr. (Modern Library).

5. PLATO. Jowett's translation, though Victorian, is classic. His version of the complete works may be found in the two-volume Random House edition, introduced by Raphael Demos. *The Portable Plato,* ed. Scott Buchanan (Viking), contains the Jowett translations of: *Protagoras, Phaedo, Symposium, Republic.* Other convenient Jowett versions: *The Works of Plato,* ed. Irwin Edman (Modern Library); *The Republic and Other Works* (Anchor); *Dialogues of Plato,* ed. Justin E. Kaplan (Washington Sq. Pr.). Other good, more modern translations: *Republic,* tr. Francis M. Cornford (Oxford Univ. Pr.); *Protagoras* and *Meno,* tr. W. K. Guthrie (Penguin); *The Last Days of Socrates* (includes *Euthyphro, Apology, Crito, Phaedo*), tr. Hugh Tredennick (Penguin).

6. ARISTOTLE. *Basic Works,* ed. Richard McKeon (Random); *Aristotle: Selections from Seven Books,* ed. Philip Wheelwright (Odyssey Pr.); *Introduction to Aristotle,* ed. Richard McKeon (Modern Library); *Ethics,* tr. J. A. Thomson (Penguin); *Nicomachean Ethics,* tr. W. D. Ross (Oxford Univ. Pr.); *Politics,* tr. J. A. Sinclair (Penguin); *Poetics,* introd. by G. F. Else (Univ. of Mich. Pr.).

7. AESCHYLUS. *The Complete Greek Tragedies,* ed. David Grene and Richmond Lattimore (4 vols., Univ. of Chicago Pr.), contains good modern versions of all the works of Aeschylus, Sophocles, and Euripides. For Aeschylus only see *Aeschylus One: Agamemnon, The Libation Bearers, The Eumenides,* tr. and introd. by Richmond Lattimore (Univ. of Chicago Pr.); *Aeschylus Two: Four Tragedies: Prometheus Bound, Seven Against Thebes, The Persians, The Suppliant Maidens,* tr. David Grene and Seth G. Benardete (Univ. of Chicago Pr.); *The Oresteia,* tr. Robert Lowell (Farrar, Straus).

8. SOPHOCLES. Highly recommended: *Oedipus Trilogy*, tr. Stephen Spender (Random); *The Oedipus Cycle of Sophocles*, tr. Dudley Fitts and Robert Fitzgerald (Harcourt). Other good editions: *Complete Plays*, ed. Moses Hadas (Bantam); *Sophocles One* (incl. *Oedipus the King, Oedipus at Colonus, Antigone*) and *Sophocles Two* (incl. *Ajax, The Women of Trachis, Electra, Philoctetes*) (Univ. of Chicago Pr.). Note also that Caedmon Records issues a sound track of W. B. Yeats's translation (transmutation is a better word) of *Oedipus Rex* as directed by Tyrone Guthrie.

9. EURIPIDES. Bantam issues *Ten Plays of Euripides*, tr. Moses Hadas and John H. McLean. University of Chicago Press publishes all the plays in five volumes in excellent translations. An interesting version of *The Trojan Women* is the adaptation by Jean-Paul Sartre (Random). Bookstores and libraries often stock translations by the great scholar Gilbert Murray. They are frequently beautiful in a turn-of-the-century manner, but the more modern versions are probably more faithful to the original.

10. LUCRETIUS. *Nature of the Universe*, tr. Ronald E. Latham (Penguin); *On Nature*, tr. Russell M. Geer (Bobbs-Merrill); *On the Nature of Things*, ed. S. Palmer Bovie (New American Library); *The Way Things Are: The De Rerum Natura of Titus Lucretius Carus*, tr. Rolfe Humphries (Indiana Univ. Pr.). Of these I prefer the last.

11. VIRGIL. *Aeneid:* tr. Rolfe Humphries (Scribner's); tr. Robert Fitzgerald (Random); tr. William F. Knight (Penguin); tr. C. Day Lewis (Anchor) ; tr. Allen Mandelbaum (Bantam). The Fitzgerald version is highly acclaimed. Note also *Georgics*, tr. S. P. Bovie (Univ. of Chicago Pr.); tr. Allen Mandelbaum (Univ. of Calif. Pr.).

12. MARCUS AURELIUS. Long's translation of the *Meditations* is contained in *The Stoic and Epicurean Philosophers*, ed. Whitney J. Oates (Modern Library Giants). It is also (bound with the *Enchiridion of Epictetus*) published by Regnery. Other versions: tr. G. M. Grube (Bobbs-Merrill); tr. Maxwell Staniforth (Penguin).

THE MIDDLE AGES

13. SAINT AUGUSTINE. The *Confessions* are included in *Basic Writings of St. Augustine*, ed. Whitney J. Oates (2 vols., Random). Paperback editions: tr. R. S. Pine-Coffin (Penguin); tr. Edward B. Pusey (Collier); tr. Rex Warner (Mentor). I like the Warner version. Note also *On the Two Cities: Selections from The City of God*, ed. F. W. Strothmann (Ungar).

14. DANTE. Among many other translations there are good versions of *The Divine Comedy* by John Ciardi (Norton); Thomas G. Bergin

(Harlan Davidson); Dorothy Sayers (Penguin); Allen Mandelbaum (Univ. of Calif. Pr.). Mandelbaum's translation is also offered in paperback by the Quality Book Club with pen and wash drawings by Barry Moser. The translation by Charles S. Singleton (Princeton Univ. Pr.) inclines to the literal, but this has its value. Note also *La Vita Nuova*, tr. Barbara Reynolds (Penguin); *On World Government* (*De Monarchia*), tr. H. S. Schneider (Bobbs-Merrill); and the excellent *Portable Dante* (Viking).

15. CHAUCER. *Complete Works*, ed. W. W. Skeat (Oxford Univ. Pr.). *Canterbury Tales*, tr. Nevill Coghill (Penguin); tr. David Wright (Vintage); (prose) tr. R. M. Lumiansky (Washington Sq. Pr.). *Portable Chaucer*, ed. Theodore Morrison (Viking). *Troilus and Crisseyde*, tr. Nevill Coghill (Penguin). *A Choice of Chaucer's Verse*, ed. Nevill Coghill (Merrimack). I like Coghill's verse translation of the Tales.

PLAYS

16. SHAKESPEARE. Many publishers offer the individual plays in paperback: Riverside, Penguin, Dell, New American Library, Harcourt Brace Jovanovich, Signet, Scott Foresman. A good one-volume complete edition, however, is the thing to buy: S. Wells et al., *William Shakespeare: The Complete Works* (Oxford Univ. Pr.); *Complete Plays and Poems*, ed. W. A. Neilson and C. J. Hill; the Hardin Craig edition, revised by Craig and David Bevington; and those published by Riverside, Signet, Penguin, and Scott Foresman. *The Portable Shakespeare* (Viking) offers good selections.

17. MOLIÈRE. Signet issues a one-volume edition of Donald Frame's reliable translation of *Tartuffe* and six other important plays; and in another volume his translation of *The Misanthrope* plus other plays. Another good, more unconventional translator is Richard Wilbur. Harcourt Brace issues his *Misanthrope* (with *Tartuffe*) and *The School for Wives* in separate volumes. Penguin has two volumes of John Wood's translations, comprising most of the better-known plays. But the best way to read Molière is to learn French first.

18. GOETHE. Oxford University Press issues an abridged version of both parts of *Faust* by the fine poet Louis MacNeice. Also recommended: the two parts tr. Walter Kaufmann (Anchor); Part 1, tr. C. F. MacIntyre (New Directions); Part 1, tr. Randall Jarrell (Farrar, Straus); Part 1, tr. David Luke (World's Classics). Avoid the antiquated Bayard Taylor version. Also useful: *Great Writings of*

Goethe, ed. Stephen Spender (New American Library); *Wilhelm Meister's Apprenticeship,* tr. Thomas Carlyle (Collier).

19. IBSEN. Virtually all the plays have been translated by Michael Meyer and are published in five paperback volumes by Methuen. Anchor publishes his *When We Dead Awaken and Three Other Plays.* Another reputable translator is James W. MacFarlane. Oxford offers three volumes comprising Ibsen's best work. Modern Library has Eva Le Gallienne's translation of six well-known plays. New American Library offers complete *Major Prose and Plays,* tr. Rolf Fjelde.

20. SHAW. *Bernard Shaw's Plays* (Norton), *Four Plays* by Shaw (Dell), and *Plays Unpleasant* (Penguin) will collectively provide you with eleven of the best plays. In separate volumes Penguin offers *Androcles, The Apple Cart, Arms and the Man, Caesar and Cleopatra, Candida, The Devil's Disciple, Heartbreak House, Major Barbara, Man and Superman, The Millionairess, Pygmalion, Saint Joan,* and *Selected One-Act Plays.* Oxford offers *Back to Methusaleh* in hardcover, as Hill and Wang does for *The Quintessence of Ibsenism.* There are many other easily procurable editions.

21. CHEKHOV. The handiest edition of the complete plays is in the Penguin Classics series, tr. and introd. by Elisaveta Fen. Another good paperback is *Plays and Letters, 1884–1904* (Norton). His short stories have appeared in a bewildering profusion of editions. Three representative volumes: *Anton Chekhov: Selected Stories,* tr. Ann Dunnigan (Signet Classics); *Ward Six and Other Stories,* tr. Ann Dunnigan (Signet Classics); *Peasants and Other Stories,* selected and with a preface by Edmund Wilson (Doubleday Anchor). Ecco Press has issued in paperback twelve volumes of *The Tales of Anton Chekhov,* using the classic version by Constance Garnett.

22. O'NEILL. Vintage has *Three Plays* (*Mourning Becomes Electra, Desire Under the Elms, Strange Interlude*); Vintage has *The Iceman Cometh;* and Yale University Press has *Long Day's Journey into Night.* For other O'Neill plays see: *Six Short Plays of Eugene O'Neill* (Vintage); *Seven Plays of the Sea* (Vintage); *Anna Christie* (bound with *The Emperor Jones* and *The Hairy Ape* [Vintage]); *Touch of the Poet* (Yale Univ. Pr.); *More Stately Mansions* (Yale Univ. Pr.).

23. BECKETT. Grove publishes all of Beckett. His *Collected Works* so far extend to twenty-five volumes, which include of course the three recommended plays. *Endgame* also includes *Act Without Words,* and *Krapp's Last Tape* includes four shorter plays and "mimes." Three of Beckett's best-known novels (*Molloy, Malone Dies, The Unnamable*) are assembled in one volume.

24. WATSON AND PRESSEY, eds. Their *Contemporary Drama* is published in four volumes by Scribner's. Here are a few good one-volume anthologies: *Contemporary Drama: Thirteen Plays,* ed. Stanley A. Clayes and David G. Spencer (Scribner's); *Drama in the Modern World,* ed. Samuel A. Weiss (Heath); *Modern Drama,* ed. Otto Reinert (Little, Brown); *Representative Modern Plays: Ibsen to Tennessee Williams,* ed. Robert Warnock (Scott Foresman); *Twentieth Century Drama: England, Ireland, the United States,* ed. Ruby Cohn and Bernard Dukore (Random).

NARRATIVES

25. BUNYAN. Paperbacks of *The Pilgrim's Progress* are easily come by: Airmont; Holt, Rinehart; and Signet (with a foreword by the formidable F. R. Leavis) all offer handy volumes.

26. DEFOE. Many paperback editions of *Robinson Crusoe* are available: among others, Signet, Dutton, and Washington Square Press. Holt, Rinehart and Dutton offer *Moll Flanders.* Oxford has *Roxana,* ed. Jane Jack.

27. SWIFT. Dell, Norton, Oxford, and Holt, Rinehart all offer good editions of *Gulliver. The Portable Swift,* ed. Carl Van Doren (Viking), contains a fine selection from Swift's miscellaneous work in both prose and verse.

28. STERNE. Editions of *Tristram Shandy*: Oxford, Penguin, Riverside, Airmont, Signet, Norton, Evergreen. The Harvard University Press edition also contains *A Sentimental Journey* and *Selected Sermons and Letters. A Sentimental Journey* is available in Everyman and Penguin.

29. FIELDING. *Tom Jones* is available in Modern Library, Signet, Norton, Airmont, Penguin. *Joseph Andrews*: Modern Library, Norton, Riverside, Penguin, Everyman, Oxford. Signet and Everyman offer *Jonathan Wild.*

30. AUSTEN. *Pride and Prejudice* can be found everywhere: among others, Holt, Dell, Signet, Penguin, Bantam, Riverside (ed. Mark Schorer, a fine scholar), Everyman. Modern Library binds it with *Sense and Sensibility,* introd. by David Daiches. Riverside's *Emma* is introduced by the brilliant critic Lionel Trilling; also available in Everyman, Airmont, Signet, Penguin. The magisterial R. W. Chapman edition (Oxford) comes in six volumes and includes the minor works.

31. EMILY BRONTË. Among the many available editions of *Wuthering Heights,* note especially: Riverside, ed. V. S. Pritchett; Penguin, ed. David Daiches. Penguin publishes a large paperback that also

contains Charlotte's *Jane Eyre* and Anne's *The Tenant of Wildfell Hall.*

32. THACKERAY. *Vanity Fair* is available generally. Good editions: Modern Library, Oxford Univ. Pr., Penguin, Riverside. Penguin has a good *Henry Esmond.*

33. DICKENS. *Pickwick*: Everyman, Airmont, Signet, Penguin. *David Copperfield*: Bantam, Airmont, Riverside, Signet, Penguin. *Bleak House*: Bantam, Riverside, Signet, Penguin, Norton. *Great Expectations*: Bantam, Airmont, Everyman, Signet, and Holt, Rinehart. *Hard Times*: Bantam, Everyman (introd. by G. K. Chesterton), Signet, Norton, Penguin. *Our Mutual Friend*: Penguin, Signet. *Little Dorrit*: Penguin, Signet, Oxford Univ. Pr. Most of the other major titles are in one or more of the better-known paperback series.

34. GEORGE ELIOT. *Mill on the Floss*: Norton, Airmont, Everyman, Signet. The Riverside edition is edited by the great Eliot scholar G. S. Haight. *Middlemarch*: Signet, Penguin, Norton, and Riverside (ed. G. S. Haight). *Daniel Deronda*: Penguin, Signet. *Adam Bede*: Airmont, Everyman, Signet, Riverside, Penguin.

35. CARROLL. The two Alice books are so readily available that editions need not be cited. Try, of course, to get one containing the Tenniel illustrations. Meridian offers a fascinating *Annotated Alice,* introd. by Martin Gardner. Dover has *Humorous Verse of Lewis Carroll* and also *Pillow Problems* (bound with *A Tangled Tale*).

36. HARDY. *Mayor of Casterbridge*: Bantam, Airmont, Riverside, Signet, St. Martin's Pr., Norton, Penguin, and others. *Jude the Obscure*: Airmont, Signet, Penguin, others. *Return of the Native*: Bantam, Norton, Penguin, St. Martin's Pr., others. *Tess of the D'Urbervilles*: Modern Library, Signet, Penguin, others. *Complete Poems*: Macmillan, *The Dynasts* (3 vols. hardbound): St. Martin's Pr.; *Wessex Tales*: St. Martin's Pr.

37. CONRAD. *Nostromo*: Signet, Penguin, Everyman, and Modern Library offer good editions. Many critics rate *Lord Jim* above *Nostromo.* It's available in Penguin, Airmont, Riverside, and other editions. Try also *The Secret Agent* (Anchor); *Heart of Darkness* (with *The Secret Sharer*) (Signet); *Nigger of the Narcissus, Typhoon and Other Stories* (Penguin).

38. FORSTER. *A Passage to India*: Harvest. *Howards End, The Longest Journey, A Room with a View,* and *Where Angels Fear to Tread* are all in Vintage. The interesting *Aspects of the Novel* is in Harvest.

39. JOYCE. The *Ulysses* to own is the new Vintage "corrected text" edition. If you're determined to try the difficult *Finnegans Wake,* it's in Penguin, which also publishes *The Portable James Joyce, Portrait of the Artist as a Young Man,* and *Dubliners.*

40. WOOLF. All four recommended titles as well as *The Common Reader, First Series* are in Harvest. Several volumes of the *Essays* and the *Letters* are published by Harcourt.

41. LAWRENCE. *Sons and Lovers* and *Women in Love* are in Penguin, as are *The Rainbow, Complete Poems,* and *Complete Short Stories* (3 vols.). The once shocking *Lady Chatterly's Lover*: Grove, Signet, Bantam. Viking publishes the *Portable D. H. Lawrence,* ed. Diana Trilling, and *Studies in Classic American Literature.*

42. HUXLEY. Perennial Library (Harper & Row) issues *Brave New World* separately and also bound with *Brave New World Revisited.* The same imprint also at one time published many of Huxley's other novels, such as *After Many a Summer Dies the Swan, Antic Hay, Crome Yellow, Point Counter Point, Eyeless in Gaza,* as well as *Great Short Works.* Consult your bookseller or library for collections of his essays.

43. ORWELL. *Animal Farm* and *Nineteen Eighty-four* are both in Signet. Harvest offers five volumes of his *Collected Essays, Journalism & Letters* as well as an *Orwell Reader,* introd. by R. H. Rovere.

44. MANN. Modern Library and Vintage offer *The Magic Mountain.* Vintage also has *Buddenbrooks* and *Doctor Faustus,* both well worth reading, as is *Death in Venice and Seven Other Stories* (Vintage).

45. KAFKA. Modern Library and Vintage offer *The Castle;* Schocken has a "definitive edition" with commentary by Thomas Mann. Vintage has *The Trial;* Schocken publishes a "definitive edition" with Kafka's own drawings. Schocken also has the *Complete Stories.*

46. RABELAIS. A good translation of *Gargantua and Pantagruel* is by John M. Cohen (Penguin). See also Penguin's *Portable Rabelais,* ed. Samuel Putnam.

47. VOLTAIRE. *Candide* is issued by Penguin, Oxford, Signet. Modern Library includes "other writings," as does Signet. Ben Redman's *Portable Voltaire* (Viking) is a good collection. You may be able to find Peter Gay's translation of the *Philosophical Dictionary* (Harvest).

48. STENDHAL. Signet's edition of *The Red and the Black* is good; and you may chance upon a Bantam edition, tr. Lowell Bair, with introd. by the author of this book. *Charterhouse* is in Penguin and Signet—I prefer the latter, tr. C. K. Scott-Moncrieff. University of Chicago Press publishes *The Life of Henry Brulard: The Autobiography of Stendhal.*

49. BALZAC. *Père Goriot* is in Airmont, Signet, and Penguin (under the title *Old Goriot*). *Eugénie Grandet* is in Penguin and Everyman. You might also try *Cousin Pons* and *Cousin Bette,* both Penguin.

50. FLAUBERT. The Modern Library edition of *Madame Bovary*, tr. Francis Steegmuller, is preferred. Other acceptable versions: Bantam, Airmont, Riverside, Signet, Penguin. Penguin also used to issue *Three Tales*, tr. Robert Baldick.

51. PROUST. The complete "definite Pléiade edition" of *Remembrance of Things Past*, tr. C. K. Scott-Moncrieff, Terence Kilmartin, and Andreas Mayor is published by Random House in three volumes. The seven parts are also available separately.

52. MALRAUX. *Man's Fate* is in Vintage; *The Conquerors* and *Man's Hope* in Evergreen. *The Voices of Silence:* (Princeton Univ. Pr.). The important *Psychology of Art* comes only hardbound.

53. CAMUS. *The Plague* is in Modern Library and Vintage; *The Stranger* in Vintage. Other Camus titles of interest: *The Fall, The Rebel, Exile and the Kingdom* (all Vintage).

54. POE. Vintage (Giant) has *Complete Tales and Poems*. Other convenient editions: Meridian, Signet, Everyman. Viking issues a good *Portable Poe.*

55. HAWTHORNE. Too many editions available to warrant listing. Penguin issues a *Portable Hawthorne* and Vintage his *Short Stories.*

56. MELVILLE. *Moby Dick* is generally available in many editions. Riverside has a good one edited by the distinguished scholar Alfred Kazin. Penguin issues a *Portable Melville* and Perennial *Great Short Works*, containing *Bartleby.* Signet and Phoenix, among other imprints, offer *Billy Budd.*

57. MARK TWAIN. *Huckleberry Finn* is available in many editions. A good one, ed. Lionel Trilling, is the Holt, Rinehart issue. Perennial has *Great Short Works*, and there are many editions of *Life on the Mississippi*, well worth reading.

58. HENRY JAMES. *The Ambassadors:* Norton, Airmont, Riverside (ed. Leon Edel, the master of James scholarship), Signet, Everyman, Penguin. Penguin has a *Portable Henry James.* Perennial offers *Great Short Works.* If you're hooked on Henry James, try *The Complete Notebooks of Henry James*, ed. Leon Edel and Lyall H. Powers (Oxford Univ. Pr.).

59. FAULKNER. *The Sound and the Fury*: Vintage and Modern Library. *As I Lay Dying*: Vintage. Viking has *The Portable Faulkner*, splendidly edited by Malcolm Cowley. Vintage issues *Collected Stories. Absalom, Absalom!*: Penguin, Vintage.

60. HEMINGWAY. All of Hemingway is published by Scribner's; they offer an omnibus *Short Stories* and also a *Hemingway Reader.* The recent *Complete Stories of Ernest Hemingway* (the so-called Finca Vigía edition) includes stories previously uncollected and is the one to read.

61. BELLOW. *Adventures of Augie March*: Avon. *Herzog*: Avon, Penguin. *Humboldt's Gift*: Avon. *Portable Saul Bellow*: Penguin. *More Die of Heartbreak*: Morrow (hardbound).

62. CERVANTES. Mentor has an acceptable abridged edition of *Don Quixote*. Penguin has a *Portable Cervantes,* containing the excellent Putnam translation. Also look for the Starkie translation (Signet) or the Cohen version (Penguin).

63. BORGES. *Labyrinths*: New Directions; *Dreamtigers*: Univ. of Texas Pr. Dutton issues *The Aleph & Other Stories, The Book of Imaginary Beings, The Book of Sand.* Evergreen has *A Personal Anthology.* The University of Texas Press offers *Other Inquisitions.* For his poetry see *Jorge Luis Borges: Selected Poems,* tr. Di Giovanni (Dell).

64. GARCÍA MÁRQUEZ. *One Hundred Years of Solitude* is in Avon. Harper & Row offers three volumes of his short stories: *Innocent Indira and Other Stories, Leaf Storm and Other Stories, No One Writes to the Colonel and Other Stories.* Interesting recent novel: *Love in the Years of Cholera* (Knopf).

65. GOGOL. *Dead Souls,* tr. B. G. Guerney (Holt, Rinehart) may be hard to find. Other good versions are issued by Norton, Airmont, Signet, Penguin. Signet has *Diary of a Madman and Other Stories;* Norton offers *The Overcoat and Other Tales of Good and Evil;* University of Chicago Press issues *The Complete Tales of Nikolai Gogol* in two volumes.

66. TURGENEV. *Fathers and Sons* is available in Modern Library (Guerney's translation), Bantam, Norton, Signet, Penguin. Penguin has *Sketches from a Hunter's Album* (another rendering of *A Sportsman's Sketches*).

67. DOSTOYEVSKY. *Crime and Punishment*: Oxford, Norton, Bantam, Everyman, Modern Library (Garnett tr.), Signet, Vintage, Airmont, Penguin (Magarshack tr.). *The Brothers Karamozov*: Penguin (2 vols.), Airmont, Vintage, Bantam, Modern Library (Garnett tr.) Try also *The Idiot*: Signet, Penguin.

68. TOLSTOY. *War and Peace*: Penguin (2 vols.), Norton (annotated), Signet, Washington Sq. Pr. (abridged). *Anna Karenina,* some good editions: Penguin, Norton, Modern Library, Oxford Univ. Pr. Perennial has *Great Short Works* and Penguin *The Portable Tolstoy.*

69. NABOKOV. *Lolita* is in Medallion Books and you may find it in the Capricorn series. McGraw-Hill has an annotated *Lolita.* Medallion Books offers *Pale Fire. Speak, Memory* is issued by Pyramid. Penguin issues a useful *Portable Nabokov.*

70. SOLZHENITSYN. *The First Cycle* (Bantam); *Cancer Ward* (Bantam, Dell); *Gulag Archipelago* (3 vols., Harper & Row); *One Day in the Life of Ivan Denisovich* (Signet).

PHILOSOPHY, PSYCHOLOGY, POLITICS, ESSAYS

71. HOBBES. *Leviathan*: Bobbs-Merrill, Everyman, Pelican (Penguin), Collier.

72. LOCKE. *Second Treatise*: Bobbs-Merrill; *Essay Concerning Human Understanding*: (2 vols., Dover), Meridian, Everyman, Collier.

73. HUME. *An Enquiry Concerning Human Understanding*: Oxford Univ. Pr., Open Court.

74. MILL. *On Liberty*: Bobbs-Merrill, Norton. Oxford has *Three Essays* (*On Liberty*, *Representative Government*, *Subjection of Women*). Columbia University Press and Riverside publish the *Autobiography*.

75. MARX and ENGELS. There are many editions of the *Communist Manifesto*; Penguin has a handy volume. International Publishing has *Selected Works of Marx & Engels*.

76. NIETZSCHE. *Thus Spake Zarathustra* is in Penguin, and you may find other editions. *Beyond Good and Evil*: Gateway, Penguin, Random. *The Birth of Tragedy* (with *The Genealogy of Morals*): Anchor. Penguin has a *Portable Nietzsche* and also a *Nietzsche Reader*.

77. FREUD. The Freud bibliography, for he was a prolific writer, is a bit intimidating. Some important works are available only hardbound. Here are some recommended paperbacks: *General Selection from the Works of Sigmund Freud* (Anchor); *Civilization and Its Discontents* (Norton); *General Psychological Theory* (Collier); *Interpretation of Dreams* (Avon); *New Introductory Lectures on Psychoanalysis* (Norton); *Psychopathology of Everyday Life* (Norton, Mentor); *Three Contributions to the Theory of Sex* (Dutton).

78. MACHIAVELLI. *The Prince*: many editions, including Airmont, Mentor, Oxford, Penguin, Everyman.

79. MONTAIGNE. *Complete Essays*, tr. Donald Frame (Stanford Univ. Pr.). Look also for the translation by John M. Cohen in Penguin.

80. DESCARTES. *Discourse on Method*: Everyman, Bobbs-Merrill, Penguin. Columbia University Press publishes a full-dress *Philosophical Work* in two volumes.

81. PASCAL. His *Thoughts* or *Pensées* are in Penguin; *Selections* is published by Harlan Davidson.

82. TOCQUEVILLE. The best edition of *Democracy in America* is that edited by Phillips Bradley (Knopf). Vintage has it in two volumes, Anchor in one. Mentor offers an abridged edition.

83. EMERSON. Good collections of the *Essays* are to be found in Penguin, Everyman, Modern Library, Signet, Riverside. Dover publishes *The Heart of Emerson's Journals*.

84. THOREAU. *Walden* is readily available in Bantam, Norton, Signet, Modern Library. Most editions include *Civil Disobedience*. Penguin

has a *Portable Thoreau* and Bantam has *Walden and Other Writings,* ed. J. W. Krutch.

85. WILLIAM JAMES. Dover publishes *The Principles of Psychology* (2 vols.); *Pragmatism* is issued by Meridian and Harvard University Press; *The Varieties of Religious Experience*: Collier, Mentor.

86. DEWEY. Modern Library offers *Human Nature and Conduct* (hardbound).

87. SANTAYANA. *Skepticism and Animal Faith* is issued by Dover in paperback. Most of his other writings are hardbound. Scribner's publishes *Persons and Places* (3 vols.) and *The Last Puritan.* MIT Press has recently announced a one-volume hardbound edition of *Persons and Places,* "the first unexpurgated version." It inaugurates a "new definitive edition of Santayana's works."

POETRY

88. DONNE. Penguin has *The Complete English Poems,* as does Hendricks House. Modern Library has *Poetry and Prose.*

89. MILTON. Mentor has *Paradise Lost and Other Poems*; Holt offers *Paradise Lost* and *Selected Poetry and Prose*; and there is a *Portable Milton* (Penguin). Other editions are easily come by.

90. BLAKE. A very good edition is Oxford's *Complete Writings of William Blake.* Penguin has the *Complete Poems,* as well as a good *Portable Blake,* ed. Alfred Kazin.

91. WORDSWORTH. The best moderately priced edition is Oxford's *Poetical Works with Introduction and Notes.* Less comprehensive but good: Riverside's *Selected Poems and Prefaces* and Modern Library's *Selected Poetry,* ed. Mark Van Doren.

92. COLERIDGE. Modern Library has *Selected Poetry and Prose*; Oxford has *Complete Poems*; Penguin has a *Portable Coleridge*; Everyman has the *Biographia Literaria.*

93. YEATS. The best edition (hardbound): *The Poems of W. B. Yeats,* ed. Richard Finneran (Macmillan). Through Collier, Macmillan also issues *Eleven Plays,* the *Autobiography,* and *Essays and Introductions. Last Poems* (Aurora); *Selected Poems* (Macmillan).

94. T. S. ELIOT. Harcourt issues hardbound volumes of the *Collected Poems* and *Collected Plays.* Some useful paperbacks: *The Waste Land and Other Poems* (Harcourt); *Four Quartets* (Harvest); *The Sacred Wood* (Methuen). Harvest also has Eliot's plays in separate volumes.

95. WHITMAN. Riverside gives you the *Complete Poetry and Selected Prose.* Penguin has a good *Portable Whitman. Leaves of Grass* is issued by Signet, Airmont, Norton, Modern Library, and Holt, Rinehart.

BIBLIOGRAPHY

96. FROST. Holt, Rinehart publishes *Collected Poems* in hardback and *Selected Poems* in paperback. Washington Square Press has Untermeyer's edition, the *New Enlarged Anthology of Robert Frost's Poems*. You may come upon other paperback editions.

97. AUDEN and PEARSON, eds. The five-volume *Poets of the English Language,* hardbound, published by Viking, may be hard to find. Volume 4 (*Romantic Poets*) is a Viking Portable.

98. ELLMANN and O'CLAIR, eds. The *Norton Anthology of Modern Poetry* (Norton) is now in paperback. See also Ellmann and O'Clair's *Modern Poems: An Introduction to Poetry* (Norton).

HISTORY, BIOGRAPHY, AUTOBIOGRAPHY

99. MORRIS; ROSSITER; eds. Morris's *Basic Documents* is published by both Krieger and Van Nostrand (Anvil Books). Rossiter's *Federalist Papers* is in New American Library. Bantam, Harvard University Press, and Modern Library also have good editions of the latter. A H M Publications offers *Selections from The Federalist,* ed. Henry S. Commager.

100. ROUSSEAU. Penguin has J. M. Cohen's excellent translation of the *Confessions*. Washington Square Press issues in one volume *The Social Contract* and *Discourse on the Origin of Inequality*.

101. BOSWELL. Penguin, Modern Library, and Signet (abridged) offer the *Life*. McGraw-Hill publishes the Boswell *Private Papers* in many hardbound volumes. Oxford publishes in paperback Boswell's interesting *Journal of a Tour to the Hebrides*.

102. ADAMS. Riverside has a fine edition of the *Education*; also Houghton Mifflin (Sentry edition). Anchor may still offer *Mont-Saint-Michel and Chartres* in paperback.

103. BRAUDEL. *Civilization and Capitalism, 15th–18th Century* (3 vols., Harper & Row). *The Mediterranean and the Mediterranean World in the Age of Philip II* (2 vols., Harper & Row). *On History* (Univ. of Chicago Pr.).

ANNEX

I. MCNEILL; the DURANTS. *The Rise of the West* is in Phoenix and University of Chicago Press, which also issues McNeill's *History of Western Civilization: A Handbook*. Scott Foresman brings you up to date with his *The Contemporary World: Nineteen Fourteen to the Present* (rev. ed. 1975). The Durants' *Story of Civilization* (Simon & Schuster) is available only in hardcover.

BIBLIOGRAPHY

II. MORISON; SMITH. Morison's *Oxford History* is in three volumes, Mentor. Page Smith's eight-volume *People's History* comes only hardbound from McGraw-Hill.

III. WHITEHEAD. *Science and the Modern World* is published by the Free Press, which also issues his interesting *Adventures of Ideas*.

IV. WHITEHEAD. *An Introduction to Mathematics* is published by Oxford in a revised edition (1959).

V. GOMBRICH. *The Story of Art* (Prentice-Hall).

VI. ADLER and VAN DOREN. The revised 1972 edition of *How to Read a Book* is in Touchstone.

Suggestions for Further Reading

The Bibliography lists editions, mostly paperback, of the original communications suggested by the Plan. It also lists other works by the Plan's authors.

The suggestions that follow, however, are limited to secondary or reference books helpful to the reader wishing to acquire a deeper knowledge of the lives, background, and historical setting of our authors. (As with the Bibliography, I have weighted the subjoined titles toward paperbacks.) For a key to the publishers of the paperback series see page 239.

You will also find listed many hardbound, more expensive books. Some may be out of print (true of paperbacks also) and available only through second-hand bookstores and libraries. In such cases the publisher's name is at times omitted.

Note to serious students: R. R. Bowker Co. (Order Dept., 245 W. 17th St., New York, New York 10011) publishes *Paperbound Books in Print,* revised annually. It is in three expensive volumes and lists more than 200,000 books, arranged by title, author, and subject. Most libraries have it. It is a marvelous aid for those who wish to build, at moderate cost, a library of both original communications and secondary works.

It is probably unnecessary to direct the reader to the Encyclopaedia Britannica for sound biographical and background information.

THE BEGINNING (1–12)

A comprehensive reference volume covering both Greece and Rome is Paul Harvey, ed., *Oxford Companion to Classical Literature* (Oxford Univ. Pr.). For mythology: Zimmerman, *Dictionary of Classical Mythology* (Bantam); Edith Hamilton, *Mythology* (Mentor); H. J. Rose, *Gods and*

Heroes of the Greeks (Meridian). Greek history: J. B. Bury, *A History of Greece* (Modern Library) is a landmark, but dated. More recent: Hatzfeld and Aymard, *History of Ancient Greece* (Norton); C. E. Robinson, *History of Greece* (Methuen); Peter Green, *Ancient Greece* (Thames & Hudson). A masterly general study of Greek culture: Werner Jaeger, *Paideia* (Oxford Univ. Pr.).

Surveys of Greek literature: Moses Hadas, *A History of Greek Literature* (Columbia Univ. Pr.); Albin Lesky, *History of Greek Literature* (Crowell); Gilbert Murray, *The Literature of Ancient Greece* (Phoenix).

For Homer: Jasper Griffin, *Homer*; Michael Silk, *Homer: The Iliad* (Cambridge Univ. Pr.); Mark Edwards, *Homer: Poet of the Iliad* (Johns Hopkins Univ. Pr.); M. I. Finley, *The World of Ulysses* (Pelican); G. S. Kirk, *Homer and the Epic* (Cambridge Univ. Pr.).

For the historians: J. B. Bury's *The Ancient Greek Historians* (Dover) covers other Greek historians as well as Herodotus and Thucydides and is a classic in its field. For Herodotus: John L. Myres, *Herodotus: Father of History* (Regnery). For Thucydides: J. H. Finley, *Thucydides*, 2d ed. (Harvard Univ. Pr.).

For the Greek philosophers: Rex Warner, *The Greek Philosophers* (Mentor); A. E. Taylor, *Plato: The Man and His Work* (Methuen); G. C. Field, *The Philosophy of Plato*; I. F. Stone's iconoclastic *The Trial of Socrates* (Little, Brown); Mortimer J. Adler, *Aristotle for Everyone* (Macmillan); Abraham Edel, *Aristotle and His Philosophy* (Univ. of N.C. Pr.).

For Greek drama: H. D. F. Kitto, *Greek Tragedy* (Anchor); C. M. Bowra, *Sophoclean Tragedy*; Gilbert Murray, *Euripides and His Age* (Oxford Univ. Pr.).

For Rome: Michael Grant, *History of Rome* (Scribner's); R. H. Barrow, *The Romans* (Pelican); Moses Hadas, *A History of Latin Literature* (Columbia Univ. Pr.). A fine essay on Lucretius is in George Santayana's *Three Philosophical Poets* (Anchor), which also contains essays on Dante (14) and Goethe (18). For Virgil see G. Highet, *Poets in a Landscape* (Knopf); T. R. Glover, *Virgil* (Macmillan). For Marcus Aurelius see Matthew Arnold's famous essay in *The Portable Marcus Aurelius*, ed. Lionel Trilling (Viking). A reasonably recent biography is Anthony Birley's *Marcus Aurelius* (Yale Univ. Pr.).

THE MIDDLE AGES (13–15)

Henry Osborn Taylor's two-volume *The Mediaeval Mind* (Harvard Univ. Pr.), though written many years ago, is still a valuable and comprehensive study of "thought and emotion in the Middle Ages." Together with Will Durant's *The Age of Faith* (volume IV of the *Story of Civilization* [I]), these books will give you a good general picture of a fascinating period. For specific writers:

13. SAINT AUGUSTINE. Martin C. D'Arcy, ed., *St. Augustine: His Age, Life and Thought* (Meridian Books); Peter Brown, *Augustine of Hippo* (Univ. of Calif. Pr.); Rebecca West's brilliant, untraditional *St. Augustine* (Nelson); Warren T. Smith, *Augustine: His Life and Thought.*

14. DANTE. Francis Fergusson, *Dante* (Macmillan); Thomas G. Bergin, *Dante* (Greenwood); Jefferson Butler Fletcher, *Dante* (Univ. of Notre Dame Pr.); the essay on Dante in George Santayana's (87) *Three Philosophical Poets* (Anchor); the essay on Dante in T. S. Eliot's (94) *Selected Essays, 1917–1932* (Harcourt); Robin Kirkpatrick, *Dante: the Divine Comedy* (Cambridge Univ. Pr.). Good biography: R. J. Quinones, *Dante Alighieri.*

15. CHAUCER. John Livingston Lowes, *Geoffrey Chaucer* (Ind. Univ. Pr.); Marchette Chute, *Geoffrey Chaucer of England* (Everyman); D. S. Brewer, *Chaucer,* 3d ed. (Longman); G. G. Coulton, *Chaucer and His England* (Dutton); S. S. Hussey, *Chaucer: An Introduction.* Donald R. Howard, *Chaucer* (Dutton) is the most recent large-scale study.

PLAYS (16–24)

16. SHAKESPEARE. To aid in your reading of Shakespeare, I list several books, each approaching the subject from a different angle, each useful in a different way.

    M. C. Bradbrook, *Shakespeare: The Poet in His World* (Columbia Univ. Pr.); A. C. Bradley, *Shakespearean Tragedy* (Fawcett); Peter Quennell, *Shakespeare; Northrop Frye on Shakespeare* (Yale Univ. Pr.); G. B. Harrison, *Introducing Shakespeare* (Penguin); Marchette Chute, *Shakespeare of London* (Dutton); Anthony Burgess, *Shakespeare* (Penguin); A. Nicoll, *Shakespeare in His Own Age* (Cambridge Univ. Pr.); S. Schoenbaum, *Shakespeare: The Globe and the World* (Oxford Univ. Pr.). Jan Kott's *Shakespeare Our Contemporary* (Norton) is a stimulating modern view, of interest to those involved in production.

17. MOLIÈRE. W. D. Howarth, *Molière: A Playwright and His Audience* (Cambridge Univ. Pr.); J. L. Palmer, *Molière: His Life and Works* (Richard West); Gertrud Mander, *Molière;* D. B. W. Lewis, *Molière: The Comic Mask* (Coward McCann).

18. GOETHE. It is worthwhile, so versatile is Goethe's mind, to get some idea of what he did and thought exclusive of *Faust.* For this purpose you might find useful *Great Writings of Goethe* (New

American Library), by Stephen Spender. This also contains Mac-Neice's excellent English translation of *Faust*, Part 1. Other suggestions: G. W. Lewes, *The Life and Works of Goethe* (Everyman); the essay on Goethe in Santayana's (87) *Three Philosophical Poets* (Anchor); and various essays on Goethe in Thomas Mann's (44) *Essays of Three Decades* (Vintage). See also: Barker Fairley, *Goethe, as Revealed in His Poetry* and *A Study of Goethe* (Univ. of Chicago Pr.); Erich Heller, *The Disinherited Mind* (Harcourt). Emil Ludwig's *Goethe: The History of a Man, 1749–1832* is a readable, popularized biography. A recent excellent study: Nicholas Boyle, *Faust*, Part 1 (Cambridge Univ. Pr.).

19. IBSEN. M. J. Valency, *The Flower and the Castle* (Octagon); James McFarlane, ed., *Henrik Ibsen: Penguin Critical Anthology* (Penguin). A slanted but brilliant essay is Shaw's (20) *The Quintessence of Ibsenism* (Hill and Wang, Dramabooks). See also: H. Clurman, *Ibsen* (Macmillan); J. Northam, *Ibsen: A Critical Study* (Cambridge Univ. Pr.). For biography see M. C. Bradbrook, *Ibsen the Norwegian*; H. Meyer, *Ibsen: A Biography*.

20. SHAW. On Shaw himself the commentaries are legion. Uninspired and indeed not very perceptive but a vast storehouse of facts is Archibald Henderson's *George Bernard Shaw: Man of the Century* (Appleton-Century-Crofts). For an interesting collection of essays by various hands try Louis Kronenberger, ed., *G. B. Shaw: A Critical Survey* (World Publishing Co.). Three quite different studies, of which Chesterton's is truly brilliant (but also highly personal), are: Eric Bentley's *Bernard Shaw* (New Directions); G. K. Chesterton's *George Bernard Shaw* (Hill and Wang, Dramabooks); and Hesketh Pearson, *George Bernard Shaw: His Life and Personality* (Atheneum). See also: Michael Holroyd, *The Genius of Shaw*; J. F. Matthews, *George Bernard Shaw* (Columbia Univ. Pr.).

21. CHEKHOV. Good biographies are: David Magarshack, *Chekhov: A Life*; Ernest J. Simmons, *Chekhov: A Biography* (Phoenix); Ronald A. Hingley, *A New Life of Anton Chekhov*; Henri Troyat, *Chekhov*, which is both recent and highly readable. See also M. J. Valency, *The Breaking String*.

22. O'NEILL. The standard biography is Arthur and Barbara Gelb, *O'Neill* (Harper & Row). See also Barrett H. Clark, *Eugene O'Neill: The Man and His Plays*, rev. ed. (Dover); Doris Alexander, *The Tempering of Eugene O'Neill*; F. I. Carpenter, *Eugene O'Neill* (Twayne).

23. BECKETT. *On Beckett: Essays and Criticism*, edited and introduced by S. E. Gontarski (Grove), is an interesting collection of writings about Beckett as writer and private man. Books on Beckett are numerous. Here are a few: Hugh Kenner, *Samuel Beckett: A*

Critical Study (Univ. of Calif. Pr.); Charles Lyons, *Samuel Beckett* (Grove); J. Fletcher and J. Spurling, *Beckett: A Study of His Plays* (Hill and Wang); R. N. Coe, *Samuel Beckett* (Grove); W. Y. Tindall, *Samuel Beckett* (Columbia Univ. Pr.); Lawrence Harvey, *Samuel Beckett: Poet and Critic*; Ruby Cohn, *Samuel Beckett: The Comic Gamut*; Deirdre Bair, *Samuel Beckett: A Biography* (Harvest); Vivian Mercier, *Beckett/Beckett* (Oxford Univ. Pr.). For a more general approach, see Martin Esslin's excellent *The Theatre of the Absurd* (Anchor).

24. WATSON and PRESSEY, eds. Post-Ibsen drama is brilliantly discussed in E. R. Bentley, *The Playwright as Thinker* (Harvest) and Robert Brustein, *The Theatre of Revolt* (Atlantic Monthly Pr.). For a survey of the whole field: Allardyce Nicoll, *World Drama* (Barnes & Noble). For general reference: J. Gassner and E. Quinn, *The Reader's Encyclopaedia of World Drama*; *Oxford Companion to the Theatre*, ed. Phyllis Hartnoll (Oxford Univ. Pr.).

NARRATIVES (25–70)

Though hardly new, perhaps the most penetrating studies of the novel still remain: E. M. Forster's (38) *Aspects of the Novel* (Harvest); Henry James's (58) *The Art of Fiction and Other Essays* and *The Art of the Novel*; Percy Lubbock's *The Craft of Fiction.*

For a good general survey of English fiction see Walter Allen, *The English Novel* (Everyman); also I. P. Watt, *The Rise of the Novel.* F. R. Leavis's influential *The Great Tradition* (Anchor) has long chapters on George Eliot, Henry James, and Joseph Conrad, as well as a general discussion of English fiction. For Dickens, Thackeray, Emily Brontë, and George Eliot see David Cecil's *Victorian Novelists* (Phoenix). On the individual novelists I list herewith a few standard works, not all of them easily found in bookstores or small libraries.

25. BUNYAN. G. B. Harrison, *Bunyan: A Study in Personality* (Shoe String); R. Sharrock, *John Bunyan,* rev. ed. (St. Martin's Pr.); O. E. Winslow, *John Bunyan* (Macmillan), perhaps the most useful biography.

26. DEFOE. The fullest biography is J. R. Moore, *Daniel Defoe, Citizen of the Modern World* (Univ. of Chicago Pr.). See also: James Sutherland, *Defoe* (Riverside); the essay by Virginia Woolf (40) in *The Common Reader* (Harvest).

27. SWIFT. For biography: I. Ehrenpreis, *Swift: The Man, His Works, and the Age* (2 vols.). See also: Carl Van Doren, *Swift* (Viking);

R. Quintana, *The Mind and Art of Jonathan Swift* (Peter Smith); David Ward, *Jonathan Swift: An Introductory Essay* (Methuen).

28. STERNE. W. L. Cross's solid but old-fashioned *Life and Times of Sterne* has been superseded by Arthur H. Cash, *Laurence Sterne* (2 vols., Methuen). For a Victorian view see Thackeray's (32) *The English Humourists of the Eighteenth Century* (Dutton), which also discusses Swift and Fielding. For a more modern appraisal see Virginia Woolf's (40) essay "The Sentimental Journey" in her *Second Common Reader* (Harvest). This also discusses, among other topics, *Robinson Crusoe* (26), Swift's *Journal to Stella* (27), and the novels of Thomas Hardy (36).

29. FIELDING. The standard biography is the two-volume *Henry Fielding: His Life, Works, and Times,* by F. Homes Dudden (Oxford Univ. Pr.). For most readers this is pretty formidable, as is the even more basic and earlier three-volume work by Wilbur L. Cross, *The History of Henry Fielding* (Russell). Thackeray's (32) estimate of Fielding is good but deeply Victorian: see his *The English Humourists of the Eighteenth Century* (Dutton). Useful also is Ronald Paulson, ed., *Fielding: A Collection of Critical Essays* (Barnes & Noble); Andrew Wright, *Henry Fielding: Mask and Feast* (Univ. of Calif. Pr.).

30. AUSTEN. The standard life is *Jane Austen: Her Life and Letters,* by W. and R. A. Austen-Leigh (Russell). See also Elizabeth Jenkins, *Jane Austen* (Farrar, Straus); essay by Virginia Woolf (40) in *The Common Reader* (Harvest); Marghanita Laski, *Jane Austen and Her World* (Viking); B. C. Southam, ed., *Jane Austen: The Critical Heritage* (Routledge & Kegan), which offers a reflection of current views; John Halperin, *The Life of Jane Austen* (Johns Hopkins Univ. Pr.); Tony Tanner, *Jane Austen* (Harvard Univ. Pr.); Mary Lascelles, *Jane Austen* (Oxford Univ. Pr.); Douglas Bush, *Jane Austen*; David Cecil, *A Portrait of Jane Austen* (Hill and Wang).

31. EMILY BRONTË. Though of course somewhat outmoded by subsequent scholarship, Elizabeth Gaskell's *Life of Charlotte Brontë* (Penguin) still offers an interesting picture of the whole family. Muriel Spark's fine study of Emily has recently been reissued. Other informative books: Irene Cooper Willis, *The Brontës* (Dufour); Thomas Winnifrith, *The Brontës* (Macmillan); A. Harrison and D. Stanford, *Emily Brontë*; Winifred Gerin, *Emily Brontë: A Biography* (Oxford Univ. Pr.); Edward Chitham, *A Life of Emily Brontë* (Blackwell).

32. THACKERAY. The standard life: Gordon N. Ray, *Thackeray: The Uses of Adversity (1811–1846)* and *Thackeray: The Age of Wisdom (1847–1863)* (McGraw-Hill). A good one-volume biography: Ann Monsarrat, *An Uneasy Victorian.* A fine critical study is Geoffrey

Tillotson, *Thackeray the Novelist* (Cambridge Univ. Pr.). See also: John Carey, *Thackeray: Prodigal Genius* (Faber & Faber); Alexander Walsh, ed., *Thackeray: A Collection of Critical Essays* (Prentice-Hall).

33. DICKENS. The comprehensive biography is Edgar Johnson, *Charles Dickens: His Tragedy and Triumph* (Penguin). The Dickens literature is formidable. Here are some interesting treatments: F. R. and Q. D. Leavis, *Dickens the Novelist* (Rutgers Univ. Pr.); Humphry House, *The Dickens World* (Oxford Univ. Pr.); Angus Wilson, *The World of Charles Dickens* (Academy Chicago Pubs.); Edmund Wilson's pathbreaking essay "Dickens: The Two Scrooges" in *The Wound and the Bow* (Farrar, Straus); J. Hillis Miller, *Charles Dickens: The World of His Novels* (Ind. Univ. Pr.); G. K. Chesterton, *Charles Dickens: A Critical Study* (Schocken), a brilliant study; George Orwell (43), "Dickens" in *Dickens, Dali & Others* (Harvest). A good specialized study: Graham Storey, *Dickens: Bleak House* (Cambridge Univ. Pr.).

34. GEORGE ELIOT. The definitive life is Gordon S. Haight: *George Eliot: A Biography* (Oxford Univ. Pr.). For acute criticism see Joan Bennett, *George Eliot: Her Mind and Her Art* (Cambridge Univ. Pr.); Barbara Hardy, *The Novels of George Eliot: A Study in Form* (Essential Books). See also: R. T. Jones, *George Eliot* (Cambridge Univ. Pr.); Marghanita Laski, *George Eliot and Her World*; Lawrence and Elizabeth Hanson, *Marian Evans and George Eliot* (Oxford Univ. Pr.). Other views of George Eliot may be found in Virginia Woolf's *The Common Reader* (Harvest), F. R. Leavis's *The Great Tradition* (Anchor), David Cecil's *Victorian Novelists* (Phoenix), and Henry James's (58) *Partial Portraits* (Univ. of Mich. Pr.). Gillian Beer, *George Eliot* (Ind. Univ. Pr.) offers an interesting feminist approach, as does Jennifer Uglow (Pantheon).

35. CARROLL. Official, dull, and reticent is S. Dodgson Collingwood's *Life and Letters of Lewis Carroll* (Richard West). It's rather hard to find, which may be a good thing. Derek Hudson's *Lewis Carroll* (British Book Centre) takes advantage of the diaries and many hitherto unpublished letters. Anne Clark's *Lewis Carroll* is also a good short biography. Florence Becker Lennon's *The Life of Lewis Carroll* offers an interesting analysis of Carroll's peculiar temperament, as refracted through his work. Shorter studies are legion, one of the best being Edmund Wilson's "C. L. Dodgson: The Poet-Logician" in his *The Shores of Light* (Farrar, Straus). For a once-over-lightly see Roger Lancelyn Green's *Lewis Carroll* (Bodley Head Monograph). Highly amusing and instructive is *The Annotated Alice*, edited by Martin Gardner (Clarkson N. Potter). For an interesting collection

of mainly modern viewpoints, some profound, some mildly lunatic, see Robert Phillips, ed., *Aspects of Alice* (Vanguard Pr.).

36. HARDY. The official life is by Florence E. Hardy, now in one volume: *The Early Life of Hardy, 1840–1891* and *The Later Years, 1892–1928* (Shoe String). Professor Guerard's introduction to *The Mayor of Casterbridge* (Pocket Books) is excellent. See also Lord David Cecil, *Hardy, the Novelist* (Appel); Douglas Brown, *Thomas Hardy* (Longmans); Virginia Woolf's (40) essay in *The Second Common Reader* (Harvest); Robert Gittings, *Young Thomas Hardy* and *Thomas Hardy's Later Years*; Irving Howe, *Thomas Hardy* (Collier).

37. CONRAD. Two standard lives: Jocelyn Baines, *Joseph Conrad: A Critical Biography* (Greenwood); F. R. Karl, *Joseph Conrad: The Three Lives* (Farrar, Straus). See also: B. C. Meyer, *Joseph Conrad: A Psychoanalytical Biography* (Princeton Univ. Pr.); Leo Gurko, *Joseph Conrad: Giant in Exile* (Collier); Zdzislaw Najder, *Joseph Conrad: A Chronicle* (Rutgers Univ. Pr.); G. Jean-Aubry, *Sea-Dreamer, A Definitive Biography of Joseph Conrad* (Doubleday); A. J. Guérard, *Conrad the Novelist* (Atheneum); F. R. Leavis, *The Great Tradition* (N. Y. Univ. Pr.); E. M. Forster (38), "Joseph Conrad: A Note" in *Abinger Harvest* (Harvest).

38. FORSTER. Lionel Trilling's *E. M. Forster* (New Directions) is the best study. The authorized biography is by P. N. Furbank. See also: Rose Macaulay, *The Writings of E. M. Forster*; Virginia Woolf (40), *The Death of the Moth and Other Essays* (Harvest); F. C. Crews, *E. M. Forster: The Perils of Humanism* (Princeton Univ. Pr.); Wilfred Stone, *The Cave and the Mountain* (Stanford Univ. Pr.).

39. JOYCE. The definitive biography is Richard Ellmann's *James Joyce* (Oxford Univ. Pr., hardbound). Excellent general studies: Harry Levin, *James Joyce: A Critical Introduction* (New Directions); W. Y. Tindall, *A Reader's Guide to James Joyce* (Farrar, Straus); Anthony Burgess, *Re Joyce* (Norton). Edmund Wilson's brilliant estimate is in his *Axel's Castle* (Scribner's). On *Ulysses* see Stuart Gilbert, *James Joyce's Ulysses* (Vintage); H. Blamires, *The Bloomsday Book* (Methuen); Frank Budgen, *James Joyce and the Making of Ulysses* (Ind. Univ. Pr.); Hugh Kenner, *Ulysses* (Allen Unwin). All the above are in paperback. If you attempt *Finnegans Wake,* take along Campbell and Robinson, *A Skeleton Key to Finnegans Wake* (Penguin). A good recent Joyce study is John Bishop, *Joyce's Book of the Dead* (Univ. of Wis. Pr.).

40. WOOLF. Quentin Bell, *Virginia Woolf* (2 vols., Harcourt) is the fullest biography. See also P. Rose, *Woman of Letters: A Life of Virginia Woolf* (Oxford Univ. Pr.). These are hardbound and

probably obtainable only through your library. For a specialized study see Eric Warner, *The Waves* (Cambridge Univ. Pr.). There is a large and increasing corpus of literature about Virginia Woolf and the Bloomsbury group of which she was the center. In connection with the latter see Michael Holroyd's life of Lytton Strachey (2 vols., Holt, Rinehart); Leon Edel, *Bloomsbury: A House of Lions* (Avon).

41. LAWRENCE. *D. H. Lawrence: A Composite Biography,* ed. Edward Nehls (Univ. of Wis. Pr.); H. T. Moore, *The Intelligent Heart* (Farrar, Straus); Keith Sagar, *The Life of D. H. Lawrence*; George J. Becker, *D. H. Lawrence* (Ungar); Richard Aldington, *Portrait of a Genius, But* ... (Collier). Critical studies: F. R. Leavis, *D. H. Lawrence, Novelist* (Phoenix); Aldous Huxley (42), *Collected Essays* (Harper & Row); Graham Hough, *The Dark Sun*; *D. H. Lawrence: A Centenary Celebration,* ed. Peter Balbert and P. L. Marcus (Cornell Univ. Pr.). Lawrence's *Letters* have been edited by both Aldous Huxley and (in two volumes) by H. T. Moore. See also *Not I but the Wind* (Southern Ill. Univ. Pr.) by his wife Frieda.

42. HUXLEY. For the formidable Huxley family see Ronald W. Clark, *The Huxleys.* Biographies: Sybille Bedford, *Aldous Huxley: A Biography,* (2 vols.); Jocelyn Brooke, *Aldous Huxley* (British Book Centre). A good recent academic study: Robert S. Baker, *The Dark Historic Pages: Social Satire and Historicism in the Novels of Aldous Huxley, 1921–1939* (Univ. of Wis. Pr.).

43. ORWELL. A good authorized biography is Bernard Crick's *George Orwell: A Life* (Little, Brown). Perhaps the most penetrating short study is Lionel Trilling's "George Orwell and the Politics of Truth," in his *The Opposing Self: Nine Essays in Criticism* (Harvest). An excellent two-volume treatment is by Peter Stansky and William Abrahams: *The Unknown Orwell* and *Orwell: The Tranformation* (both Academy Chicago Pubs.). Various points of view are represented in *George Orwell: A Collection of Critical Essays,* ed. Raymond Williams (Prentice-Hall). Other useful books: Raymond Williams, *George Orwell* (Columbia Univ. Pr.); Christopher Hollis, *A Study of George Orwell: The Man and His Works* (Regnery); *The World of George Orwell,* ed. Miriam Gross (Simon & Schuster).

44. MANN. Hans Buergin and Hans-Otto Mayer, *Thomas Mann: A Chronicle of His Life* (Univ. of Ala. Pr.); Richard Winston, *Thomas Mann: The Making of an Artist, 1875–1911* (Knopf). The reader may find useful commentary in *The Stature of Thomas Mann,* ed. Charles Neider (Books for Libraries); J. G. Brennan's *Thomas Mann's World* (Russell); my own paperback anthology *Reading I've Liked* (Simon & Schuster); Hermann J. Weigand, *Thomas Mann's Novel*

"Der Zauberberg" (AMS Pr.); Erich Heller, *The Ironic German* (Gateway). For an interesting Marxist approach see Györgi Lukács, *Essays on Thomas Mann.*

45. KAFKA. The Kafka literature is approaching industrial proportions. For biographies see Max Brod, *Franz Kafka: A Biography* (Schocken); Ronald Hayman, *Kafka: A Biography* (Oxford Univ. Pr.); Ernst Pawel, *The Nightmare of Reason*, a remarkable book. Critical studies: Erich Heller, *Franz Kafka* (Princeton Univ. Pr.); Heinz Politzer, *Franz Kafka, Parable and Paradox* (Cornell Univ. Pr.); Ronald D. Gray, ed., *Kafka: A Collection of Critical Essays* (Prentice-Hall); Angel Flores, ed., *The Kafka Problem* (Gordian).

46. RABELAIS. The best one-volume life I know is the translation by Louis P. Roche of Jean Plattard's *The Life of François Rabelais* (International Scholastic Book Service), but this is hard to come by. Samuel Putnam's *Rabelais, Man of the Renaissance* (Books for Libraries) is good too. D. B. Wyndham Lewis's *Doctor Rabelais* (Sheed & Ward), by a Catholic and a humorist, offers a sympathetic interpretation of both these aspects of Rabelais. Donald Frame's *François Rabelais: A Study* is a good introductory book, and Mikhail Bakhtin's *Rabelais and His World* (Ind. Univ. Pr.) a penetrating one.

47. VOLTAIRE. The best biography in English is probably Theodore Besterman, *Voltaire* (Harcourt). See also Richard Aldington, *Voltaire* (Richard West); Ira O. Wade, *The Intellectual Development of Voltaire* (Princeton Univ. Pr.); Virgil W. Topazio, *Voltaire: A Critical Study of His Major Works* (Random); W. Andrews, *Voltaire* (New Directions); H. N. Brailsford, *Voltaire* (Oxford Univ. Pr.). A. J. Ayer's *Voltaire* (Random) deals brilliantly with his lesser-known works. Peyton E. Richter and Ilona Ricardo's *Voltaire* is a good introductory biography.

48. STENDHAL. For a sound biography in English see Matthew Josephson's *Stendhal* (Russell). Martin Turnell's brilliant *The Novel in France* (Vintage) offers penetrating analyses of Balzac (49), Flaubert (50), and Proust (51). The excellent Lowell Bair translation of *The Red and the Black* (Bantam) contains a longish introduction by Clifton Fadiman. See also: Wallace Fowlie, *Stendhal* (Macmillan); Harry Levin, *The Gates of Horn: A Study of Five French Realists* (Oxford Univ. Pr.); Victor Brombert, ed., *Stendhal: A Collection of Critical Essays* (Prentice-Hall); Storm Jameson, *Speaking of Stendhal.*

49. BALZAC. Some good biographies and studies: V. S. Pritchett, *Balzac*; André Maurois, *Prometheus: The Life of Balzac* (Harper & Row); Herbert J. Hunt, *Honoré de Balzac*; Stefan Zweig, *Balzac.* Shorter

studies are to be found in Harry Levin's *Toward Balzac* (New Directions) and particularly Henry James's (58) "The Lesson of Balzac" in *The Future of the Novel* (Vintage), ed. Leon Edel. The latter also contains estimates of Flaubert (50), Turgenev (66), Tolstoy (68), and Conrad (37).

50. FLAUBERT.   An adequate biography in English is P. Spencer's *Flaubert: A Biography* (Grove). Enid Starkie's *Flaubert: The Making of the Master* and Francis Steegmuller's *Flaubert and Madame Bovary* (Phoenix) are good studies. See also B. F. Bart's *Flaubert* (Syracuse Univ. Pr.). University of Chicago Press has published Jean-Paul Sartre's brilliant but idiosyncratic and unfinished *The Family Idiot: Gustave Flaubert, 1821–1857.*

51. PROUST.   An excellent brief biography is André Maurois's *Proust* (Meridian). Another is Richard H. Barker's *Marcel Proust* (Criterion). George D. Painter's *Marcel Proust* (2 vols., Atlantic Monthly Pr.) is a detailed, comprehensive, well-researched classic biography. For a brief but masterly appreciation see Edmund Wilson's *Axel's Castle* (Scribner's). See also: Germaine Brée, *Marcel Proust and Deliverance from Time* (Rutgers Univ. Pr.); Roger Shattuck, *Proust's Binoculars: A Study of Memory, Time, and Recognition in À la recherche du temps perdu* (Random); Germaine Brée, *The World of Marcel Proust* (Houghton Mifflin); Samuel Beckett (23), *Proust* (Grove).

52. MALRAUX.   W. M. Frohock, *André Malraux and the Tragic Imagination* (Stanford Univ. Pr.). See also: Janet Flanner, *Men and Monuments* (Harper & Row); Wallace Fowlie, *A Guide to Contemporary French Literature* (Meridian); Henri Peyre, *The Contemporary French Novel* (Oxford Univ. Pr.); Denis Boak, *André Malraux* (Oxford Univ. Pr.), a highly critical assessment; Charles Blend, *André Malraux: Tragic Humanist*; C. M. Jenkins, *André Malraux.* You may be able to find the abridged English translation of the comprehensive biography by Jean Laconture, *André Malraux.*

53. CAMUS.   Herbert Lottman, *Albert Camus: A Biography* (Braziller); Germaine Brée, *Camus* (Rutgers Univ. Pr.); Philip Thody, *Albert Camus 1913–1960* (Macmillan); Adele King, *Camus* (Putnam); P. H. Rhein, *Albert Camus*; R. Quilliot, *The Sea and Prisons*; Patrick McCarthy, *Camus: A Critical Study of His Life and Work.*

54. POE.   The standard authority is Arthur H. Quinn's *Edgar Allan Poe: A Critical Biography* (Appleton-Century-Crofts). See also Joseph Wood Krutch's excellent *Edgar Allan Poe: A Study in Genius* (Russell). One of the finest critical works (but it requires close attention) on the major American writers of the mid-nineteenth

century is F. O. Matthiessen's *American Renaissance* (Oxford Univ. Pr.). While this discusses Poe, the major emphasis is on Melville (56), Thoreau (84), Hawthorne (55), and Whitman (95). It may be consulted in connection with these four writers particularly. See also: Edward Wagenknecht, *Edgar Allan Poe: The Man Behind the Legend* (Oxford Univ. Pr.); Constance Pope-Hennessy, *Edgar Allan Poe, 1809–1849: A Critical Biography*; Perry Miller, *The Raven and the Whale* (Greenwood); William L. Howarth, ed., *Twentieth Century Interpretations of Poe's Tales* (Prentice-Hall); Roger Asselineau, *Edgar Allan Poe* (Univ. of Minn. Pr.).

55. HAWTHORNE. Two excellent short treatments: Mark Van Doren's *Nathaniel Hawthorne: A Critical Biography* (Compass); Randall Stewart's *Nathaniel Hawthorne: A Biography* (Yale Univ. Pr.). See also: Henry James's (58) pioneering study (1879), *Hawthorne*; Hyatt H. Waggoner, *Hawthorne: A Critical Study* (Harvard Univ. Pr.); B. Bernard Cohen, ed., *The Recognition of Nathaniel Hawthorne* (Univ. of Mich. Pr.), a collection of critical essays from various hands; J. R. Mellow, *Nathaniel Hawthorne and His Times* (Houghton Mifflin); Arlin Turner, *Nathaniel Hawthorne: A Biography.*

56. MELVILLE. The literature is vast and various. Some interesting treatments: Leon Howard's *Herman Melville: A Biography* (Univ. of Calif. Pr.); Newton Arvin's *Herman Melville* (Compass); Richard Chase's *Herman Melville: A Critical Study* (Macmillan); W. E. Sedgwick, *Herman Melville: The Tragedy of Mind*; Lewis Mumford, *Herman Melville*; A. R. Humphreys, *Melville*; Van Wyck Brooks, *The Times of Melville and Whitman* (Dutton); Richard Chase, ed., *Herman Melville: A Collection of Critical Essays* (Prentice-Hall). Jay Leyda's *The Melville Log: A Documentary Life of Herman Melville* (Gordian) is just what the title suggests.

57. MARK TWAIN. The (highly) official biography is Albert B. Paine, *Mark Twain, A Biography: The Personal and Literary Life of Samuel Langhorne Clemens* (3 vols., Chelsea House). Two quite different interpretations: Van Wyck Brooks, *The Ordeal of Mark Twain* (Meridian); Bernard De Voto, *Mark Twain's America* (Houghton Mifflin). See also: H. N. Smith, *Mark Twain: The Development of a Writer* (Atheneum); Charles Neider's remarkable edition of *The Autobiography of Mark Twain* (Harper & Row); Justin Kaplan, *Mister Clemens and Mark Twain* (Touchstone); Walter Blair, *Mark Twain and Huck Finn* (Univ. of Calif. Pr.).

58. HENRY JAMES. One of the great biographies of our time is Leon Edel's *The Life of Henry James* (5 vols., Avon). For the best commentator on Henry James see his own *The Art of the Novel* (Scribner's).

Other excellent studies: F. W. Dupee, *Henry James* (Morrow); F. O. Matthiessen, *Henry James: The Major Phase* (Oxford Univ. Pr.) and *The James Family: A Group Biography* (Vintage); Edmund Wilson in *The Triple Thinkers* (Farrar, Straus); Gordon Pirie, *Henry James*; F. R. Leavis, *The Great Tradition* (N.Y. Univ. Pr.). See also a study of *The Princess Casamassima* in Lionel Trilling's highly recommended *The Liberal Imagination* (Anchor).

59. FAULKNER. The authorized life is J. L. Blotner, *William Faulkner: A Biography* (2 vols., Random). Faulkner may end by having more commentators than readers. Here are a few excellent studies: Michael Millgate, *The Achievement of William Faulkner* (Bison); Cleanth Brooks, *William Faulkner: The Yoknapatawpha County* and *William Faulkner: Toward Yoknapatawpha and Beyond* (Yale Univ. Pr.); F. J. Hoffman, *William Faulkner* (Twayne); Irving Howe, *William Faulkner: A Critical Study* (Phoenix). For shorter critical estimates see: F. J. Hoffman and O. W. Vickery, eds., *William Faulkner: Three Decades of Criticism* (Harcourt); Robert Penn Warren, ed., *Faulkner: A Collection of Critical Essays* (Prentice-Hall). Perhaps the finest short estimate remains Malcolm Cowley's classic introduction to *The Portable Faulkner* (Viking).

60. HEMINGWAY. The standard biography: Carlos Baker, *Ernest Hemingway: A Life Story* (Avon). See also: Philip Young, *Ernest Hemingway: A Reconsideration* (Univ. of Minn. Pr.); Carlos Baker, *Hemingway: The Writer as Artist* (Princeton Univ. Pr.); Scott Donaldson, *By Force of Will*; Peter Griffin, *Along with Youth: Hemingway, The Early Years* (Oxford Univ. Pr.); Jeffrey Meyer, *Hemingway* (Harper & Row); K. S. Lynn, *Hemingway: The Life and Work* (Simon & Schuster). This last, a recent work, is fairly full-dress, stresses his early years, and treats Hemingway's darker side. For other insights see: Alfred Kazin, *On Native Grounds* (Harvest); F. J. Hoffman, *The Modern Novel in America* (Gateway); Edmund Wilson's essay in *Eight Essays* (Anchor); Denis Brian, *The True Gen: An Intimate Portrait of Hemingway by Those Who Knew Him* (Grove).

61. BELLOW. J. J. Clayton, *Saul Bellow: In Defense of Man* (Ind. Univ. Pr.); Malcolm Bradbury, *Saul Bellow*; Earl Rovit, *Saul Bellow* (Univ. of Minn. Pr.); Earl Rovit, ed., *Saul Bellow: A Collection of Critical Essays* (Prentice-Hall).

62. CERVANTES. The bibliography is of course enormous. Gerald Brenan's *Literature of the Spanish People* has a fine Cervantes chapter and is well worth reading complete. The old standard biography is still authoritative: F. Fitzmaurice-Kelly, *Miguel de Cervantes Saavedra: A Memoir*. See also: J. W. Krutch, *Five*

Masters (Ind. Univ. Pr.); Mark Van Doren, *Don Quixote's Profession* (Columbia Univ. Pr.); A. F. G. Bell, *Cervantes* (Univ. of Okla. Pr.); Salvador de Madariaga, *Don Quixote: An Introductory Essay in Psychology* (Oxford Univ. Pr.); Rudolph Schevill, *Cervantes*; R. L. Predmore, *Cervantes*; William Byron, *Cervantes*; M. McKendrick, *Cervantes*.

63. BORGES. Ana Maria Barrenechea, *Borges, The Labyrinth Maker* (N. Y. Univ. Pr.); Ronald Christ, *The Narrow Act: Borges' Art of Illusion* (N. Y. Univ. Pr.); Emir Rodríguez Monegal, *Jorge Luis Borges: A Literary Biography* (Paragon House); G. H. Bell-Villada, *Borges and His Fiction: A Guide to His Mind and Art* (Univ. of N.C. Pr.); M. S. Stabb, *Jorge Luis Borges* (St. Martin's Pr.).

64. GARCÍA MÁRQUEZ. G. H. McMurray, *Gabriel García Márquez*.

65. GOGOL. As you read Gogol, Turgenev, Tolstoy, Dostoyevsky, and Chekhov, you may find useful Mark Slonim's *Outline of Russian Literature* (New American Library). Fuller treatments of Gogol: Vladimir Nabokov's somewhat eccentric but interesting *Nikolai Gogol* (New Directions); J. Lavrin, *Gogol*; V. Erlich, *Gogol* (Yale Univ. Pr.); Jesse Zeldin, *Nicolai Gogol's Quest for Beauty: An Exploration into His Works*; V. Setchkarev, *Gogol: His Life and Works* (N.Y. Univ. Pr.); D. Magarshack, *Gogol: A Life* (Grove).

66. TURGENEV. Three reliable biographies: A. Yarmolinsky, *Turgenev, the Man, His Art and His Age* (Orion Pr.); L. B. Shapiro, *Turgenev: His Life and Times*; D. Magarshack, *Turgenev: A Life* (Grove). Edmund Wilson contributes an interesting, lengthy introduction to a Turgenev collection, *Literary Reminiscences and Autobiographical Fragments* (Evergreen). A fine study is V. S. Pritchett's *The Gentle Barbarian: The Life and Work of Turgenev* (Vintage).

67. DOSTOYEVSKY. R. Hingley, *Dostoyevsky: His Life and Work*; Henri Troyat, *Firebrand: The Life of Dostoevsky*; E. H. Carr, *Dostoevsky* (Richard West); Avrahm Yarmolinsky, *Dostoevsky, His Life and Art* (Criterion Books). Perhaps the best treatment: Janko Lavrin, *Dostoevsky* (Russell).

68. TOLSTOY. Perhaps the most readable life is Henri Troyat, *Tolstoy* (Crown). The standard biography is Aylmer Maude, *The Life of Tolstoy*, (2 vols., World's Classics). For shorter biographies Janko Lavrin, *Tolstoy: An Approach* (Russell); Ernest Simmons, *Leo Tolstoy* (Peter Smith); and Martine de Courcel, *Tolstoy: The Ultimate Reconciliation*. Special interpretations of high interest: D. S. Merezhkovski, *Tolstoi as Man and Artist* (Scholarly); Isaiah Berlin, *The Hedgehog and the Fox: An Essay on Tolstoy's View of History* (Touchstone); George Steiner, *Tolstoy or Dostoevsky: An Essay in the Old Criticism* (Knopf); Edward Crankshaw, *Tolstoy:*

The Making of a Novelist; Alexandra Tolstoy, *Tolstoy: A Life of My Father* (Nordland).

69. NABOKOV. Two interesting works by Andrew Field supplement each other: *Nabokov: His Life in Art* and *Nabokov: His Life in Part* (Viking). See also: Peter Quennell, ed., *Nabokov: A Tribute* (Morrow); D. E. Morton, *Vladimir Nabokov* (Mod. Lit. Monographs, Unger); J. Moynihan, *Vladimir Nabokov* (Univ. of Minn. Pr.).

70. SOLZHENITSYN. Hans Bjorkgren, *Aleksandr Solzhenitsyn: A Biography*, tr. Kaa Eneberg (Third Pr.); John B. Dunlop et al., *Aleksandr Solzhenitsyn: Critical Essays and Documentary Materials* (Macmillan); Györgi Lukács, *Solzhenitsyn*, tr. William D. Graf (MIT Pr.); Abraham Rothberg, *Aleksandr Solzhenitsyn: The Major Novels* (Cornell Univ. Pr.); Michael Scammell, *Solzhenitsyn* (Norton); *Solzhenitsyn: A Pictorial Autobiography* (Farrar, Straus); D. Burg and G. Feifer, *Solzhenitsyn* (Stein & Day).

PHILOSOPHY, PSYCHOLOGY, POLITICS, ESSAYS (71–87)

Bertrand Russell's *History of Western Philosophy* (Touchstone) covers the entire period from the Greeks to our own day, not always to the satisfaction of academic minds. Will Durant's *Story of Philosophy* (Simon & Schuster) remains a highly readable account, particularly strong on the biographical side. Mentor publishes five useful little books: Giorgio De Santillana's *The Age of Adventure* (Renaissance philosophers); Stuart Hampshire's *The Age of Reason* (seventeenth century); Isaiah Berlin's *The Age of Enlightenment* (eighteenth century); Henry D. Aiken's *The Age of Ideology* (nineteenth century); Morton White's *The Age of Analysis* (twentieth century).

71. HOBBES. Richard Peters, *Hobbes* (Penguin); D. D. Raphael, *Hobbes*. Basil Willey's *The Seventeenth Century Background* (Anchor) discusses, in addition to Hobbes, Milton (89), Descartes (80), Locke (72).

72. LOCKE. D. J. O'Connor, *John Locke*, good introduction (Peter Smith); R. I. Aaron, *John Locke* (Oxford Univ. Pr.); Maurice Cranston, *John Locke: A Biography* (Macmillan), a fine job. See also: *Locke Reader*, ed. J. W. Yolton (Cambridge Univ. Pr.); *Locke Selections*, ed. S. P. Lamprecht (Scribner's).

73. HUME. E. C. Mossner's *The Life of David Hume* (Oxford Univ. Pr.) is the definitive biography. J. Y. T. Greig's *David Hume* (Richard West) is shorter. See also: Barry Stroud, *Hume* (Routledge & Kegan); *David Hume: Many-Sided Genius*, ed. K. R. Merrill and

R. W. Shahan (Univ. of Okla. Pr.); A. J. Ayer, *Hume* (Hill and Wang).

74. MILL. Maurice Cranston, *J. S. Mill*; Michael St. John Packe, *The Life of John Stuart Mill* (Macmillan), the fullest account; E. R. August, *John Stuart Mill*; J. Plamenatz, *The English Utilitarians.*

75. MARX (and ENGELS). Standard life: Franz Mehring, *Karl Marx: The Story of His Life* (Univ. of Mich. Pr.). See also: S. K. Padover, *Karl Marx: An Intimate Biography* (Mentor); Isaiah Berlin, *Karl Marx: His Life and Environment* (Oxford Univ. Pr.), a brilliant short account; Sidney Hook, *Marx and the Marxists* (Anvil). For insight into Marx and his connection with thought in general see: R. H. Heilbroner, *The Worldly Philosophers* (Touchstone); Jacques Barzun, *Darwin, Marx, Wagner* (Anchor); J. K. Galbraith, *The Evolution of Economics* (Houghton Mifflin). An excellent recent study is Bruce Mazlish, *The Meaning of Karl Marx* (Oxford Univ. Pr.).

76. NIETZSCHE. Walter Kaufmann's *Nietzsche: Philosopher, Psychologist, Antichrist* (Princeton Univ. Pr.) is a learned work defending Nietzsche against the kind of charges made by such critics as Bertrand Russell. See also: Ronald Hayman, *Nietzsche: A Critical Life*; Richard Schacht, *Nietzsche,* a recent interpretation; Karl Jaspers, *Nietzsche* (Regnery); Janko Lavrin, *Nietzsche: A Biographical Introduction* (Scribner's); *Nietzsche Reader* (Penguin); Alexander Nehamas, *Nietzsche: Life as Literature* (Harvard Univ. Pr.).

77. FREUD. The standard biography, a classic, is Ernest Jones's *Life and Works of Sigmund Freud* (3 vols., Basic). Basic Books also has this in an abridged edition edited by Lionel Trilling and Steven Marcus. In *An Autobiographical Study* (Norton) Freud himself offers a brief account. See also: Philip Rieff, *Freud: The Mind of the Moralist* (Phoenix); Ralph Steadman, *Sigmund Freud* (Touchstone); Lionel Trilling, *Freud and the Crisis of Our Time* (Beacon Pr.); R. W. Clark, *Freud: The Man and the Cause.*

78. MACHIAVELLI. Best biography: R. Ridolfi, *Life of Niccolò Machiavelli* (Univ. of Chicago Pr.). More recent: Quentin Skinner, *Machiavelli* (Hill and Wang).

79. MONTAIGNE. Best biography in English: Donald M. Frame, *Montaigne* (Harcourt). Marvin Lowenthal's *The Autobiography of Michel de Montaigne* (Vintage) arranges excerpts from the *Essays* so as to follow the course of Montaigne's life. Frame's *Montaigne's Discovery of Man* (Columbia Univ. Pr.) is a serious, scholarly work. Two first-class essays: Virginia Woolf's (40) in *The Common Reader* (Harvest) and Ralph Waldo Emerson's (83) in *The Portable Emerson* (Viking).

80. DESCARTES. Full account: J. R. Vrooman, *René Descartes: A Biography* (Putnam). See also: Bernard Williams, *Descartes: The Project of*

Pure Enquiry (Pelican); and the relevant chapters in Durant, *Story of Philosophy* (Touchstone) and Bertrand Russell, *History of Western Philosophy* (Touchstone).

81. PASCAL. Jean Mesnard's *Pascal: His Life and Works* (Philosophical Library) and *Pascal* (Univ. of Ala. Pr.) are authoritative. Morris Bishop's *Pascal: The Life of Genius* (Greenwood) is a sound biography; also A. G. Krailsheimer's *Pascal* (Hill and Wang). See also T. S. Eliot's (94) essay on Pascal in his *Selected Essays* (Harcourt).

82. TOCQUEVILLE. Good standard biography: J. P. Mayer, *Alexis de Tocqueville: A Biographical Essay in Political Science*. Recommended: a careful reading of Phillips Bradley's long and thoughtful introduction to his monumental two-volume edition of *Democracy in America* (Vintage). See also: G. W. Pierson, *Tocqueville in America*, abridged by Dudley C. Lunt (Anchor); J. P. Mayer, *Alexis de Tocqueville: Journey to America* (Yale Univ. Pr.).

83. EMERSON. Standard biography: R. L. Rusk, *The Life of Ralph Waldo Emerson* (Columbia Univ. Pr.). See also: Lewis Leary, *Ralph Waldo Emerson: An Interpretive Essay*; Van Wyck Brooks, *The Flowering of New England* (Houghton Mifflin); F. O. Matthiessen, *American Renaissance* (Oxford Univ. Pr.); Bliss Perry, ed., *The Heart of Emerson's Journals* (Dover); George Santayana's (87) essay on Emerson in *Interpretations of Poetry and Religion* (Harper & Row); Kenneth Walter Cameron, *Emerson the Essayist*; Stephen E. Whicher, *Freedom and Fate: An Inner Life of Ralph Waldo Emerson* (A. S. Barnes).

84. THOREAU. Good biography: Walter Harding, *The Days of Henry Thoreau* (Dover). See also Richard Lebeaux, *Young Man Thoreau*; R. T. Richardson, Jr., *Henry Thoreau: A Life of the Mind* (Univ. of Calif. Pr.); Sherman Paul, *The Shores of America: Thoreau's Inward Exploration* (Univ. of Ill. Pr.); H. S. Canby, *Thoreau* (Beacon Pr.).

85. WILLIAM JAMES. The basic account is Ralph Barton Perry's *The Thought and Character of William James* (2 vols., Harvard Univ. Pr.), of which there is a good one-volume abridgement (Braziller). See also: Jacques Barzun, *A Stroll with William James* (Univ. of Chicago Pr.); C.H. Grattan, *The Three Jameses* (N. Y. Univ. Pr.); Gay Wilson Allen, *William James* (Univ. of Minn. Pr.); G. Santayana's (87) chapter on James in *Character and Opinion in the United States* (Norton); R. B. Perry, *In the Spirit of William James* (Ind. Univ. Pr.). *The Letters of William James* have been edited by his son Henry in two volumes (Kraus Reprint); and his brother, Henry, offers *Notes of a Son and Brother* (Scribner's).

86. DEWEY. *Intelligence in the Modern World: John Dewey's Philosophy*

(Modern Library) contains excellent selections from most of Dewey's major works, plus a long, professional philosopher's introduction by the editor, Joseph Ratner. See also Sidney Hook's *John Dewey: An Intellectual Portrait* (Greenwood); P. A. Schilpp, ed., *The Philosophy of John Dewey* (Open Court); Irwin Edman, *Philosopher's Holiday* (Viking); George Dykhuizen, *The Life and Mind of John Dewey.*

87. SANTAYANA.   Sympathetic portrait: Daniel Cory, *Santayana: the Later Years* (Braziller). Cory has also edited *The Letters of George Santayana* (Scribner's). See also: Willard Arnett, *Santayana and the Sense of Beauty* (Ind. Univ. Pr.); G. W. Howgate, *George Santayana* (A. S. Barnes); P. A. Schilpp, ed., *The Philosophy of George Santayana* (Tudor Pub. Co.). Most recent: John McCormick, *George Santayana: A Biography* (Knopf).

POETRY (88–98)

88. DONNE.   Definitive biography: R. C. Bald, *John Donne: A Life* (Oxford Univ. Pr.). See also: Wilbur Sanders, *John Donne's Poetry* (Cambridge Univ. Pr.); J. B. Leishman, *The Monarch of Wit: An Analytical and Comparative Study of John Donne* (Hutchinson); Edmund Gosse, *Life and Letters of John Donne* (2 vols., Peter Smith); H. I. Faussett, *John Donne, A Study in Discord* (Russell); George Williamson, *The Donne Tradition* (Noonday Pr.); Theodore Spencer, ed., *A Garland for John Donne* (Peter Smith); T. S. Eliot's (94) influential essay on "The Metaphysical Poets" in his *Selected Essays* (Harcourt).

89. MILTON.   Comprehensive biography: W. R. Parker, *Milton* (2 vols., Oxford Univ. Pr.). Shorter biographical treatments: J. H. Hanford, *John Milton, Englishman* (Crown); Rose Macaulay, *Milton* (Macmillan). See also: David Daiches, *Milton* (Norton); E. M. W. Tillyard, *Milton* (Macmillan); Basil Willey, *The Seventeenth Century Background*, Chapter 10 (Anchor); and the two interesting Milton essays in T. S. Eliot's (94) *On Poetry and Poets* (Noonday Pr.).

90. BLAKE.   Mona Wilson, *The Life of William Blake* (Oxford Univ. Pr.); S. Foster Damon, *William Blake: His Philosophy and Symbols* (Peter Smith); Mark Schorer, *William Blake* (Vintage); essay on Blake in T. S. Eliot's (94) *Selected Essays* (Harcourt); Jacob Bronowski, *William Blake and the Age of Revolution* (Harper & Row); Northrop Frye, *Fearful Symmetry: A Study of William Blake* (Princeton Univ. Pr.). An investigation in depth by a fine Blake scholar is Kathleen J. Raine's *Blake and Tradition* (2 vols.,

Princeton Univ. Pr.). See also her *William Blake* (Oxford Univ. Pr.).

91. WORDSWORTH. Standard biography: G. McL. Harper, *William Wordsworth, His Life, Works, and Influence* (2 vols, Russell). See also Mary Moorman's *William Wordsworth: A Biography* (2 vols., Oxford Univ. Pr.) and the more recent Hunter Davies, *William Wordsworth* (Atheneum). For diverse critical appraisals see: H. I. Faussett, *The Lost Leader, A Study of Wordsworth* (Harcourt); H. W. Garrod, *Wordsworth: Lectures and Essays* (Oxford Univ. Pr.); Coleridge's (92) *Biographia Literaria* (Everyman); J. Wordsworth, *The Music of Humanity* (Nelson); Matthew Arnold's essay in *Essays in Criticism,* 2d series (Dutton).

92. COLERIDGE. The most recent full biography: Oswald Doughty, *Perturbed Spirit: The Life and Personality of Samuel Taylor Coleridge.* Another good modern brief biography is W. J. Bate's *Coleridge* (Macmillan). E. K. Chambers's *Samuel Taylor Coleridge* (Oxford Univ. Pr.) is fuller, but dated. See also Lawrence Hanson's *The Life of Samuel Taylor Coleridge* (Russell). The finest book on Coleridge's genius and a masterpiece in its own right is John Livingston Lowes's *The Road to Xanadu* (Vintage). See also: Thomas De Quincey, *Reminiscences of the English Lake Poets* (AMS Pr.), for a firsthand glimpse; I. A. Richards, *Coleridge on Imagination* (Ind. Univ. Pr.); Kathleen Coburn, ed., *Coleridge: A Collection of Critical Essays* (Prentice-Hall); Basil Willey, *Samuel Taylor Coleridge* (Norton); S. Prickett, *Coleridge and Wordsworth: The Poetry of Growth* (Cambridge Univ. Pr.).

93. YEATS. Standard biography: J. M. Hone, *William Butler Yeats (1865–1939)* (Haskell). See also: T. R. Henn, *The Lonely Tower* (Pellegrini & Cudahy); Richard Ellmann, *Yeats: The Man and the Masks* (Norton); Douglas Archibald, *Yeats* (Syracuse Univ. Pr.); Denis Donoghue, *Yeats* (Viking); Harold Bloom, *Yeats* (Oxford Univ. Pr.); essays on Yeats in Arland Ussher's *Three Great Irishmen* (New American Library); Edmund Wilson, *Axel's Castle* (Scribner's); T. S. Eliot (94), *On Poetry and Poets* (Farrar, Straus).

94. T. S. ELIOT. Good biography: Peter Ackroyd, *T. S. Eliot: A Life* (Simon & Schuster). See also: F. O. Matthiessen, *The Achievement of T. S. Eliot* (Oxford Univ. Pr.); George Williamson, *A Reader's Guide to T. S. Eliot* (Noonday Pr.); Hugh Kenner, *The Invisible Poet: T. S. Eliot* (McDowell, Obolensky); Helen Gardner, *The Art of T. S. Eliot* (Faber & Faber); essay on Eliot in Edmund Wilson's *Axel's Castle* (Scribner's); Elizabeth Drew, *T. S. Eliot: The Design of His Poetry* (Scribner's); E. Martin Browne, *The Making of T. S. Eliot's Plays* (Cambridge Univ. Pr.). Two good essay collections are: Hugh

Kenner, ed., *T. S. Eliot: A Collection of Critical Essays* (Prentice-Hall); Allen Tate, ed., *T. S. Eliot: The Man and His Work* (Penguin). A sympathetic interpretation of Eliot as conservative is Russell Kirk's excellent *Eliot and His Age* (Random).

95. WHITMAN. Good standard biography: Gay Wilson Allen, *The Solitary Singer* (Wayne St. Univ. Pr.). Other good book-length treatments: Justin Kaplan, *Walt Whitman: A Life* (Simon & Schuster); H. S. Canby, *Walt Whitman: An American* (Greenwood); Emory Holloway, *Whitman: An Interpretation in Narrative* (Biblio and Tannen). See also: Richard Chase, *Walt Whitman* (Univ. of Minn. Pr.); D. H. Lawrence (41), "Whitman," in *Studies in Classic American Literature* (Penguin); Paul Zweig, *Walt Whitman: The Making of the Poet* (Basic Books).

96. FROST. Lawrence Thompson's *Robert Frost* (3 vols., Holt, Rinehart) is official but not reverent. Qualifying Thompson's interpretation of Frost's character is W. H. Pritchard's *Frost: A Literary Life Reconsidered* (Oxford Univ. Pr.). See also: E. S. Sergeant, *Robert Frost: The Trial by Existence*; Sidney Cox, *A Swinger of Birches: A Portrait of Robert Frost* (N. Y. Univ. Pr.); R. L. Cook, *The Dimensions of Robert Frost*; R. A. Brower, *The Poetry of Robert Frost* (Oxford Univ. Pr.); J. M. Cox, ed., *Robert Frost: A Collection of Critical Essays* (Prentice-Hall); Richard Poirier, *Robert Frost: The Work of Knowing* (Oxford Univ. Pr.).

97. AUDEN and PEARSON, eds. There are dozens of good general anthologies of English and American verse. The Auden and Pearson anthology seems as good as any, but you may also wish to consult Richard Aldington, ed., *The Viking Book of Poetry of the English-Speaking World* (2 vols., Viking); *The Oxford Book of English Verse* (Oxford Univ. Pr.); J. F. Nims, *The Harper Anthology of Poetry*. Louis Untermeyer's *Lives of the Poets* (Fireside) is a good, readable compendium of biography plus critical summary. It deals with English and American poets from Beowulf to Dylan Thomas. Obviously the bulk of the world's great poetry is in languages other than English. See D. Weissbort and Ted Hughes, eds., *Modern Poetry in Translation* (Persea). If you can search out a copy of Mark Van Doren's out-of-print *An Anthology of World Poetry*, you will be well repaid. Hubert Creekmore's *A Little Treasury of World Poetry* (Scribner's), though built on a smaller scale, is also excellent.

For translations from the Greek: Dudley Fitts, *Poems from the Greek Anthology* (New Directions); Higham and Bowra, *The Oxford Book of Greek Verse in Translation* (Oxford Univ. Pr.); *Greek Lyrics,* tr. Richmond Lattimore (Univ. of Chicago Pr.); *Poems from the Greek Anthology*, tr. Kenneth Rexroth (Univ. of Mich. Pr.); Constantine A. Trypanis, ed., *The Penguin Book of Greek Verse* (Penguin).

From the Latin: L. R. Lind, *Latin Poetry in Verse Translation* (Riverside). A delightful book on the Latin poets, containing some superb translations, is Gilbert Highet's *Poets in a Landscape* (Knopf).

From the Middle Ages (fourteen languages): Hubert Creekmore's *Lyrics of the Middle Ages* (Grove).

From the French: Broome and Chesters, eds., *Anthology of Modern French Poetry* (Cambridge Univ. Pr.); B. Woledge et al., eds., *The Penguin Book of French Verse* (Penguin); C. F. MacIntyre, *French Symbolist Poetry* (Univ. of Calif. Pr.); Wallace Fowlie, *Mid-Century French Poets* (Evergreen); Angel Flores, *An Anthology of French Poetry from Nerval to Valéry in English Translation* (Anchor).

From the Spanish: J. A. Crow, ed., *Anthology of Spanish Poetry from the Beginnings to the Present Day, Including Both Spain and Spanish America* (La. St. Univ. Pr.); J. M. Cohen, ed., *The Penguin Book of Spanish Verse* (Penguin).

From the Italian: George Kay, ed., *The Penguin book of Italian Verse* (Penguin).

From the German: Angel Flores, ed., *An Anthology of German Poetry from Hölderlin to Rilke* (Anchor); *The Penguin Book of German Verse*, ed. Leonard Forster (Penguin); *Anthology of German Poetry through the 19th Century*, ed. Gode and Ungar (Ungar).

From the Irish: *Penguin Book of Irish Verse*, ed. Brendan Kennelly (Penguin); *Kings, Lords, and Commoners*, ed. and tr. by Frank O'Connor (Knopf).

From the Russian: *New Russian Poets*, ed. and tr. by George Reavey (Merrimack Bk. Service).

From the Chinese: A. R. Davis, ed., *Penguin Book of Chinese Verse* (Penguin).

From the Arabic: *Modern Poetry of the Arab World*, ed. and tr. by Abdullah al-Udhari (Penguin).

Books *about* poetry are not generally very helpful. There are exceptions. One is Mark Van Doren's *Introduction to Poetry* (Hill and Wang). This precedes a good general anthology with 135 pages of sharp, intelligible, no-nonsense commentaries on thirty varied examples of first-rate verse. See also the excellent *How Does a Poem Mean*, by Ciardi and Williams (Houghton Mifflin).

98. ELLMANN and O'CLAIR, eds. This is an entirely serviceable collection of modern verse. But others may do as well. A first-rate collection is *Modern Verse in English, 1900–1950* (Macmillan), ed. David Cecil and Allen Tate. It contains splendid introductions by the distinguished editors. A few inexpensive small anthologies of modern verse: *New Poets of England and America*, ed. Hall, Pack, and Simpson (Meridian); *The Pocket Book of Modern Verse*, ed. Oscar Williams (Washington Sq. Pr.); *100 Modern Poems*, ed. Selden Rodman (New American Library); *Faber Book of 20th Century Verse*, ed. Heath-Stubbs and Wright (Merrimack Bk. Service). For a comprehensive history of British and American poetry, *A History of Modern Poetry*, ed. David Perkins (Belknap).

HISTORY, BIOGRAPHY, AUTOBIOGRAPHY (99–103)

99. MORRIS; ROSSITER; eds. For a wider sampling and discussion of American historical records, see Richard Hofstadter's *Great Issues in American History* (2 vols., Vintage). For the Declaration see Carl Becker's *The Declaration of Independence* (Vintage). For the making of the Constitution see: Carl Van Doren, *The Great Rehearsal* (Viking); C. D. Bowen, *Miracle at Philadelphia* (Little, Brown).

100. ROUSSEAU. Recommended biography: Jean Guéhenno, *Jean-Jacques Rousseau* (Columbia Univ. Pr.). See also: Peter France, *Rousseau: Confessions* (Columbia Univ. Pr.); Maurice Cranston, *Jean-Jacques: The Early Life and Work of Jean-Jacques Rousseau, 1712–1754*. For a classic attack on Rousseau see Irving Babbitt's *Rousseau and Romanticism* (Univ. of Tex. Pr.).

101. BOSWELL. The multivolume *Yale Editions of the Private Papers of James Boswell* is published by McGraw-Hill, edited in the main by Frederick Pottle; some volumes have collaborative editors. On these papers Pottle based his important *James Boswell: The Earlier Years, 1740–1769*. The first volume of the Yale series, the fascinating *Boswell's London Journal 1762–1763*, is available in paperback (McGraw-Hill).

Other studies of this curious flawed genius: Hesketh Pearson, *Johnson and Boswell* (Harper & Row); Wyndham Lewis, *James Boswell: A Short Life* (Eyre & Spottiswoode); C. B. Tinker, *Young Boswell*. See also J. L. Clifford, ed., *Twentieth Century Interpretations of Boswell's Life of Johnson* (Prentice-Hall); W. J. Bate, *Samuel Johnson* (Harvest).

102. ADAMS. The letters are important, if you find yourself interested in Adams. Worthington Chauncey Ford has edited three volumes of them: *A Cycle of Adams Letters, 1861–1865*; *Letters of Henry*

Adams, 1858–1891; *Letters of Henry Adams, 1892–1918* (Peter Wolff). The definitive biography (a fine one) is Ernest Samuels's three-volume life: *The Young Henry Adams*; *Henry Adams: The Middle Years*; *Henry Adams: The Major Phase* (Harvard Univ. Pr.). Other admirable studies: J. C. Levenson, *The Mind and Art of Henry Adams* (Houghton Mifflin); Elizabeth Stevenson, *Henry Adams: A Biography* (Macmillan); R. A. Hume, *Runaway Star: An Appreciation of Henry Adams* (Cornell Univ. Pr.); William Dusinberre, *Henry Adams: The Myth of Failure.*

103. BRAUDEL. Braudel appeared so recently on the scene that I know of no comprehensive commentary or biography in English. The best short appreciation, a brilliant one, is to be found in *The Great Ideas Today, 1983* (Encyclopaedia Britannica). It is a long review by Charles Van Doren of Braudel's *Mediterranean*. In 1972 the *Journal of Modern History* published a special issue on Braudel.

ANNEX (I–VI)

I.   MCNEILL; THE DURANTS. A reading of these twelve volumes should suffice for most of us. Here, however, are some good alternates: Crane Brinton et al., *History of Civilization: Prehistory to 1715* and *History of Civilization: 1715 to Present* (Prentice-Hall); Hugh Thomas, *History of the World* (Harper & Row); Joseph Reither, *World History: A Brief Introduction* (McGraw-Hill); Bryce Lyon et al., *History of the Western World* (3 vols., Random); John A. Garraty and Peter Gay, *History of the World* (3 vols., Harper Classics). Also: Herbert A. Davies, *An Outline History of the World* (Oxford); John Bowle, *Man through the Ages* (Little, Brown); Goldwin Arthur Smith, *The Heritage of Man* (Scribner's); Chester G. Starr et al., *A History of the World* (2 vols., Rand McNally).

Handsome: *Life's Picture History of Western Man* (Simon & Schuster). For reference: William R. Shepherd, *Historical Atlas* (Barnes and Noble); William Langer, ed., *An Encyclopedia of World History* (Houghton Mifflin).

II. MORISON; SMITH. These two cover the ground pretty well, but there are any number of good histories of our country in paperback. Here are four: J. A. Garraty, *The American Nation* (2 vols., Harper & Row) and *Short History of the American Nation* (Harper Classics); Hofstadter and Miller, *The United States, Parts 1 and 2* (Prentice-Hall); R. N. Current and G. J. Goodwin, *History of the United States,* (2 vols., Knopf). For reference: Richard B. Morris, ed., *Encyclopedia of American History* (Harper & Row). D. W. Brogan's *The American Character* (Knopf) is a brilliant short book that you may wish to compare with Tocqueville (82). See also: Bernard Bailyn et al., *The Great Republic* (2 vols., Little, Brown); G. B. Tindall, *America: A Narrative History* (2 vols., Norton).

III. WHITEHEAD (as philosopher). His *Essays in Science and Philosophy* includes some autobiographical notes and sketches. For interpretation see Victor Lowe's *Understanding Whitehead* (Johns Hopkins Pr.). A delightful picture of the philosopher emerges from *Dialogues of Alfred North Whitehead* (New American Library) as recorded by Lucien Price.

IV. WHITEHEAD (as mathematician). The most interesting, most varied reading *about* mathematics I know of is to be found in James R. Newman's magnificent four-volume anthology *The World of Mathematics* (Simon & Schuster). At least half of it is perfectly comprehensible to anyone who has had two years of high school math. A somewhat similar and splendid anthology is Campbell and Higgins, eds., *Mathematics: People, Problems, Results* (Wadsworth International). Somewhat more difficult: Aleksandrov et al., eds., *Mathematics: Its Contents, Methods, and Meanings* (MIT Pr.). These two latter collections are in paperback, as is Morris Kline's fine *Mathematics and the Search for Knowledge*. For fascinating biographies of the great figures see E. T. Bell's *Men of Mathematics* (Fireside). A delightful, offbeat book is Kasner and Newman's *Mathematics and the Imagination* (Touchstone). Another is the brief *A Mathematician's Apology* by the great G. H. Hardy (Cambridge Univ. Pr.). A brilliant little book that connects literature and mathematics is Scott Buchanan's *Poetry and Mathematics* (Univ. of Chicago Pr.). Two more advanced histories: E. T. Bell, *The Development of Mathematics* (McGraw-Hill); D. J. Struik, *A Concise History of Mathematics* (Dover).

V. GOMBRICH. There are a great many fine histories of art, and you may prefer one of them to Gombrich. A splendid one is H. W. Janson's *History of Art* (Harry Abrams), third edition, updated by A. F. Janson. Erwin O. Christensen's *History of Western Art* (New American Library) will cost you very little. It is clear, concise, illustrated, and has a bibliography. The same publisher also offers his *Pictorial History of Western Art* in paperback. Helen Gardner's *Art Through the Ages* (Harcourt) is a standard text, well illustrated, rather pedagogical. The same is true of Upjohn, Wingert, and Mahler's *History of World Art* (Oxford Univ. Pr.) and Michael Levey's *History of Western Art* (Oxford Univ. Pr.). Germain Bazin's *History of Art from Prehistoric Times to the Present* (Houghton Mifflin) has a good bibliography and authoritative text. See also Dr. Frederick Hartt's *A History of Art in the Western World* (Scribner's). For those who wish to learn more about modern art a notable work is John Canaday's *Mainstreams of Modern Art: David to Picasso* (Simon & Schuster). See also Sara Newmeyer's *Enjoying Modern Art* (New American Library). Most good art books are pretty expensive, but you get something for your money in the way of format and illustrations.

VI.   ADLER and VAN DOREN.   For our purposes Adler and Van Doren's book is the best I know. Alfred Stefferud, ed., *The Wonderful World of Books* (New American Library) contains many short essays on the joys of reading, with occasionally some good concrete advice, plus useful bibliographies. See also I. A. Richards, *How to Read a Page: A Course in Efficient Reading, with an Introduction to 100 Great Works* (Beacon Pr.).

Index

INDEX

INDEX

INDEX

About the Author

Clifton Fadiman was born in New York City and was graduated from Columbia University in 1925. With a wide range of interests and a broad spectrum of talents, he has been involved in almost every facet of the world of literature. He has been a high school teacher; book critic for various publications, including *The New Yorker*; book editor; columnist; lecturer; consultant; contributing editor of several magazines, including *Saturday Review*; host of "Information Please" and "The Quiz Kids," among other TV and radio programs; and judge of the National Book Award for Children's Books. He is the author of essays, criticism, and numerous introductions to classic works of literature and juvenile books, as well as editor of many anthologies.

Currently on the Board of Editors of the Encyclopaedia Britannica and a member of the Editorial Committee of the Book-of-the-Month Club, Mr. Fadiman is also on the Editorial Board of *Cricket*, a magazine for children, and is Associate Editor of *Great Books of the Western World*. He is on the Advisory Board of the Center for the Study of Children's Literature at Simmons College and Director Emeritus of the Fromm Institute for Lifelong Learning at the University of San Francisco.

He has been frequently recognized for his contributions to literature. His most recent awards include the Dorothy C. McKenzie Award for a Distinguished Contribution to the Field of Children's Literature in 1985 and the Santa Barbara Writers' Conference Award for Distinguished Service to Literature in 1987.

Mr. Fadiman's most recent anthologies include *The World Treasury of Children's Literature*; *The Little, Brown Book of Anecdotes*; and *The World of the Short Story.* He lives in Santa Barbara, California.